Developing
Adult Literacy

Oxfam GB

Oxfam GB, founded in 1942, is a development, humanitarian, and campaigning agency dedicated to finding lasting solutions to poverty and suffering around the world. Oxfam believes that every human being is entitled to a life of dignity and opportunity, and it works with others worldwide to make this become a reality.

From its base in Oxford in the United Kingdom, Oxfam GB publishes and distributes a wide range of books and other resource materials for development and relief workers, researchers and campaigners, schools and colleges, and the general public, as part of its programme of advocacy, education, and communications.

Oxfam GB is a member of Oxfam International, a confederation of 13 agencies of diverse cultures and languages, which share a commitment to working for an end to injustice and poverty – both in long-term development work and at times of crisis.

For further information about Oxfam's publishing, and online ordering, visit www.oxfam.org.uk/publications

For information about Oxfam's development, advocacy, and humanitarian relief work around the world, visit www.oxfam.org.uk

Developing Adult Literacy

Approaches to Planning, Implementing,
and Delivering Literacy Initiatives

Juliet McCaffery, Juliet Merrifield, and Juliet Millican

First published by Oxfam GB in 2007

© Oxfam GB 2007

ISBN 978-0-85598-596-7

A catalogue record for this publication is available from the British Library.

The information in this publication is correct at the time of going to press.

Available from:

Bournemouth English Book Centre, PO Box 1496, Parkstone, Dorset, BH12 3YD, UK
tel: +44 (0)1202 712933; fax: +44 (0)1202 712930; email: oxfam@bebc.co.uk

USA: Stylus Publishing LLC, PO Box 605, Herndon, VA 20172-0605, USA
tel: +1 (0)703 661 1581; fax: +1 (0)703 661 1547; email: styluspub@aol.com

For details of local agents and representatives in other countries, consult our website:
www.oxfam.org.uk/publications
or contact Oxfam Publishing, Oxfam House, John Smith Drive, Cowley, Oxford, OX4 2JY, UK
tel +44 (0) 1865 473727; fax (0) 1865 472393; email: publish@oxfam.org.uk

Our website contains a fully searchable database of all our titles, and facilities for secure online ordering.

Published by Oxfam GB, Oxfam House, John Smith Drive, Cowley, Oxford, OX4 2JY, UK

Printed by Information Press, Eynsham

Oxfam GB is a registered charity, no. 202 918, and is a member of Oxfam International.

Foreword

It is surprising that this book has not been written before. It provides a definitive overview of the work and ideas involved in developing adult literacy that nicely bridges theory and practice – serving both as a handbook for adult literacy practitioners and as a review of the state of the art for researchers and policy makers. It is surprising because many of the issues signalled here have been separately recognised by different participants – practitioners, researchers, policy makers – but the parts have not previously been brought together so readably and clearly.

The publication of this book is timely since literacy is undergoing something of a revival of interest. Various international bodies are attempting to come to grips with the problems faced in previous attempts to 'improve the literacy rate' or to bring literacy to the 'illiterate'. Recent approaches, as the book indicates, have adopted a more sophisticated perspective on what counts as literacy and how it might be learned. The Global Monitoring Report 'Literacy for Life' (UNESCO 2005a) collated knowledge from the field and nicely disposed of the limitations of these earlier approaches and terms – but it is a lengthy and fairly comprehensive document that summarises a wide range of literature and is not easy to use for immediate or practical purposes. The present volume, then, in a way mediates that larger enterprise for the general reader, providing a work that can be kept at hand and referred to in the immediate pressures of programme development and of facilitating adult learning.

Other current developments also complement the authors' encapsulation of the state of play and how we should proceed. The International Benchmarks on Adult Literacy developed by ActionAid International and the Global Campaign for Education (2005) offer standards for adult literacy based on an extensive survey. These standards, as the present volume makes clear, should not be interpreted as a 'one size fits all' approach in the manner of previous approaches to literacy policy, but should rather be adapted according to context. The Abuja Call for Action (2007) makes the case for renewed commitment to adult literacy, calling for new momentum among national and local governments and civil-society actors, as well as new investments by national governments in an international context. At the same time, national initiatives are attempting to bring these wider positions to bear on their own governments. In the UK the Literacy Working Group (LWG), an amalgam of NGOs in the field of adult education, literacy, and development, has produced a position paper drawing upon these various recent studies and initiatives in order to offer support to the Department for International Development (DFID). There are, then, big players making big calls in the field. What the present volume offers, in that context, is an account of how such commitments might be actualised, and what exactly is involved in putting adult literacy on the agenda and developing programmes that could be more effective than in the past.

In order to accomplish this, the authors (all of whom have significant experience as practitioners, facilitators, researchers, programme directors etc.) set out the practical as well as the conceptual issues involved in addressing adult literacy. They are careful to speak directly to the reader, avoiding the imposition of a template for action and instead laying out the terrain and helping the reader to assess which of many answers best suit their own situation. They start by locating adult literacy work in the broader international context, citing the various programmes and policy perspectives in past years, coming up to date with the Global Monitoring Report. They note the previous assumption that literacy acquisition and the consequent raising of the literacy 'rate' in a given country would lead to the attainment of wider development goals, such as economic take-off, health improvement, or gender equality. It is now recognised that these grand ambitions are too one-dimensional – literacy may be a necessary but it is not a sufficient cause for such developments. Moreover, it must be recognised that literacy varies from one context to another, both across countries but also for individuals as they move between different tasks, institutions, and relationships (Street 2001). 'One size fits all' won't do, and programmes based on uniform 'delivery' are doomed to failure. But how can this more complex situation be navigated by programme developers and adult literacy facilitators without their getting bogged down in minute details of local culture? The authors prove to be helpful companions in addressing such difficult questions, carefully mapping the different approaches and the different consequences of adopting them.

Having set out the broader international context, they then identify specific topics necessary to understanding literacy and to implementing programmes.

In doing so they adopt a useful strategy of laying out a position that has been influential in the field, citing the critiques of that position, and then offering a clear and balanced perspective of their own. With respect to gender and development, for instance, they indicate the importance of the shift from Women in Development (WID) to Gender and Development (GAD) that has characterised the field in recent years, but then indicate some of the critiques of both positions that call for further moves. Their own considered position at this point is for 'mainstreaming gender', locating gender issues in relation to other aspects of inequality such as race, class, and age. Men as well as women may be disadvantaged in certain circumstances and by certain perspectives on programme development, and the larger picture will always need to be taken into account. This larger perspective is also apparent in the authors' approach to 'understanding literacy'. They clearly describe the different approaches, with apt reference both to scholars and to actual programmes. The approaches are usefully labelled as skills, tasks, social practice, and critical reflection. In each case there have been critiques, and in practice different positions frequently overlap. The authors' own position – 'What we think' – sees the four approaches not so much as alternatives but as boxes nested inside each other. Their idea of literacy, then, is that it 'has many layers', and subsequent chapters address each 'layer' in turn, looking at how each has been put into practice in literacy learning programmes. The aim is to help planners and facilitators be aware of the alternatives and of the consequences of adopting particular favoured positions.

This may sound like a rather academic survey of the field, but the authors are uniquely able to draw authoritatively on academic knowledge without sinking into academic discourse, which can often be obscure and esoteric, putting off both facilitators and policy makers. The book instead contrives to keep readers fully engaged while at the same time providing us with the benefit of the best thinking in the field. Since the acquisition of literacy itself is often claimed to achieve such a synthesis – to provide 'ordinary' people in their everyday lives with the benefit of what thinkers have written in more specialised circumstances – it is important that the authors of this volume meet such a high goal. That they do so where others have failed is perhaps itself proof of their thesis – that it is not literacy itself that achieves such insight but the way it is done.

Brian Street, Professor of Language in Education, King's College London

Acknowledgements

We wrote this book because we felt that there was no existing book which clearly explained the theoretical and conceptual framework behind different models of adult literacy for development. Most work of this nature is highly academic and not easy to read for people in other countries whose first language is not English. We wanted to produce something that explained the different models of literacy to planners and policy makers in order to help them decide on the type of programme they wanted to develop. Juliet Millican first contacted Oxfam and actually got the three of us to sit down and write, and we are very grateful to her for taking this initiative.

In writing this book we have utilised the experience of all those in adult literacy with whom we have worked over many years. It is their knowledge, commitment, and enthusiasm that led to the writing of this book. We wanted to share what we have learnt from our colleagues, students, tutors, and academics working in many parts of the world – in Nigeria, South Africa, Zambia, Pakistan, India, Egypt, Nepal, the USA, Canada, England, Scotland, and the Irish Republic. We would like to offer special thanks to our referees, who read and commented on drafts of the book and made many useful suggestions.

Each adult literacy programme is different, with its own individual characteristics. We have drawn on this richness and diversity to provide policy makers and planners of adult literacy programmes with a range of examples and ideas gleaned from the practical experience and the theoretical analysis of those working in the field.

For further information on our work, please visit our website at www.3jmliteracy.com

Juliet McCaffery, Juliet Merrifield, and Juliet Millican

Contents

Foreword (*by Professor Brian Street*) v

Acknowledgements viii

List of acronyms x

About the authors xii

Part I: Understanding the Context

    1. Introduction 2

    2. The international context 7

    3. Mainstreaming gender 18

Part II: Understanding Literacy

    4. What do we mean by literacy? 32

    5. Literacy as skills 43

    6. Literacy as tasks 57

    7. Literacy as social practice 72

    8. Literacy as critical reflection 87

Part III: Understanding the Preparation Process

    9. Planning for literacy 108

    10. The language of literacy 123

    11. Monitoring and evaluating literacy programmes 135

Part IV: Understanding the Learning Process

    12. How people learn to read and write 152

    13. Approaches to curriculum 169

    14. Resources for literacy 186

    15. Training and supporting literacy educators 207

    16. Assessing literacy learning 232

Part V: Making Sense of Adult Literacy

    17. Conclusions 254

References 264

Index 280

List of acronyms

ABET	Adult Basic Education Training (South Africa)
ALBSU	Adult Literacy and Basic Skills Unit (UK)
CELL	Capacity Enhancement for Lifelong Learning
CEP	Community Education Project (Nigeria)
CLPN	Community Literacies Project Nepal
DFID	Department for International Development (UK)
EFA	Education for All
EWLP	Experimental World Literacy Programme
FENTO	Further Education National Training Organisation (UK)
GAD	Gender and Development
GALAE	General Authority for Literacy and Adult Education (Egypt)
GCSE	General Certificate of Secondary Education (UK)
IALS	International Adult Literacy Study
ICT	information and communication technology
LABE	Literacy and Adult Basic Education
LGMs	learner-generated materials/locally generated materials
LOCAL	Learner Oriented Community Adult Literacy
MDGs	Millennium Development Goals
MLJ	Mapping the Learning Journey
NALA	National Adult Literacy Agency (Ireland)
NCSALL	National Center for the Study of Adult Learning and Literacy (USA)
NGO	non-government organisation

NLS	New Literacy Studies
NRDC	National Research and Development Centre on Adult Literacy and Numeracy (UK)
ODPM	Office of the Deputy Prime Minister (UK)
OECD	Organisation for Economic Co-operation and Development
PCD	participatory curriculum development
PRA	participatory rural appraisal
REFLECT	Regenerated Freirean Literacy using Empowering Community Techniques
SOLO	Sudan Open Learning Organisation
UNDP	United Nations Development Programme
UNESCO	United Nations Educational, Scientific and Cultural Organization
WID	Women in Development
ZPD	zone of proximal development

About the authors

Juliet McCaffery worked for over 20 years on adult literacy programmes in the voluntary sector in Brighton and in the statutory sector in the London Borough of Lambeth. She then worked as the first gender and development officer for the British Council. She is now a freelance consultant and has worked in Egypt, Nigeria, Nepal, Pakistan, Sierra Leone, South Africa, Sudan, and Yemen, designing and evaluating literacy programmes as well as training literacy educators. She has published teaching materials and training guides, written a number of articles, and promoted and published student writing.

Juliet Merrifield has 25 years experience in adult education as both a researcher and practitioner. She is Principal of the Friends Centre, an independent adult education centre in Brighton, and was formerly Director of the Learning from Experience Trust in London. She worked in the USA for 20 years, first at the Highlander Center promoting education for social change, and later as Director of the Center for Literacy Studies. She is particularly interested in evaluation, assessment, and planning.

Juliet Millican has worked for more than 20 years in the field of adult literacy and community education while maintaining a fractional post at a university in the UK. She has worked in a project management capacity in Egypt, Senegal, The Gambia, South Africa, Nepal, and India, and on short-term contracts in other parts of the world. She was lead author on the Oxfam publication *Adult Literacy: A Handbook for Development Workers* published in 1995. She is particularly interested in participatory approaches to curriculum design, materials development, and experiential and reflective learning.

Part I
Understanding Context

1
Introduction

This book is written for people who plan, develop, and deliver literacy programmes and initiatives. It sets out some of the concepts of literacy and the main approaches to adult literacy education that have been used in different parts of the world, and uses these to show different ways to develop and manage programmes.

There is little doubt that literacy is important. Chapter 2 places literacy in the international context, including the Education for All initiative and the Millennium Development Goals (MDGs), and the underlying major development issues they are trying to address. The role literacy can play in development is not a simple one. Literacy can be an important element in addressing deep social problems, but is never a quick-fix solution. Becoming literate can be part of a process of empowerment, but literacy on its own does not confer power. Literacy is intricately bound up with other aspects of society including gender, class, and ethnicity (see Chapter 3).

As Chapter 4 outlines, the word 'literacy' means different things to different people. It is not an easy concept to define, and definitions often fail because they try to simplify something that is complex and changing. Our own idea of literacy has several layers. Literacy is rooted in the *skills* of reading and writing. These skills are used by individuals to accomplish *tasks* in their daily lives. These tasks are part of their literacy *practices*, socially and culturally rooted in the communities in which they live and work. Literacy can be a means for *critical reflection* on the world as part of a process of change. Chapters 5 to 8 describe in more detail these four aspects of literacy and their associated programmes of learning.

We believe that a more literate world has the potential to be a better place for those who live in it. The sociologist Johan Galtung once said that if the whole world became literate nothing much would change: 'But if the whole world consisted of literate, autonomous, critical, constructive people, capable of translating ideas into action, individually or collectively – the world would change' (Galtung 1976, quoted by Limage 2004: 16).

This book is intended to help staff in government or non-government organisations (NGOs) who are charged with developing adult literacy initiatives. There are many things to think about. Programme managers must:

- identify needs and appropriate ways to offer learning activities in communities;
- plan for the recruitment and training of adult literacy teachers;
- develop curriculum and teaching materials;
- make decisions about how to assess learning and evaluate programmes.

None of these plans can be made in isolation, without thinking about all the others. None of the decisions are value-free or merely 'technical': all require an understanding of ideas, values, and principles. Chapters 9 to 16 offer support in the process of thinking through the issues, making practical planning decisions, and delivering adult literacy initiatives.

It may be tempting to think that a solution has already been developed somewhere, which can simply be adapted and implemented 'as is'. But 'off-the-shelf' solutions don't often work for complex phenomena like literacy, which are shaped by cultural and social factors. Literacy initiatives must take into account the local context, resources, scale, and most importantly the purposes of learners, the local community, and other key stakeholders. These will inevitably differ by place and time.

The book's outline

Part I: Understanding the Context.
This section sets the scene for beginning to work on adult literacy.
Chapter 2 places literacy in the international context and Chapter 3 treats literacy in the gender context.

Part II: Understanding Literacy.
Chapter 4 outlines four key concepts of literacy that have shaped much of literacy learning over the last 30 years. These concepts and their associated learning programmes are used throughout the book to outline alternatives and decisions to be made. Chapters 5 to 8 describe approaches based on these concepts of 'literacy as skills', 'literacy as tasks', 'literacy as practices', and 'literacy as critical reflection'.

Part III: Understanding the Preparation Process.
This section provides support for the decisions to be made in planning literacy programmes. Chapter 9 provides an overview of essential considerations in planning. Chapter 10 addresses issues in the language of literacy teaching and learning. Chapter 11 outlines what needs to be considered in planning monitoring and evaluation of literacy programmes.

Part IV: Understanding the Learning Process.
This section offers practical guides for each key element of literacy-programme development. Chapter 12 reviews research on how people learn to read and write and provides an essential backdrop to planning teaching. Chapter 13 focuses on developing curriculum and Chapter 14 on developing materials. Chapter 15 reviews issues in the selection and training of facilitators. Chapter 16 describes approaches to assessment of literacy learning and evaluation of programmes.

In Part V, Chapter 17 we draw together some common themes and principles and outline key issues and opportunities for literacy programmes.

The aim of the book is to help programme managers think through the decisions they have to make in setting up and running a literacy programme. We do not offer a template or a single way of doing things. There are many answers to the questions and readers will choose what works for them in their particular context with the resources available.

While we want readers to be aware of concepts about literacy and learning, we also want this to be a practical book. We make use of case studies to illustrate how the ideas have been put into practice in particular contexts. We offer checklists that may help to clarify decisions to be made. We do not expect readers to start at the beginning and work their way through, but to dip in and out of the book as needed.

Language and terms in this book

The authors are aware that the words we use carry associations for readers that we may not intend. The word 'teacher' for example is often associated with a certain status in the community, with qualifications and training, and most importantly with assumptions about a hierarchical relationship with students. Teachers may be expected to use what Freire called the banking method of education, filling the empty vessels of students' heads with the knowledge the teacher possesses. No matter that teachers may not be that kind of person or take this approach to education: when we use that term we run the risk that readers will think they know what we mean.

We have a different image in mind for adult literacy programmes. We see teachers as working in collaboration with their students, in dialogue with them about their learning needs and interests, learning from them the ways that literacy might play a role in their daily lives and in their communities. While teachers certainly need good training in order to be able to take this active and constructive approach to teaching and learning, they don't need to be so different in status and class from their students. For this reason we often use the term *facilitator* or *tutor* in this book to identify the particular kind of teacher we have in mind.

The term 'student' is another one that carries particular images – of children sitting in rows in school, of passive learning, receiving knowledge and wisdom from teachers. Using the term for adults risks them being treated as children, their life experience and knowledge ignored, their only role to receive learning. Again, we have a different picture in mind. We see students as working collaboratively with other students and with their teacher, contributing actively to the learning process, connecting new knowledge to what they already know and applying it in their lives. For this reason we use the term *learner* or *participant* in this book to identify the particular kind of adult student we have in mind.

The term 'classroom' conjures up different images depending on where you are. That image often includes children sitting and a teacher standing, symbolising the hierarchy of the relationship. It is a separate world from the rest of life. We need a better word for the kind of setting in which adults learn, a place that is part of everyday life and connected with it, and one in which people learn together to meet their own purposes. We use the terms *literacy group* or *learning group* to identify the particular kind of learning environment we have in mind.

We use the term *literacy programme* to identify one or more literacy groups that have been planned as part of the same initiative or project. Within any one country there may be different programmes, using different approaches. A literacy programme may be very small and local or even international in scope. While within a programme the aims and methods may be unevenly put into practice, we assume that a programme does have common aims, methods, and approaches.

As authors we recognise and support the importance of numeracy. Numeracy is a parallel concept to literacy: it is based on a set of mathematics skills (like estimating, measuring, and calculating) but needs to be viewed much more broadly as these are applied in life and shaped by the social and cultural environment. While we support the importance of numeracy, and sometimes discuss it with literacy in this book, as authors it is not our area of expertise and so is not our focus here.

Finally, this book is intended for people who are charged with developing literacy programmes in particular contexts. While we hope the book will be of use to people in all parts of the world, we are aware that contexts differ in terms of infrastructure and resources and we are particularly interested in those countries where literacy is intended to have an impact on poverty reduction. We therefore use the term *global South* or *South* to refer to non-industrialised (or partly industrialised) countries of what has in the past been called the developing world. We are all developing in different ways and at different rates and so we consider the term 'developing world' inappropriate. However, in this sense the South or global South is more of an economic than a geographic term and would not for instance include Australia or New Zealand. These countries may have more in common with Europe or America and countries broadly referred to as the *North* or the *global North*.

2

The international context

In a speech at a major literacy conference in Cairo in 2005, Dr Mir Asghar Hussain, the Director of UNESCO's Education and Planning Division, set out clearly the reasons for the world's focus on literacy:

> *Literacy is a fundamental human right and a prerequisite to the empowerment of the individual and development of society. Literacy is at the heart of learning, the core of Education for All (EFA) and central to the achievement of the Millennium Development Goals (MDGs). Access to quality literacy learning opportunities and the development of literate environments are essential components of strategies for poverty reduction, equality, economic development and environmental protection, in general a prerequisite for achieving democracy.*
> (Hussain 2005)

Literacy is viewed as essential to the reduction of poverty, to economic development, and to democracy.

This chapter considers the external and macro factors that impact at the micro level of literacy programmes. It provides a brief overview of the current global situation and draws attention to some of the global disparities in literacy levels. It notes that literacy is a comparatively new phenomenon and presents current international policies on adult literacy.

Organisational frameworks

A group of adults sitting together in a community centre or under a tree to learn to read, write, and calculate seems far removed from the world of international politics. Yet the women and men who have chosen or been persuaded to attain or improve their literacy and numeracy skills are at the centre of what can be conceptualised as a series of circles (see Figure 2.1).

Assisting these women and men to learn is a very clear objective, but our capacity to do this is framed by a range of external factors: culture, tradition, employment opportunities, regional and local government policies, national government policies, international policies and the state of the global economy all impact on what is provided at local level.

Local culture, tradition, and social mores will impact on the nature of the literacy group, as will who attends and what time it meets. National government policies will determine regional and local policy. International policies in terms of the global economy, and international policies for education will impact on national government policies. If the global economy is strong, a greater proportion of the richer countries' gross national product will be contributed to aid programmes. Aid policies and priorities are determined not only by politicians but also by academics, educators, and economists.

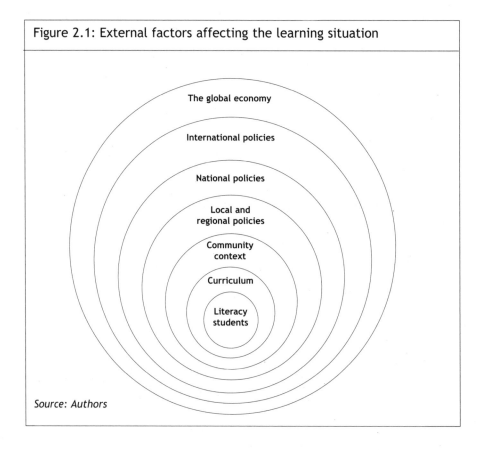

Figure 2.1: External factors affecting the learning situation

The global economy

International policies

National policies

Local and regional policies

Community context

Curriculum

Literacy students

Source: Authors

Currently the reduction of poverty is the highest priority on the aid agenda. Improvements in education are thought to assist in achieving this. The idea that high literacy levels lead to economic growth is commonly held, as wealthier countries tend to have higher literacy levels than poorer countries, but whether high levels of literacy are a causal factor in economic growth or the result of such growth is far less clear. There are areas with very high levels of literacy but low economic growth such as the state of Kerala in South India.

Statistics on literacy levels

The statistics on levels of literacy are largely estimates. Different countries collect statistics in different ways. Some base them on information from household censuses, others on school enrolment or completion rates. People may be literate in a minority language or the language of religious texts, such as Koranic Arabic, but not in the dominant language (for example the low level of literacy for nomadic Fulani pastoralists does not take into account their ability to read the Arabic of the Koran). Their literacy therefore may not be included in assessments of literacy levels. Though they provide an excellent overview of the situation, statistics on literacy levels should be treated with some care. The statistics and much of the comment on the current situation in this section is drawn from the UNESCO (2005a) Education for All Global Monitoring Report 'Literacy for Life'.

Based on statistics gathered between 2000–2004, UNESCO estimated that 771 million adults over the age of 15 were not literate – that is 18 per cent of the world's adult population. Table 2.1 presents estimates of literacy across the world, broken down into developed, developing, and in-transition countries.

Table 2.1: UNESCO estimates of literacy population	
Area	% of population literate
World	81.9
Countries in transition	99.4
Developed countries	98.7
Developing countries	76.4
Source: UNESCO 2005a: 166	

The lowest literacy rates in the world are in sub-Saharan Africa at 58.7 per cent, the Arab states at 62.7 per cent, and South and West Asia at 58.6 per cent.

In these regions 40 per cent of the population is illiterate (UNESCO 2005a). There is a great variation within countries in these regions. Table 2.2 shows some of the lowest literacy rates and some of the highest rates in these regions. The contrast between countries is stark.

Table 2.2: Regional differences (2000-2004)			
Region	Average (%)	Male (%)	Female (%)
Sub-Saharan Africa			
Chad	25.5	40.6	12.7
Mali	19.0	26.7	11.9
Niger	14.4	19.6	9.4
Botswana	78.9	76.1	81.5
Congo	82.8	88.9	77.1
Zimbabwe	90.0	93.8	86.3
South and West Asia			
Nepal	48.6	62.7	34.9
Pakistan	48.7	61.7	35.2
Islamic Republic of Iran	77.0	83.5	70.4
Sri Lanka	90.4	92.2	88.6

Source: UNESCO 2005a: 280-7

Though the average rate is slightly higher in the Arab states, there are similar large disparities in this region: the rate in Jordan is 89.9 per cent, the United Arab Emirates 77 per cent, Morocco only 50.7 per cent, and Yemen 49 per cent, with a female literacy rate of 29.5 per cent, though this figure is 17 per cent higher than in 1990. In many other countries there have been similar improvements of between 10–20 per cent since 1990. There are many reasons for these differences; the higher levels in each region demonstrate that with the necessary financial resources, sound policies, and effective administration, high levels of literacy can be achieved in all regions of the world.

Disparity and exclusion

People most likely to be less literate are women, older people, people in rural areas, and sometimes those from larger households. The strongest correlation to literacy is the number of years schooling adults have received (UNESCO 2005a: 175).

In all the examples cited above the female literacy rate is lower than the male literacy rate. As well as this gap between the male and female rates discussed further in the next chapter, there are also significant urban rural divides with much higher levels of literacy in urban centres and very low levels in some remote rural areas. This reflects greater access to education and higher quality education in urban areas. For example in Ethiopia the literacy rate in the Addis Ababa region is 83 per cent, but it is 25 per cent in the Amahara region (UNESCO 2005a: 171).

There are also groups of people who for social, cultural, or political reasons have been largely excluded from mainstream education. In the global North such exclusion would apply to the Roma in Europe (Ringold *et al.* 2004) and the Gypsies in the UK (ODPM 2004), the Aborigines in Australia, and to indigenous peoples in many countries. In New Zealand a significantly higher percentage of Maoris than non-Maoris scored below the minimum level required for the demands of everyday life and work. This exclusion may result from 'a lack of recognition or respect for a certain group's cultural heritage, or from negative stereotypes that characterise group members as in some way inferior, primitive, backward or uncivilised' (UNESCO 2005a: 178).

Reduced access to formal education traps such groups of people in a cycle of illiteracy in addition to stigma and exclusion. Data on these groups is limited as 'population censuses disregard, or are not allowed to assess, the ethnicity of their populations' (UNESCO 2005a). Important exceptions are Bolivia, Brazil, Mexico, and Peru. Namibia is the only country to calculate literacy by linguistic group (UNDP 2004).

Language can be a significant barrier to access and achievement even when education is available. Approximately 300 to 350 million indigenous people across the world speak between 4000 and 5000 languages, live in 70 countries, and account for five per cent of the world's population. Over 60 per cent of tribal or indigenous people live in Asia, 17 per cent in Latin America, and eight per cent of the population in India are indigenous people, belonging to 400 tribes or groups. The literacy rates of indigenous women are the lowest in the world – in Cambodia among the Ratanakiri and Mondulkin communities, the literacy rate is two per cent for women and 20 per cent for men; it is eight per cent for women in Rajasthan, India (Rao and Robinson-Pant 2003). Nomadic pastoralist people are another group with very low literacy levels: less than one per cent among nomadic Fulani in north-eastern Nigeria (Ezeomah *et al.* 2006) and eight per cent in the Afar region of Ethiopia. In some countries governments have attempted to reach such groups by establishing boarding schools and hostels. Possibly with the best of intentions, attendance at these schools is sometimes enforced, rather than voluntary, as in the case of the San in Southern Africa (Le Roux 1999). Education can be part of an overt or covert policy of sedentarisation, settlement, and eventual assimilation.

Other excluded groups include low caste groups in India and Dalits in Nepal, and those excluded for being of a minority religion. Other groups live 'outside' society such as street children, homeless people, internally displaced people and refugees, illegal immigrants, and those in institutions such as prisons.

International policies

Universal literacy is now an international goal. The year 1990 was declared International Literacy Year and the decade from then until 2000 the International Decade for Literacy. Two important conferences were held at the beginning and at the end of the decade. In 1990 the encompassing vision in the Declaration on Education for All at Jomtien, Thailand, was one of universal basic education and education as a fundamental right for all people.
As UNESCO stated: 'For the first time policy makers and representatives of the world of education and civil society agreed on a world strategy to promote universal basic education for children, and to reduce massive illiteracy rates among young people and adults, especially women', (UNESCO 2000: 7).
In practice this broader vision narrowed. Donor agencies and national governments focused on achieving ten years of basic education for all children by 2015.

At the end of the decade in 2000, the conference in Senegal agreed the Dakar Framework for Action. This reaffirmed the vision agreed at Jomtien and reasserted education as a fundamental human right. The goals were:

1. Expanding and improving early childhood education

2. Ensuring that all children have access to free and compulsory primary education by 2015

3. Ensuring that the learning needs of all young people and adults are met through equitable access to appropriate learning and life skills programmes

4. Achieving a 50 per cent improvement in levels of adult literacy by 2015, especially for women, and equitable access to basic and continuing education for all adults

5. Eliminating gender disparities in primary and secondary education by 2005 and achieving gender parity by 2015

6. Improving the quality of education

Importantly two of these six goals, goals 3 and 4, reassert the importance of adult education.

To achieve these goals governments and organisations pledged to mobilise strong national and international political commitment, develop national action plans, and significantly enhance investment in basic education. The international community would develop strategies and mobilise resources and increase external finance for education, particularly basic education. At the heart of the initiative was support for national policies with aid delivered through a sector-wide framework – that is multilateral and bilateral aid to support national government initiatives in education. It was also agreed to monitor progress towards these goals, and a series of Education for All Global Monitoring Reports is being produced. The report on 'Literacy for Life' (UNESCO 2005a) provides an extremely useful comprehensive view of the current situation.

The increased focus on adult literacy was unfortunately not reaffirmed in the goals agreed at the UN Millennium Summit in September 2000, at which world leaders agreed the following MDGs:

1. Eradicate extreme poverty and hunger

2. Achieve universal primary education

3. Promote gender equality and empower women

4. Reduce child mortality

5. Improve maternal health

6. Combat HIV/AIDS, malaria, and other diseases

7. Ensure environmental sustainability

8. Develop a global partnership for development

Only goal 2 refers to education and none to adult literacy, though goal 3 on gender equality has implications for the education of adult women.

Though primary education is included, 'Literacy for Life' notes that despite the agreements reached at the conference on Education for All, few bilateral donors and development banks make explicit reference to literacy in their aid policies. Most refer to literacy as an instrument for reaching other ends (UNESCO 2005a).

The importance of adult literacy

The concept of universal basic education agreed at Jomtien included adults as well as children, yet the education of children has dominated the agenda and literacy for adults has become the 'Cinderella of the education system' (Swift 2006). It is ignored and attracts minimal resources both at national and international level. The theory understandably is that if every country can provide good schooling, all children and therefore all adults will eventually become literate. This ignores the fact that 104 million children are out of school; access to school is far from universal; and very high rates of withdrawal are common, leading to a low rate of school completion. In a third of the countries for which data is available, less than two-thirds of the pupils who enter currently complete primary education. Though the situation is improving, low school-survival rates are found in nearly 70 per cent of the countries in sub-Saharan Africa as well as in a number of countries in Asia and Latin America (UNESCO 2005a: 47).

Four years of sustained schooling is generally thought to ensure a reasonable level of literacy but it should be remembered that even in the richer countries many adults have only limited literacy and numeracy skills after 11 years of schooling. In many poor countries the quality of teaching and of teaching materials leaves much to be desired. Civil unrest and internal strife also disrupts the education system. Survival rather than education becomes the priority. When the national government is weak, if those opposing the government have the opportunity to indoctrinate young minds, schools can be part of the problem as well as the solution (Sommers 2002).

One of the key factors in children's attendance at school, particularly the attendance of girls, is the amount of schooling the parents received, particularly the mother. An understanding and knowledge of the education system by their parents is a determining factor in the education of children. Similarly when educational opportunities arrive for their children, many parents, particularly non-literate women, demand the opportunity to learn (personal observation on the DFID-funded Ammal project in the North West Frontier Province, Pakistan – Ammal is an Urdu word meaning 'practice').

Many people believe adult education is and will continue to be an essential element in the goal to achieve universal literacy, and that a twin-track approach of both adult and primary education should be adopted as a strategy to achieve universal literacy.

Current trends

One of the tensions in adult literacy is the difficulty of assessing the outcomes of financial investment in the area. A World Bank Report (Oxenham 2004) which reviewed World Bank programmes in five countries found the structures, programmes, and evaluations were not comparable, so it was impossible to identify best practice. The need to evaluate outcomes and, to date, the difficulty in doing so in adult literacy, has led to a greater emphasis on measuring levels of attainment and certification, and on the accreditation of training, in a general move towards the professionalisation and institutionalisation of adult literacy.

At the same time there is a move away from the learning of the technical skills divorced from the ways literacy and numeracy are used. There is greater awareness of the need to ground programmes in the reality of their social and cultural contexts and to focus on the literacy and numeracy required by individuals in their community. Thus the tools of ethnography and participatory rural appraisal (PRA; see Chapter 8) are being used to identify the social, political, cultural, and economic situation of the community in which the programme will operate, to ensure that the programme is relevant.

Innovative ways of teaching and learning are being developed. Foremost among these is the ActionAid REFLECT programme and Yo Si Puedo (see Chapter 8). Both have been introduced into many countries throughout the world. In REFLECT, the programme of learning is drawn up by local educators in the local context (Archer and Cottingham 1996). In Yo Si Puedo, developed in Cuba, a pre-determined programme using broadcast media and video trains student and educator simultaneously (UNESCO 2005a: 228). It claims that a learner can acquire a basic level of literacy in 65 sessions over two months.

Another trend is greater consideration of combining literacy with other adult training. Women's income-generation programmes have done this for a number of years but greater thought is now being given to how to include literacy and numeracy in a range of different areas at both basic and more advanced levels.

Perhaps the greatest innovation in the last ten years is the introduction of learning literacy and numeracy skills through information and communication technology (ICT). One example is the Open Basic Education Project in India run by the National Open School in 1998–9 on which some 130,000 students enrolled (UNESCO 2005a: 228). ICT has proved a popular introduction to literacy and numeracy in the UK, particularly among men.

In Egypt the ICT Trust Fund developed a project to train literacy educators to use ICT in their classes. Also in Egypt a mobile technology club overcame the problem of computer scarcity in remote areas by equipping two caravans and two buses with computers and taking them round the communities. However popular these programmes are, it has to be recognised that the use of ICT even in mobile units is far from a reality in many parts of the world.

Implications for planners

Designing and implementing effective literacy and numeracy programmes is not simple. Effective management and evaluation procedures are essential. Policy makers and programme managers will need to be aware of groups and communities who are not in the mainstream, those who are hard to reach for both geographical and cultural reasons. The solutions to these issues may not be easy, but unless they are addressed, the situation of those already excluded will become more severe. The aim of the declarations of EFA is for universal literacy; literacy for all, not just the few.

The publication of the report 'Literacy for Life 2006' (UNESCO 2005a) raised the profile of adult literacy. This provides an excellent summary of the situation in the first years of the 21st century. It re-emphasises the importance of providing opportunities for young people and adults to acquire the skills now considered essential for participation in most societies. The report recommends three priorities for action to meet the EFA goals:

- making youth and adult education a higher priority on national and international agendas;
- focusing on literate societies, not just on literate individuals;
- defining government responsibility for youth and adult literacy.

Such a substantial and detailed report contributes significantly to advocating an increase in national and international resources for adult literacy and youth programmes. The current policy of international donors is to respond to the priorities expressed by recipient governments. In some countries adult education and literacy is included in national development plans for education; in others it is not. It is therefore important that those involved in adult literacy advocate for adult literacy to be included in national development plans and national education plans as an integral part of any educational provision. It is also important to know which international policies governments have signed up to and how these are reflected in national educational policies.

Further reading

There are few books which provide an overview of adult literacy in the context of development. These resources provide readers with an understanding of the field:

B. V. Street, *Literacy in Theory and Practice*, Cambridge: Cambridge University Press, 1984.

D. A. Wagner, R. L. Venezky, and B. V. Street (eds.), *Literacy: An International Handbook*, USA: Westview Press, 1999.

H. Abadzi, 'What We Know About Acquisition of Adult Literacy – is there Hope?', World Bank Discussion Paper 245, Washington, DC: World Bank, 1984.

T. L. Harris, International Reading Association, and R. E. Hodges, *The Literacy Dictionary: The Vocabulary of Reading and Writing*, The International Reading Association, 1995.

UNESCO, Education for All Global Monitoring Report 'Literacy for Life', Paris: UNESCO, 2005.

3
Mainstreaming gender

Gender is a key concept in all aspects of development including education. This chapter explains international policy, and describes the social and economic disparities between men and women. It outlines the concepts underlying gender polices, gives a brief overview of the two major policy approaches to gender issues – 'Women in Development' and 'Gender and Development' – and stresses the importance of integrating a gender perspective into literacy programmes. Gender-mainstreaming issues are considered throughout the book and Chapter 9 includes a detailed section on planning for gender-integrated programmes.

What is 'mainstreaming gender'?

Mainstreaming gender means ensuring that the impact on both women and men is identified in all aspects of the programme:

- policy
- implementation strategies, curriculum
- materials
- monitoring
- evaluation
- staffing
- training and support.

The statistics in Chapter 2 give a clear indication of the disparity in the literacy rates of women and men. In all the countries cited, women have significantly lower levels of literacy than men. In Niger the female literacy rate was only 9.4 per cent in 2004. In Mali it was less than half the male rate and in Chad a quarter of the male rate. In all three countries, the literacy rate was exceptionally low, but in all three the female rate was even lower. Of the 104 million children worldwide who are out of school, 57 per cent are girls (UNESCO 2003/4: 6). Therefore when considering establishing policies for literacy or planning literacy programmes, it is essential to ensure that the policy clearly promotes literacy for women, and that implementation is female-friendly and overcomes the barriers to women attending. These barriers may be external to the programme – such as restrictions on movement and mixing with the opposite sex, or heavy domestic duties like child care and fetching water – or internal to the programme, due to unsuitable timing of classes or irrelevant curricula. In many countries, women are also the mainstay of subsistence economies and marketing activities in addition to their child-care and domestic duties.

Men can also be adversely affected if policies and programmes do not take into account their particular difficulties and needs. Ensuring that all staff in the organisation carrying out the literacy initiative take account of the situation of both women and men, ensuring equal benefits, is 'mainstreaming gender'.

The international declarations

The international declarations relating to gender include: The Convention on the Elimination of All Forms of Discrimination Against Women, 1979; The Forward Looking Strategies on Women, Nairobi, 1985; the Convention on the Rights of the Child, 1989; The World Declaration on Education for All, Jomtien, Thailand, 1990; The Vienna Declaration on Human Rights,1993; The Platform for Action agreed at the Fourth UN Conference for Women, Beijing,1995; The World Summit for Social Development, Copenhagen, 1995; Education for All, the Dakar Framework for Action, Dakar, Senegal, 2000; and the MDGs. Dates given are those when the declarations were adopted. There is clearly now a strong international commitment to educate women and girls which is enshrined in these international declarations of commitment to human rights, including women's human rights and the right of women and girls to education.

One of the first international declarations to address gender issues was The Convention on the Elimination of All Forms of Discrimination Against Women (CEDAW 1979); it condemned all forms of discrimination against women and promoted women's access to education and training. The Vienna Declaration on Human Rights (1993) recognised for the first time that the human rights of women and girls are 'an inalienable, integral and indivisible part of universal human rights'.

These declarations drew attention to the unequal opportunities experienced by women and by men. They recognised that patriarchy, a form of social organisation in which the father or eldest male is the head of the family and holds most or all of the power, can result in women having very little control over their lives. Societies and religions differ and they respect and oppress women in different ways.

Gender disparity

Decision-making structures worldwide are dominated by men at household, community, and national level. Representation in parliament reveals an extraordinary commonality across countries. In 2005 women comprised 17.9 per cent of MPs in the UK, 9.1 per cent in Thailand, 10.1 per cent in Chile, and two per cent in Bangladesh. Women comprised more than 30 per cent of MPs in only 14 countries (UNDP 2005).

It is easy to forget the conditions which women face in both industrialised and non-industrialised societies. Such conditions can include extreme forms of domestic violence including murder and wife burning, the destruction of female foetuses, the abandonment of infant girls, and trafficking women for the sex trade. Nearly 50 per cent of all female murder victims in the UK are killed by a partner or ex-partner (Amnesty International 2004). A high priority should be given both to preventing these abuses and punishing those who commit them. Very few men are convicted of wife burning in India despite repeated 'accidents'. Women may also face the absence of health care and maternity services, often severely exacerbated by the absence of female medical staff. In Nepal, for example, only 11 per cent of births are attended by trained staff (UNDP 1995). In some countries the desire to control women's sexuality and reproduction has led to honour killings, seclusion, purdah, female circumcision, forced and early marriage, and restriction on women's movement and freedom of choice. This denial of women's human rights in many situations has tended to lead those involved in international development to focus exclusively on women. However, the gender debate also analyses the situation of men and notes their disadvantage in the labour market at different times in different places, and the pressure of supporting sometimes very large numbers of people.

Disparity in male and female earnings

The labour market varies across continents and cultures, but everywhere women earn less than men. In the UK women's average earned income per year is a third of men's, in Turkey half as much, and in Pakistan a third as much (see Table 3.1).

Table 3.1: Average earnings in US$ per year		
Country	Female	Male
UK	20,790	33,713
Turkey	4,276	9,286
Pakistan	1,050	3,082
Uganda	1,169	1,751

Source: UNDP 2000

Women receive less training and have fewer opportunities for promotion. In addition, the labour market frequently places women in low-paid, low-skilled mechanised jobs producing goods for richer countries, or as home workers making low-cost garments for export to Europe and North America.

In some countries women are excluded from the labour force. This exclusion of 50 per cent of the working age population from the labour market has been seen by many as an inefficient use of human resources:

> *Among the weaknesses of society is the fact that the majority of its members are not involved in productive processes…in every society women constitute half the population. To condemn them to be ignorant and inactive occasions the loss of half the society's productive potential and creates a considerable drain upon society's resources.*
> (Abu-Hamid al Ghazali and Ihya Ulum al-Din, quoted in McCaffery 1999)

Other writers, such as Kabeer (1994) noted the value of women's non-waged productive work, and this is now more frequently recognised. However, the focus remains on production and efficiency and this is reflected in many literacy programmes.

Gender disparity in education

Of 771 million adults who cannot read and write, two-thirds are women. Despite international efforts to improve the level of education of girls and women, the percentage of women who are literate has risen by only one per cent since 1990 (UNESCO 2006: 67). The low level of literacy among women is due to the fact that fewer girls than boys attend school. The highest number of out-of-school girls, 23 million, is in sub-Saharan Africa, followed by 21 million in South and West Asia (*ibid*).The gender difference in literacy levels is greatest in South and West Asia and sub-Saharan Africa, though the situation has improved significantly in many countries (*ibid*: 63).

International declarations focus on education. The MDGs sought to eliminate gender disparity in primary education by 2005 and achieve gender equality throughout education by 2015. The goals in the Education for All Dakar Framework for Action specify adult literacy. Goal 4 seeks to achieve a 50 per cent improvement in levels of adult literacy, especially for women (UNESCO 2003/4: 27).

In a few countries the gender disparity is in favour of women. In Botswana, Lesotho, and Jamaica more women than men are literate (*ibid*: 67). In 2004 in the United Arab Emirates female literacy was 80.7 per cent and male literacy 75.6 per cent. In some countries including the UK, there is concern that girls are surpassing boys in educational attainment at almost all levels in almost all subjects. Gender policies also seek to redress this.

Gender concepts

The debates and discussions around women's development and empowerment are complex and the vocabulary has its own particular meanings. Different theories have different perspectives and have developed different frameworks. The debates and frameworks are briefly summarised below. The particular gender perspective and theoretical framework adopted by a literacy programme will affect its design and implementation.

Whichever concepts underlie a literacy programme, it is extraordinarily easy to overlook the particular needs of women even though most policy makers, donors, and governments are committed to women's development. The direction and detail of a literacy programme is determined at the planning stage. If gender issues are overlooked at this stage, the programme is likely to be gender neutral and will assume that the issues and the challenges are the same for women and men. As the majority of those who are not literate are women, they are more likely to be disadvantaged by a gender-neutral approach, but men can also be disadvantaged if their particular literacy and numeracy needs are not specifically addressed.

When discussing gender issues, particular words have particular meanings. 'Sex' and 'gender' are often confused. Ann Oakely (1972) defined sex as the biological attributes and gender as the psychological and cultural attributes. The gender roles of women and men are thought by many researchers to be socially constructed; that is, different societies ascribe different roles to women and men in the home, in the community, and in public life.

Gender disparity, as referred to earlier, is the gap between the involvement, achievement, and agency of women and men in social, political, educational, and economic spheres. In education it is the difference in the levels of enrolment and achievement between boys and girls. In literacy it is the difference in the numbers of literate women and men over 15 years of age. The aim is for gender parity – equal numbers of women and men who are literate.

We also have to consider the concepts of gender equality and gender equity, words which are often used interchangeably. Gender equality has a much broader meaning; it refers to the rights of both women and men to live a full life without restrictions due to their sex or social role in society and is therefore not confined to educational or institutional settings.

Gender equity refers to the organisation of social institutions; where there is no gender equity the institution does not have the same structures for employment or service delivery for women and men. Most institutions and educational organisations can be critiqued for lack of gender equity (Aikman and Unterhalter 2005: 3).

Policy approaches: WID and GAD

Within the debate about the education of girls and boys and the levels of literacy of women and men, different policy approaches have developed over the last 30 years. These define how women are perceived by predominantly male policy makers, planners, and donors. They are briefly summarised in Box 3.1.

Box 3.1: Policy approaches to gender

Policy	Description
Welfare 1950-70 (but still widely used)	Social welfare model following on from a colonial model in which women were seen as passive beneficiaries to be helped. Focused on women's child-bearing and domestic roles. Did not challenge women's subordinate position in society.
Equity 1975-85	Original approach to address the failure of modern aid policies to benefit women resulted in the declaration of the UN Decade for Women. Women seen as active participants in development. Challenged the subordinate position of women. Interventions aimed at reducing inequality with men. Critiqued as 'western'.
Anti-poverty 1970 onwards	Focused more on reducing poverty, less challenging in part due to criticism of the equity approach. Aimed to increase women's productivity and reduce poverty. Introduced small-scale income-generating projects. Critiqued as ignoring women's subordinate role, but still popular.
Efficiency 1980 onwards	Importance of women's economic contribution to development recognised. Inclusion of women seen to improve efficiency and effectiveness of development policies. Yet women also viewed as primary family carers. Approach popular with governments.
Empowerment 1975 onwards	Women develop greater confidence, and are empowered to take greater control over their own lives and decision-making processes. Emphasis on women's self-reliance is potentially challenging for men who hold power.
Post-structuralism 1990 onwards	Difference in the organisation of societies is recognised; all are relative thus no universal single answer but many different answers.
Human development 1990 onwards	Human capabilities approach. Emphasis on rights, capabilities, and freedoms.

Source: adapted from Moser 1989 and Unterhalter 2005

These approaches are not necessarily distinct. They overlap and many programmes have elements of each in them, but they all see women's education as essential to achieving their development aims.

Women in Development (WID)

The 'Women in Development' (WID) framework was for many years the dominant framework in which women's inequality was addressed. The WID framework was developed in the 1970s following an analysis by Boserup (1970) showing that the impact of agricultural development programmes on women was largely negative. A body of literature developed which showed many instances when women were excluded from the development process. Influential writers, including Brydon and Chant (1989), Ashfar (1985), and Kabeer (1994) addressed economic and agricultural spheres. WID was first developed as a policy initiative by the US Agency for International Development and it gradually began to impact on development policy more widely. Donors began to realise that the benefits to development did not necessarily accrue equally to women and men. Guidelines for project and programme planning were developed by several organisations.

An early guide was the European Commission's 'The Integration of Women in Development' (Commission of the European Communities 1991). The Overseas Economic Co-operation Fund of Japan produced 'Guiding Principles on Women in Development' (1991). One of the major outcomes of WID policy was the development by many governments of Departments of Women's Affairs, Women's Units, and Women's Bureaux. However, their success was limited. Research has shown that they were understaffed, under-funded, marginalised, and without access to the decision-making structures.

WID can be critiqued for viewing women in isolation, divorced from their domestic and social situation. It was gradually realised that the total situation needed to be addressed, that the strategies to improve women's situation affected their families and communities, who needed to be incorporated. However, the approach was instrumental in raising the profile and importance of women in development processes.

Gender and Development (GAD)

A different approach is that of 'Gender and Development' (GAD). This approach rejects a focus which looks solely at the position of women. Instead it focuses on social structures in which women have been systematically subordinated. 'Gender' refers to the social relationships between women and men and the roles they play in society which are socially, not biologically, constructed – and which change over time. The starting point is the social construction of gender, the concept that:

> Men and women play different roles in societies, their gender differences being shaped by the ideological, historical, religious, ethnic, economic and cultural determinants. Their roles show similarities and differences between classes and societies, and…the way they are socially constructed is always temporary and spatially specific.
> (Moser 1989:180)

Thus change is always part of the development of human societies and the position of women in any society is not fixed or immutable but rather changes over time.

GAD takes a very different theoretical position to WID. The GAD approach insists that focusing on women in isolation ignores their real problem which is their subordinate status to men. By seeking to reduce gender inequity, gender policies address the disparities experienced by either sex and therefore include rather than exclude men. Though in the vast majority of situations it is women who are disadvantaged in relation to men, gender policies also seek to redress disadvantage experienced by men.

Analysing the social construction of gender – the different roles women and men play in society – the GAD approach identifies four roles for women:

- *reproductive* – child bearing, child and family caring, and domestic tasks
- *productive* – paid work, subsistence farming, marketing and self-employment
- *community* – voluntary participation for the benefit of the community
- *political* – decision-making in the community and at regional and national level.

Practical and strategic gender needs

A key element in the GAD approach is the concept of practical and strategic gender needs (see Box 3.2).

> ### Box 3.2: Practical and strategic gender needs
>
> **Practical gender needs** are needs identified by women and men which arise out of their traditional social roles – their immediate practical needs for food, shelter, income, and health care.
>
> **Strategic gender needs** imply change in the relationships of power and control, with women challenging their subordinate position or men challenging their exclusion from roles traditionally occupied by women such as child care.

Women's education is not always welcomed. Fathers sometimes think it is unnecessary for daughters to attend school; husbands sometimes feel threatened if their wives are educated – so it is important to understand the distinction between practical and strategic gender needs. Some literacy programmes do address women's rights and their subordinate position in society, yet most, possibly the majority, do not aim to change women's position in society. They aim to address women's practical gender needs to enhance their traditional roles as mothers, wives, carers, unpaid and sometimes paid workers.

Challenging the traditional roles of women and men is rarely the stated aim of any literacy programme, but learning to read and write provides women with the ability to access previously inaccessible information and to communicate with others outside their immediate environment. Literacy can open up a world of different ideas and to that extent can change women's view of themselves and the society in which they live. There is also considerable evidence from research project evaluations that participating in literacy programmes increases women's self-confidence (Bown 1991).

Some considerations regarding GAD

GAD provides a practical way of addressing gender disparity but it also has its critics. Judy El Bushra (2000) argues that there are problems with the concept of gender as it is used in development planning and practice. According to her there are three main difficulties. Firstly there is confusion over the concept of gender, secondly a general assumption that gender transformation equals women's economic empowerment, and thirdly over-simplification of complex issues (El Bushra 2000: 56).

She argues that the distinction between 'sex' and 'gender' does not always apply. Though there is a fundamental difference in chromosomes (males x and y, females xx), not all individuals can be 'unambiguously identified as male or female at birth' (*ibid*: 58). Having the sexual organs of one sex or another does not always mean that people identify psychologically with that sex – hence people are bisexual, gay, lesbian, and trans-sexual. Divisions are not as clear-cut as the GAD framework suggests.

El Bushra contends that in equating women's economic empowerment with equality empowerment, GAD overlooks the fact that women are dominated in many areas of life and also do not always control the resources they earn. It is often argued that two-thirds of the world's work is done by women (World Bank 1985) but this figure is an average of very different situations. In some cultures limitations are placed on women working outside the home; in others the opportunities for work may be very limited for both women and men.

There is always a danger when complex theoretical ideas are systematised and translated into practice. Naila Kabeer (1994) suggests a social development framework in which the 'interconnectedness of women and men's roles are accepted and interlinked and how these operate in terms of power relations dominate all interactions'.

Gender equality requires institutional analysis in terms of rules and structures, resources, activities, who decides, and whose interests are served. Rao notes that:

> *Northern agencies and development banks demonstrate greatest resistance to approaches that stress gender as a power relation and the need for change at personal level: national development agencies, particularly those working with grass roots constituencies, appear more open to this transformatory agenda.*
> (Rao 1991)

It is also important to remember that gender is not the only aspect of social differentiation and possibly not even the most important one. Fundamental to how women experience and live their lives are race, class, and age. A high-caste Indian woman will have a very different life experience to a woman peasant farmer in Kenya or a nomadic Bedouin woman. The context in which any literacy programme will operate must be carefully analysed and these differences identified when undertaking a gender analysis. A young woman who has never been to school or who had to drop out for early marriage will need a programme very different in content and timing than an older woman will need. The timing, location, and content of the programme will need to take account of women's different life experiences and expectations in order to be successful.

Implications for planners

The GAD approach facilitates the implementation of the concept of gender mainstreaming by demonstrating the practical steps that can be taken. Gender mainstreaming is now accepted by many governments and organisations as an important way to maintain an equal focus on women and men. Policy makers and planners need to consciously consider how the programme will affect both women and men, and to keep images of women, as well as men, in mind when planning the literacy programme. Mainstreaming gender into programmes is not easy. Even those who are gender-aware often overlook the way different aspects of the programme relate to and impact on women and men differently. However, if a few clear and straightforward principles are followed, pitfalls can be avoided:

1. Ensure national, regional, or NGO policies are not gender neutral. They should relate clearly to both women and men.

2. State the intended outcomes in relation to both women and men; some outcomes will be the same and some will be different.

3. Monitor and evaluate the programme in relation to both women and men.

4. Implement programmes so that both women and men have equal access to all aspects of the programme – adapting programmes to particular circumstances.

5. Ensure curriculum and materials address the needs and aspirations of both sexes and portray both sexes positively.

6. Avoid gender-neutral language such as adults, people, tutors, and trainers, and instead refer to women and men trainers or female and male trainers.

7. Employ women and men at all levels of the programme and include women at senior management levels and as trainers.

8. In culturally traditional areas, work with community leaders and opinion formers.

9. Include an analysis and discussion of gender issues in all training.

This chapter has drawn attention to the importance of conceptualising gender as an integral part of the planning, implementation, and monitoring of literacy programmes, whichever approach to literacy is used. Developing a gender-integrated programme relies as much on men being gender-aware as on women. In north-east Nigeria, in Egypt, and elsewhere male organisers played a crucial role in addressing gender issues in their literacy programmes. Gender equality means just that: both women and men playing equal roles and achieving and assisting others to achieve their full potential.

Further reading

C. O. N. Moser, 'Gender planning in the third world: meeting practical and strategic gender needs', *World Development* 17 (11): 1799–825, 1989. This article lays out the principles of gender planning on which all the future debates are based.

C. Sweetman, *Gender in the 21st Century*, Oxford: Oxfam, 2000. This book contains a number of in-depth but easy to read chapters on women in development.

Department for International Development, *Gender Manual: A Practical Guide for Development Policy Makers and Practitioners*, London: DFID, 2002. This is an essential tool for planners.

L. Bown, *Preparing the Future: Women, Literacy and Development. The impact of female literacy on human development and the participation of literate women in change*, London: ActionAid, 1991. This very useful report identifies the positive impact literacy has on women's lives.

UNESCO, *Gender and Education for All: The Leap to Equality*, Education for All Global Monitoring Report, Paris: UNESCO, 2003/4. This is an excellent review of the situation of women and girls in education at the beginning of the twenty-first century.

Part II
Understanding Literacy

4

What do we mean by literacy?

This chapter outlines briefly the ways in which literacy has come to mean more than reading and writing, and how it is seen as embedded in life and communities. It describes four 'big ideas' about literacy as a framework for understanding the concepts and their associated programme approaches (our framework is based on original thinking by Lytle and Wolfe 1989). Each of the four main concepts of literacy – as skills, tasks, practices, and critical reflection – is described, the criticisms outlined, and our own views as authors set out. The four chapters after this one describe in more detail the ways in which each concept of literacy has been applied in literacy programmes.

Words and meanings

The word 'literacy' has taken on many meanings. Originally literacy simply meant reading and writing (sometimes as little as writing one's own name). But the term has expanded far beyond reading and writing. People often use terms like 'computer literacy' to mean the ability to use computers for tasks like word processing and email, and 'political literacy' to mean understanding how the political system works and how to take part in it. A Google search turns up many more contexts in which the term literacy is used:

- environmental literacy (for example www.enviroliteracy.org)

- information literacy (for example www.infolit.org)

- media literacy (for example www.medialit.org and www.medialiteracy.com)

- financial literacy (for example www.mymoney.gov and www.jumpstart.org)

- science literacy (for example www.project2061.org)

- emotional literacy (for example www.antidote.org.uk)
- cultural literacy (for example www.readfaster.com/culturalliteracy.asp)
- visual literacy (for example www.ivla.org)
- health literacy (for example www.hsph.harvard.edu/healthliteracy)
- business literacy (for example www.business-literacy.com)

The term 'something-literacy' is often used to mean a sense of mastery of skills and knowledge in the 'something'. This use of the term literacy has some key elements in common with the original use of the term:

- an element of obtaining *access* to information, which is often not so much about skills or knowledge as about power and participation;
- a sense of two-way *communication* – for every 'reader' there is a 'writer'. In areas like health and financial literacy there is as much emphasis on helping the creators of information materials to make them accessible, as on educating people to be able to read them;
- the concept of not just having skills but also *understanding* a topic well enough to be able to apply it and use it in one's own life;
- an aspect of *critical* awareness (for example being aware of the source of the information, the potential bias, how it might be used).

This book focuses on literacy in its original association with reading and writing, but the broadening of the term and the common elements above emphasise that literacy is more than a technical skill. Our own concept as authors is close to that adopted by the 'Equipped for the Future' framework in the USA (http://eff.cls.utk.edu/default.htm), also used as the basis for the 'Literacy and Community Empowerment Program' in Afghanistan. This takes literacy to include the wide range of communications, problem-solving, and interpersonal and lifelong-learning skills that people use in their daily lives.

Sometimes the overall concept of literacy includes numeracy, the application of mathematical activity in social and cultural contexts. Numeracy is a parallel concept to literacy: it is based on a set of mathematical skills (like estimating, measuring, and calculating) but needs to be viewed much more broadly in terms of how these are applied in life and shaped by the social and cultural environment. While we support the importance of numeracy, and sometimes discuss it with literacy in this book, it is not our focus.

Literacy learning through life

Adults use literacy for many purposes and acquire literacy in many ways. The motivation to improve literacy in adult life is frequently connected to change, whether in personal life or in society. Adults may recognise a need to improve their literacy skills when they start a new job, when their children start school and want help with homework, when a relationship ends, or when they lose their usual forms of employment. Societal changes demanding new skills in literacy and numeracy may include economic or forced migration, industrialisation and the passing of subsistence economies and traditional forms of labour, social and economic development, and deepening of democracy. Worldwide, fewer women than men are literate, as fewer girls attend school. When women become literate the power dynamics between women and men change.

What it means to be 'literate' has shifted over the years. Where once it was enough to be able to write one's name, by the late twentieth century it was clear that more was needed in industrialised countries. Governments around the world have at different times identified the need to increase the educational level of their population, primarily through schooling but also through adult literacy programmes.

These programmes have different ideological and political bases. Many are designed to up-skill the workforce, whether directly or through improving the educational level of women and consequently their influence on the family and therefore the future workforce. Some have had social or political purposes like embedding revolutionary change, changing the power dynamics between women and men, and extending democratic participation.

Concepts of literacy

Within the history of adult literacy education there are competing ideas of what literacy is and what should be done about it. There are at least four broad kinds of responses to the question of what is literacy:

1. Literacy means the ability – or the *skills* – to read and write (often called the competency approach).
2. Literacy means engaging in *tasks* that require the written word and are considered essential for life and work (often called the functional approach).

3. Literacy means a set of social and cultural *practices* linked by the use of the written word (often called the social practices approach).

4. Literacy means a tool for *critical reflection* and action for social change (often called the radical approach).

The rest of this chapter describes these four concepts of literacy, and the following chapters treat each one in more detail. They are not just abstract ideas, only relevant to academic study. Different ideas about literacy lead to different approaches to literacy education. Depending on what you think literacy is, you may design a different curriculum, train people to teach in specific ways, and create particular kinds of learning materials and assessment tools. The first step in developing literacy initiatives is to clarify what you mean by literacy, and the purposes of your literacy initiative.

Literacy as skills

The idea of 'literacy as skills' underpins much traditional schooling, where the focus is on skills such as phonics (sound–letter association) and knowledge like spelling and grammar rules. In adult literacy, these are generally found in primer-based approaches. Definitions of literacy based on skills are often called 'competency' approaches. The term is sometimes used loosely and confused with 'functional' literacy (described in the next chapter). To be clear, the term 'literacy as skills' is used in this book.

In the Organisation for Economic Co-operation and Development's (OECD) International Adult Literacy Study (IALS) and similar recent initiatives, literacy is conceived as a set of 'information-processing competencies' or skills. The literacy definition used in IALS surveys conducted between 1996–2000 has a primary focus on skills, but recognises the uses of skills in daily life:

> *The ability to understand and employ printed information in daily activities, at home, at work and in the community – to achieve one's goals, and to develop one's knowledge and potential.*
> (OECD 2000)

The skills are viewed as generic and independent of the context in which they are used, so a skill used in one setting can be applied in another and can be measured though tests. Indeed, the IALS uses common test items to measure literacy in different countries, providing comparative data across social, cultural, and economic boundaries. While the IALS has been the dominant measure of literacy skills in the North, it has also spawned similar kinds of literacy surveys in countries in the South.

The IALS has given new life to skills-based approaches to adult literacy education in countries of the North including the UK and USA. In England the Skills for Life strategy is a skills-based approach reflecting the continued dominance of school-based understandings of literacy. In the USA many adult basic education programmes have a similar focus on skills. The drive for performance accountability as part of New Public Management, widely adopted in such countries, requires measures of performance; the skills approach focuses on the kinds of skills that can be easily measured in standardised tests.

Critics

Critics of such approaches argue that literacy activities never exist in isolation but always within social and cultural contexts, and that these shape particular patterns of reading and writing (Street 1984). The literacies associated with different domains within a single society are different, and so are the literacies of different cultural and social groups within and between societies. If this is the case then international comparisons are inappropriate and misleading, and 'skills' cannot usefully be taught on their own.

As anthropologist Brian Street says, literacy is never simply a neutral and generic set of skills (*ibid.*). Literacy is always 'ideological' in the sense of being embedded in social, cultural, and political systems and reflecting issues of power and identity. The literacy of schools and government offices may seem more important than the literacy of the market-place. Power relationships mean that some literacy practices become dominant and others less visible and valued because they are associated with less powerful groups – like indigenous peoples, women, lower castes, or ethnic minorities.

Literacy is also linked to language and identity. For example, many indigenous communities with their own languages find it problematic to access the language of power. Literacy instruction in their own language may be more comfortable, and may reinforce their cultural identity, but may not address their ability to engage in the mainstream and with holders of power.

What we think

We accept the importance of mastering the skills and knowledge of reading and writing in literacy education, but recognise that these are not a single set of skills applicable in all circumstances. Learning the skills is not enough: the focus of literacy education must be on application of skills in the lives of learners.

Literacy as tasks

The recognition that literacy is more than an abstract set of skills to manipulate text led to a more contextualised view of literacy as the ability to accomplish tasks in daily life. This approach has generally been described as 'functional literacy'. However, as with competency the term has sometimes been used loosely. The term 'functional literacy' was first coined by the United States Army during the Second World War to indicate 'the capability to understand written instructions necessary for conducting basic military functions and tasks'. In functional literacy approaches, the abstract ability to decode text is less important than the ability to carry out life tasks – most often those related to work.

The definition of functional literacy adopted at the UNESCO General Conference in 1978 is still in use, almost 30 years after it was created:

> *A person is functionally literate who can engage in all those activities in which literacy is required for effective functioning of his [sic] group and community and also for enabling him to continue to use reading, writing and calculation for his own and the community's development.*
> (UNESCO 2005a: 30)

UNESCO's Experimental World Literacy Programme (EWLP) in the 1970s was intended to promote functional literacy for specific groups of adults in key growth sectors of the economy within certain countries designated as ready for economic 'take-off'. It was intended to distinguish this approach from one focusing on individual needs or aspirations – the important 'functional tasks' were to be defined by government. Thus the 'literacy as tasks' approach to literacy education as promoted by UNESCO and many national governments from the 1970s onward has a specific ideological connotation.

Later programmes taking a functional literacy approach incorporated a wider array of tasks in spheres beyond work, including citizenship, families, and community involvement. Nevertheless the functional literacy approach usually defines the important tasks in advance and from the outside.

Critics

Critics say that task-based literacy programmes have had limited success (Rassool 1999). They have failed to engage with the cultural and social complexities of literacy and by defining literacy so narrowly have failed to engage learners or achieve lasting changes in their lives. Functional approaches to literacy tend to ignore differences and impose a uniform set of literacy activities on everyone – the use of 'he' in the definition is no accident. However, within any society different groups and individuals perform different kinds of literacy tasks – women's and men's literacies may be different, rural and urban dwellers, market traders and farm-workers may all engage in different literacy tasks. One size cannot fit all.

What we think

Functional literacy approaches take an important step toward focusing on application, not just possession, of skills. However, functional literacy programmes have often taken a narrow and top-down view of literacy tasks. They have ignored important differences rooted in social and cultural contexts. By starting from the outside in defining what is important to learn, they fail to nurture autonomous and reflective learners. Learning to carry out literacy tasks is not enough: literacy education needs to be more responsive to the full range of literacy practices.

Literacy as social practices – social-contextual approaches

More recently, international development agencies have broadened their view of literacy to incorporate 'literacy as practices'. The report of the sixth meeting of the Working Group on Education for All, for example, upholds literacy as 'a broad range of continually evolving competencies and practices' (UNESCO 2005b: 11).

The social practices view of literacy has been shaped by the substantial base of research and theory built up in New Literacy Studies. In this concept, reading and writing does not simply involve the skills of encoding and decoding words, or carrying out specific tasks in isolation. Literacy involves values, attitudes, and social relationships – not just skills and activities. Different literacy practices (or literacies) are associated with different domains of life – home and family, school, the workplace, communities, religious institutions, politics. Some of these domains are dominated by males, especially the public domains. Others relate more to domestic and family spheres of life and more often involve women.

Reading and writing activities are embedded within social and cultural structures and help form these. Literacy practices are shaped by 'social rules that regulate the use and distribution of texts, prescribing who may produce and have access to them' (Barton and Hamilton 1998: 7). Reading and writing vary in their functions and uses across history and cultures. In some cultures, different literacies may have very specific contexts and uses: for example the Vai in north-west Liberia have different literacies for religious and market purposes (Scribner and Cole 1981).

The concept of 'literacy as social practice' has been adopted in the Nigeria Community Education Programme, using a method called Learner Oriented Community Adult Literacy (LOCAL). Facilitators identified with learners what they needed literacy for, and brought materials related to these needs into the learning group. The Community Literacies Project Nepal (CLPN) used a similar 'real materials' approach (see Chapter 7 for a more detailed discussion of these two initiatives).

Critics

Critics say that social practices approaches are too complex to be useful, especially in the global South. These approaches may require ethnographic research in advance in order to identify local literacy practices. They require extensive training of literacy teachers to prepare them to work in a responsive way. Social practices literacy can be difficult to assess and evaluate, with no simple tests.

What we think

Social practices approaches to literacy education may still be in their infancy but there has been enough experience to provide the basis for future programmes. Simplistic concepts of literacy have not proved successful in transforming lives and communities. Effective programmes will work with tutors and learners to understand 'literacy as social practice' and to create teaching and learning that is sensitive to the cultures and social groups for which they are designed.

Literacy as critical reflection – radical approaches

Literacy is often claimed to be a tool for 'empowerment' by those who engage in all of the approaches to literacy education. However, the development of literacy skills *on their own* does not necessarily lead to empowerment or social change. But literacy can be a tool for working towards transformation at both the individual and societal level. It can be geared towards combating poverty and deprivation, the enhancement of social justice, and the promotion of equal opportunities. Radical approaches to literacy engage people in actively constructing literacy as a tool for change. They incorporate experiential learning, critical analysis, and problem solving in the programme.

Freire was perhaps the most important influence on adult literacy in the last century. His theoretical analysis and teaching methodologies provided an alternative concept of adult literacy in both the industrialised world and the global South, showing how it could contribute to changing society rather than adapting to it. He defined the central purpose of education as 'reflection and action upon the world in order to transform it' (Freire 1972: 28). For Freire, the purpose of education is not to help people fit in and conform, not just to get a job or engage in economic activity, not only to enable women and men to read a voting paper or help their children in school. It is above all to enable people to engage actively in developing their communities and the world.

REFLECT is the most extensive current programme based on Freire's ideas, and has been implemented in some 350 organisations in over 60 countries. The programme follows in a long tradition of adult education creating a democratic space for questioning, analysing, and creating. REFLECT begins with social development and moves on to literacy 'at the point of need' and when there is a purpose for reading and writing within that development. REFLECT practitioners see the process of analysis and articulation of issues as an important part of literacy, and reading and writing as an element within this. This is in contrast to other development programmes that see literacy as an 'entry point' or a way of mobilising people into development activities following on from this (see Chapter 8 for a more detailed discussion of the REFLECT initiative).

Critics

Critics say that radical approaches to literacy education often focus more on social development than on learning to read and write. They say that facilitators are often inadequately trained as literacy teachers and as a result participants do not learn the reading and writing skills that would enable them to be independent and critical learners.

What we think

Literacy education does not have to be overtly political to take the radical approach of developing critical and reflective learners. While radical approaches to literacy can sometimes be another form of orthodoxy, taking a 'critical reflection' approach to literacy means being responsive to individual and community needs. It means encouraging learners to look beyond 'reading the word' to 'reading the world', as Freire put it. It supports learners to become actors in developing their own communities and societies.

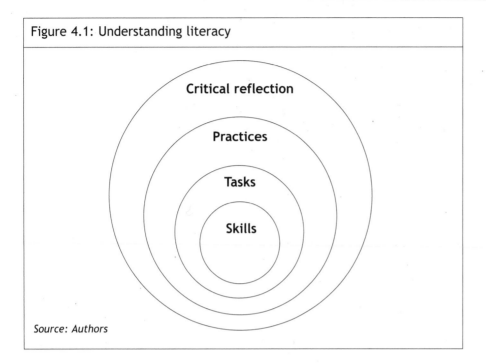

Figure 4.1: Understanding literacy

Critical reflection

Practices

Tasks

Skills

Source: Authors

Understanding literacy

The four broad concepts of literacy outlined here can be seen not so much as alternatives but as circles that nest inside one another (see Figure 4.1). All four approaches are part of the process of literacy learning, with the emphasis on each varying at different times and for different purposes.

Our idea of literacy has several layers. Literacy is rooted in the *skills* of reading and writing. These skills are used by individuals to accomplish *tasks* in their daily lives. These tasks are part of their literacy *practices*, socially and culturally rooted in the communities in which they live and work. Literacy can be a means for *critical reflection* on the world as a necessary part of becoming capable of creating change.

The next four chapters will look at how each of these layers of the concept of literacy has been put into practice in literacy learning programmes. Throughout the book our intention is to use these ideas to illustrate different ways to think about the crucial elements of designing literacy initiatives. Our hope is to encourage planners to be aware of alternatives and conscious of their assumptions and rationale.

Further reading

U. Papen, *Adult Literacy as Social Practice: More than Skills*, Abingdon, Oxon: Routledge, 2005. This is a review of literacy, language, and numeracy teaching and takes a social rather than a skills-based view and draws on recent research. It is a readable and practical guide to understanding literacy concepts and using them in education.

5

Literacy as skills

In Chapter 4 we outlined four broad concepts of literacy that have shaped many of the adult literacy programmes developed around the world. Now we will examine these concepts further and describe some examples of how they have been put into practice.

This chapter reviews 'literacy as skills' and examines the primer-based approaches that for some time have dominated literacy programmes in the global South, and the competency approaches that have become the key driver of national programmes in many industrialised countries. The advantage of both these 'literacy as skills' approaches is that they are tightly structured, uniform, and can be delivered on a large scale. The content of different learning sessions is pre-determined, and teachers have clear materials or set guidelines to follow. It is for these reasons that they have often been used in government or large-scale national programmes.

Primer-based approaches

A primer is a workbook especially designed to teach reading and writing, hence it will probably include reading exercises and sometimes ruled 'write on' lines with short words or sentences for students to copy. Primers are used predominately in the global South, where distribution networks are scarce, materials few, and teachers have limited education, preparation, or support for their task. Primers are a key resource for teachers and learners, because they organise language into elements that can be taught in different lessons. They are in many ways similar to primary school exercise books, and will usually have a number of simple images, drawn to reflect local culture and to illustrate the text.

In many ways the use of a primer provides a method for teaching rather than an approach. Primers can be based on a sound–letter association, recognition of word shapes, or on a broader Freirian approach with images for discussion, key phrases, words, and syllabic pairs. Primers generally assume a basic level of visual literacy, use a large amount of images, often in a codified format, and present each lesson or chapter in a similar way. Even when they are written and designed by people familiar with local culture and local issues they tend to be written *for* learners rather than *with* them. As such there is a danger that texts will use symbols or line drawings that might be difficult for people to recognise if they are unfamiliar with books. While all primers fix lesson content in advance (and some are even accompanied with a teacher's workbook giving a line-by-line script for what the teacher should say), different primers approach language in different ways.

An alphabetic approach

Many primers use an alphabetic approach (starting with individual letters) or ideographic approach (starting with ideograms, as in Chinese or Japanese). Individual letters or ideograms tend to focus on letter shapes, and attach these to images as a way of remembering them (such as a duck drawn into the letter d, a snake into an s, etc.). By starting with individual letters the focus is on reading and writing in parallel (rather than on learning to read first and to write later), and the early pages of the primer may contain lines for practising drawing curves or vertical, horizontal, or slanted parallel lines, as elements that make up individual letters.

Letter pairs

Some primer-based approaches may start by teaching syllabic pairs or phonemes, the smallest unit of sound (be, bi, bo etc. – see Figure 5.1). These primers may still contain images, short texts, and use key sentences, but the focus of the lesson is on learning to write and to read syllables made from a consonant and a vowel. The early lessons will start by teaching vowels or vowel sounds, and later lessons work through the alphabet, attaching vowels to different consonants. In practice this often leads to a lot of oral repetition as the teacher points to the syllable on the board and the class sound it out, repeating the new letter with each new vowel sound. Whole lessons might be spent echoing 'na, ne, ni, no, ta, te, ti, to' with little sense of what these mean. While this method might have some relevance for syllabic languages

(Portuguese, Spanish, and many African languages), it has sometimes been wrongly applied to languages which are not phonetic and have a less direct relationship between letter and sound such as English, Gaelic, and French.

Figure 5.1: Zulu primer

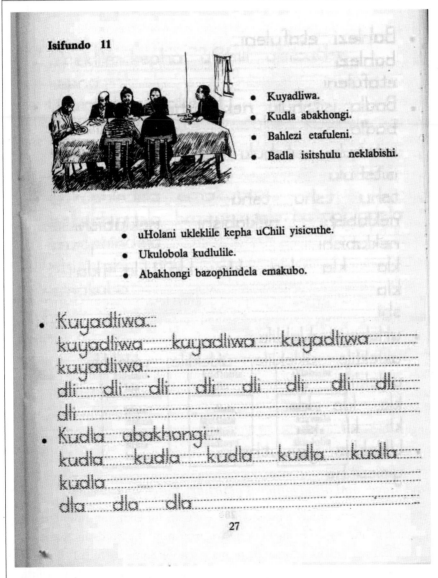

An example of a Zulu primer using a syllabic approach in which learners copy individual syllables related to images; sentences describing these, and individual words.

Source: The Bureau of Literacy and Literature in Johannesburg 1970, prepared under the direction of M. E. Whyte.

Whole word approach

Other primers start with a whole word approach. Tutors or facilitators are shown how to introduce words through pre-prepared cards with the chosen words written on them. The class is taught to recognise word shapes before going on to recognise letter shapes. Individual words – generally common nouns – might be illustrated with pictures. Spaces may be left in the primer for a student to practise writing the words themselves, or to add pictures of words they would like to write. Each new lesson in the primer might begin with a short text (for the tutor to read aloud, and the learners to try and follow) centred on the words to be learned that lesson. Primers based around whole words build up vocabulary, but this tends to be centred on the names of things, and there is less opportunity for learning grammatical terms or abstract nouns. It may take some time for students to progress to writing sentences about things they need to communicate, or using literacy in any meaningful way.

Key sentences

Some primers are organised around a new sentence for each lesson and start by presenting a whole phrase for students to learn, accompanied by a picture for discussion. The sentence might convey a short development message that programme planners feel their students ought to learn, such as 'Clean water is essential for health' or 'Cutting firewood destroys forests'. Students learn the meaning of the phrase or sentence first, and time may be spent debating it or deducing it from a picture drawn to convey its meaning. Through repetition in class they then learn to read it as a whole sentence, and gradually to recognise individual words. Primers organised in this way might go on to break the words down to individual syllables, and eventually to a 'letter of the day'. They might then take students through different steps of identifying that letter in longer words, writing it in the air, and eventually tracing it on a line in their primer.

Advantages and disadvantages of primer-based approaches

Primers have been heavily criticised in recent years for taking an autonomous approach to literacy, for being prescriptive in terms of the words and phrases that are learned, and for simulating primary school. Some are full of meaningless texts, designed only to introduce letters or words and having little relevance to learners beyond that. Others contain didactic development messages that can be seen as patronising to learners – instructing them how to 'live their lives better'. Primers are criticised for allowing very little or no scope for reflection on the needs of the learners, and for being artificial in that they are created only for learning literacy, rather than for using literacy outside the classroom. They are put together by programme planners, designers, or academics who, as literate people, may not fully identify with the needs and problems of literacy learners. Primers assume people will progress with the same needs and at the same pace.

An increased focus on the local and contextual significance of reading and writing from Brian Street and others has discounted primers as providing a neutral view of language, and de-contextualising literacy by fixing literacy learning in step-by-step, skills-based lessons. As a result some programmes have begun to abandon primer-based approaches in favour of other more creative ways of working. This has created additional difficulties. Without a primer or a class text more pressure is placed on facilitators to plan classes and to generate materials, often with very little back-up and in difficult conditions. (In rural areas there are generally no photocopiers, limited means for reproducing text, large classes, low light, and teachers who have had limited education themselves). And while teachers or programme planners often feel students will not want to 'be treated like they are in school', in some cases adults who have not had the chance to go to school as children want a school-type experience to feel they are 'really learning'.

While there are obvious dangers in using primers, there are other difficulties in abandoning them. Attempting to reproduce and circulate locally produced materials or real texts without infrastructural support is fraught with difficulties; classes with no materials have to be kept working at the same pace; and students who have no books to take home can feel cheated, as well as having fewer opportunities to practise what they have learned in areas where text is scarce. A primer is one way of 'fixing a lesson in advance' so that a teacher with limited training can take a step-by-step approach to working through it. While a creative and able teacher can respond to the needs of a class, a less confident teacher will flounder, and probably resort to ways in which they were taught in school. These methods are often far worse than the exercises written down in primers and can include meaningless repetition, rote learning, and copying of blackboard texts.

Facilitator/learner ratios vary hugely in many literacy classes, and are recorded as 1:8 in a programme in Mali, but 1:93 in programmes in Bangladesh and Zambia (*International Benchmarks on Adult Literacy* produced for the EFA Global Monitoring Report in November 2005). Benchmarks set by the EFA goals in 2005 recommend a ratio of at least one facilitator to 30 learners, but with numbers like these it is impossible to work entirely responsively and without some systemisation of classes.

Research shows that some learners do not apply what they learn in the primer to texts seen in everyday life; they see what happens inside a classroom as discrete from any reading that happens outside. A group of women learners in Nepal were baffled when asked if they could read signs written over a shop in a street. On further questioning about what they found difficult they replied 'I learn to read my primer and that is what I can read, our teacher teaches from the primer so that is what we know' (field notes, pre-project research for Community Literacies Project, Sankhusaba, Nepal, 1996). However, it has also been said that 'a good primer is better than a bad teacher with no primer at all' (Elda Lyster, consultant, Muthande HelpAge International project, 1999), and primers may have suffered a lot of bad press, particularly from new, more ideological approaches.

The survey conducted for the EFA Report on Adult Literacy (UNESCO 2005a) of 67 different literacy programmes cited primers as fifth in a list of 17 important sources of reading material, under newspapers, NGO-produced and learner-generated materials. In the end it may be easier to train teachers to work creatively with a well-written series of relevant reading material, and intersperse this with other kinds of discussions and exercises, than to aim for no pre-set materials at all. While the value of mass literacy campaigns and teaching learners in large groups to read outside of broader adult education programmes is heavily debated, these are still strongly advocated as EFA goals for 2015. If such classes are the way forward they will need to be supported by good quality materials.

Essentially, good practice should and does include a range of writing, reading, communication, and problem-solving activities, and students often feel more secure if they have some of these recorded in workbooks. Experiences of only producing teaching handbooks or teaching materials (rather than learning materials) in recent years have often led to students having almost nothing to read. Primers can supplement 'real books' or 'real language' with images, short texts, and examples of phoneme/grapheme relationships, or phonics. Providing they are not the only material used, and they are thoughtfully produced in consultation with learners, there is no real reason to avoid them.

Competency-based approaches and skills for life

Competency-based approaches to literacy start from the idea of literacy as a set of skills related to the interpretation or use of written language and symbols. They attempt to identify domains or types of skills and then organise these into different literacy levels. These skills are described in terms of the smallest elements associated with reading, writing, and counting – for example the ability to identify letters, to sound out words, or to read aloud a simple sentence. Key skills used to assess literacy are: reading and writing material written in the official language, reading and writing material written in the local language, oral mathematics, and written mathematics.

Different skills or competencies are carefully outlined in order to provide clear directions to tutors concerning what to teach. They are then arranged on a series of scales, ranging from low to high, or less to more literate. This means that any individual learner can be placed at a point on the scale according to what they are able to do. The skills are represented independently of context or use and are assumed to be transferable from one situation to another. It is therefore up to tutors to try and relate these to the lives and work of the participants with whom they are working.

Competency-based approaches to literacy have been most common in schools that provide set curricula with clear indications of learning for each school year. They were formally adopted in the North for adult literacy towards the end of the twentieth century. An individual's skills are measured through a series of different tests and this approach uses regular assessment to identify someone's progress according to the new skills that they have learned.

The English Competency approach

The English adult literacy core curriculum for literacy and numeracy draws heavily on the National Curriculum for English and Maths for schools. It includes speaking and listening, reading, writing, and numeracy, and in this way has some similarities with those primer-based approaches that seek to copy primary school textbooks. However, whereas primers produce set texts for learners to read, the competency approach describes the kinds of skills needed for texts of different levels. Consequently while primers pre-determine what learners will read about, a competency approach leaves space for a tutor to select appropriate material according to both its function and the kind of language within it.

The Australian approach

Australia also uses a competency-based approach and defines skills relating to language as well as literacy. This is not surprising, given their history as a country of immigrants, many of whom have needed to learn the English language. Competency-based training in Australia has especially focused on the skills of the workforce and follows nationally defined standards. It is based on an elaborate picture of the kinds of skills that make up literacy and language (known as 'communication'). The six aspects of communication are described as:

1. *Procedural* communication for performing tasks – e.g. giving instructions, or applying and following steps or procedures in order to complete a task.

2. *Technical* communication for using technology – related to the use of tools or machines.

3. *Personal* communication for expressing identity – related to expressing personal identity and goals (which includes such things as personal finances).

4. *Co-operative* communication for interacting in groups – related to understanding and playing roles in groups.

5. *Systems* communication for interacting in organisations – for both understanding and interacting in organisations, including educational institutions.

6. *Public* communication for interacting with the wider community – e.g. involvement in educational institutions, local community, or employment groups.

Levels range from a very basic understanding of giving instructions to quite complex levels, though the main focus of literacy programmes is on levels one to three. Beyond that, the competencies begin to address areas such as academic or specialised work-based reading tasks which in many countries is no longer understood as adult literacy.

Both the UK and the Australian approach talk about language rather than giving examples, but while the UK approach classifies this according to what a learner needs to do (e.g. use phonic or graphic knowledge to decode words), the Australian approach describes it in terms of the functions of different forms of language (e.g. communication for interaction in groups).

The International Adult Literacy Survey

The International Adult Literacy Survey (IALS) is a large, international survey of adult literacy that was carried out in 20 industrialised countries between 1994 and 1998, and attempted to draw comparisons between levels of literacy in different places. In order to do this the survey organised literacy skills in three different groups: 'prose' (continuous text), 'document' (specialised types of literacy such as forms, timetables, plans etc.), and 'quantitative' (often understood as numeracy). IALS defined literacy as 'the ability to understand and employ printed information in daily activities, at home, at work and in the community – to achieve one's goals, and to develop one's knowledge and potential' (Human Resources and Social Development Canada 2001 – see Box 5.1). While IALS took a neutral view of literacy skills by arranging these in groups according to their use, it also acknowledged different types of literacy, and in this sense has something in common with Street's concept of literacies discussed in Chapter 4. In describing language in terms of its different domains and then categorising people's abilities in these domains in terms of levels, IALS has also taken a competency approach to measuring literacy ability.

Box 5.1: The International Adult Literacy Survey

IALS domains of literacy skills

Prose literacy – the knowledge and skills needed to understand and use information from texts including editorials, news stories, brochures and instructional manuals.

Document literacy – the knowledge and skills required to locate and use information contained in various formats, including job applications, payroll forms, transportation schedules, maps, tables and charts.

Quantitative literacy – the knowledge and skills required to apply arithmetic operations, either alone or sequentially, to numbers embedded in printed materials, such as balancing a chequebook, figuring out a tip, completing an order form or determining the amount of interest on a loan from an advertisement.

IALS levels of literacy

Level 1 – persons with very poor skills, for example unable to determine the correct dose of medicine from information on the packet.

Level 2 – can deal only with material that is simple, clearly laid out, and in which the tasks involved are not too complex.

Level 3 – considered a suitable minimum for coping with the demands of everyday life and work in a complex, advanced society. It denotes roughly the skill level required for successful secondary school completion and college entry.

Levels 4 and 5 – describe respondents who demonstrate command of higher-order information processing skills.

Source: Human Resources and Social Development Canada (2000) Applied Research Bulletin, Volume 6.

Advantages and disadvantages of competency-based approaches

The danger of a list of competencies is that it breaks down tasks into meaningless elements that, while learners may be able to do them individually, do not necessarily make someone confident in dealing with written texts. The approach has been heavily criticised, particularly by those who take a more 'social practices' view of literacy. It does however provide a guide for tutors to work with. Even highly trained teachers, committed to responding to the needs of individual learners, can benefit from an organised framework to help them identify learners' needs. Working within this structure, teachers can decide with learners where to start, look at priorities, and identify gaps in skills and understanding. A confident tutor will see a list of competencies as a reference, and work from this to design a flexible and responsive programme. In many ways this is more useful than a primer-based programme which fixes the language to be used in advance: however, it does require a far more developed sense of literacy, and a familiarity with a range of different texts on the part of the teacher. Less experienced tutors may feel tied to this list of competencies, teach them mechanically and in order, and fail to adapt them to the needs and the context of those who will use them. In areas where there is poor infrastructure, or where programmes are dependent on tutors who have limited literacy themselves, attempting to respond to complex descriptions of language, and to find and utilise texts that fit these descriptions, is probably not realistic.

School equivalency

School equivalency is a term used particularly in South Africa, but also in other situations where adult literacy seeks to emulate standards set by school. Literacy progress is measured by a series of exams that are designed to be equivalent to the end-of-year exams set by primary and secondary schooling. In South African schools, end-of-year exams allow access to the next academic level, and children do not automatically progress with their chronological peer group. Consequently school equivalency is tied to year grades rather than to chronological age.

However in some European countries and in the USA there is also a process which determines 'reading age' through diagnostic testing, set according to an equivalent norm in child development. While now no longer used within adult literacy in England, special education still determines the reading age of an adult with special needs against this norm (and may for example assess them as having a reading age equivalent to a child aged 7 or 11), and this is also still the norm in the USA. The adult literacy curriculum standards in England are also calibrated against the equivalent key stages in schools, and newspaper headlines commonly comment on the number of adults 'with a reading age of 11'. Numeracy ability in England on the other hand, tends to be related to the national school curriculum, and work completed within a particular school year (for example year 6, end of primary, or year 10, pre-GCSE in the UK).

Access to higher education programmes

Perhaps the most radical school equivalency programmes are the Access to Higher Education courses that grew up in the UK in the late 1980s and early 1990s. There was relative freedom for different colleges to design their own courses, some of which applied to general discipline areas (arts, humanities, sciences), some of which were designed around specific degree courses, and some around unifying themes. Access students are taught to write the kind of academic essays they will need to produce on an undergraduate university programme, to reference books and articles correctly, and to read academic texts. In short, they focus on the academic literacy needed in university.

Access courses challenged traditional impersonal academic approaches, by beginning with individual experience, and looking at how academic discipline areas can help someone to make sense of their life experience. They provided a bridge from being an adult in twentieth-century Britain to questions raised in psychology, or sociology, or marine biology. As such they sought to demystify academia and make learning relevant while inspiring a passion and an enthusiasm for learning. They were the first in a series of programmes designed to widen participation in higher education and to appeal to the needs, interests, and lived experience of adults.

Box 5.2 describes the programme of equivalency education in Indonesia.

Box 5.2: Indonesia: 'Equivalency education'

Equivalency education in Indonesia has been designed for people who left school early for different reasons, those who wish to improve their knowledge and skills in order to get work, and those who need to update their technological skills. Equivalency education is part of the non-formal education system and consists of Packages (A and B) which are equivalent to primary education and junior secondary education, and lead to a certificate equivalent to the Junior Secondary School certificate. Package C is equal to the Senior Secondary School certificate.

The curriculum was designed by teachers and staff who were already involved in formal school-curriculum development, and was intended to help learners attain a similar target to formal schooling in terms of Minimum Competency standards. A range of skills and abilities are assessed including academic standards, moral development or behaviour management, and religious education and life skills, (local economy, work ethics, employable skills, and household management).

The equivalency programme is implemented through community institutions trained to carry out community-based non-formal education activities. The scheme is managed by the Department of National Education. Personnel include tutors, skills-based resource persons, Intensive Village Facilitators, and field staff from the Directorate of Community Education.

Teaching for all packages is carried out by tutors who are also teachers in formal schools, and learning materials consist of a series of competency-based modules, containing objectives, expected learning outcomes, activities, practices, and evaluation. These are designed to integrate academic principles with day-to-day life experiences, customised in principle to meet the different learning needs of diverse target groups. Learning outcomes are evaluated both through individual self-assessment integrated into each module and a final examination.

Learners can measure their performance by responding to problems posed in the exercises and by completing the learning activities provided in the modules. Examinations are organised nationally by the Assessment Centre responsible for examinations in the formal school system. The examinations are intended to ensure quality control and provide recognition to the graduates of the equivalency programmes. Examinations are held twice a year and those who pass are given a letter of successful completion. School books and other sources of learning materials such as printed media, multimedia services, and resource persons are also produced centrally.

Source: UNESCO 2006

Implications for planners

Approaches that focus primarily on the skills of literacy have tended to dominate traditional or large-scale literacy programmes. In the global North where infrastructure is good and tutors have generally had several years of education themselves, approaches have taken the form of describing competencies. They break skills down into the smallest describable element and specify in detail what these are. They are able to control what happens in literacy classes and offer a reasonably consistent experience in different parts of the country.

In the global South where materials are scarce, a skills approach has generally been implemented through the production of a primer which specifies what someone needs to learn when, and takes a teacher and a learner step by step through the learning process. While competency-based approaches and primer-based approaches vary – some starting with the alphabet and some with whole words or letters – they have in common the view that literacy consists of a series of separate but interrelated skills, and that these can be listed in the order in which they should be taught. Some competency-based approaches are tied into the formal school system and look for ways of integrating literacy graduates back into formal schooling. Others might provide a nationally recognised certificate of achievement that can be presented to potential employers.

Competency-based approaches do allow more scope for interpretation than primer-based approaches, so while individual skills are carefully specified, these can with competent teachers be applied to the different life tasks that people in different contexts need to undertake. However, primers have to specify not only the order in which people need to learn but also the material they learn with. As such they often misinterpret the needs of learners and provide them with material that has less relevance to their everyday lives.

A skills-based approach sits within an approach which sees literacy as a series of tasks. If links can be made between these, and skills are tied to the actual tasks that people need and want to undertake, they will have relevance to the literacy that exists outside the classroom. If a large-scale programme opts to take a skills-based approach, it is important to find ways of linking skills taught in the classroom with those that people need to use in their daily lives.

Further reading

A. Rogers, 'Some contemporary trends in adult literacy from an international perspective' on www.iiz-dvv.de/englisch/Publikationen/ Ewb_ausgaben/56_2001/eng_rogers.htm, also in *Adult Education and Development*, published by Des Deutschen Volkshochschul-Verbandes (DVV), volume 66, 2006.

M. A. Halvorson, *Literacy and Lifelong Learning for Women,* New York: Intermedia, UNESCO,1992. This is a guide to primer writing for women.

The website for the UK Skills for Life Campaign: www.dfes.gov.uk/readwriteplus/

Resources for Skills for Life tutors to use: www.skillsforlife.com/

Literacy Net: http://literacynet.dest.gov.au/ provides details of Australia's adult literacy programme.

6

Literacy as tasks

This chapter outlines an approach that conceptualises literacy as a series of tasks. While a competency approach defines the individual skills needed for reading and writing (and sometimes speaking, listening, and calculating) a 'tasks' approach begins by identifying the different tasks that people use these skills for. One of the best-known task-based approaches is functional literacy that starts with the functions (often economic) that literacy might fulfil.

A task-based approach links literacy to a particular purpose, acknowledging that different settings and different areas of work have different tasks associated with them. In some places these tasks are defined according to communities, with the recognition that one person can carry them out on behalf of others. In others a task-based approach focuses on the individual, and concentrates on what they can't do rather than what they can. This is measured against what it is assumed adults need to 'function' in a particular society or workplace, with the implication that every adult needs to do this for themselves. This approach can ignore the interdependence or skill sharing that is more often the norm.

Functional literacy

Functional literacy is, perhaps, the most dominant task-based approach, although this term has been used in many different ways at different times. What kind and level of literacy is needed in order for people to function in society is understood differently in different places, but a definition of this tends to be based around the activities of the dominant group. Consequently there are a variety of different definitions of what it means to be literate that range from simply signing your name, to being at a comparable level to children completing primary school, to being able to deal with complex form filling or lengthy instructions. Group memberships, social environment, and culture are rarely taken into account in the assessment and definition of literacy, and a functional approach, like a competency approach, aims to bring everyone to a similar basic standard.

As a concept, functional literacy emerged in the UK and USA in the 1970s, with the realisation that an increasing number of adults found it difficult to deal with some of the reading and writing tasks they met in their everyday lives. An early definition appeared in a statement made by UNESCO in 1962, and describes a literate person as someone who:

> can engage in all those activities in which literacy is required for effective functioning of his [sic] group and community and also for enabling him to continue to use reading, writing and calculation for his own and the community's development.
> (written by Gray in 1956, adopted by UNESCO in 1978, and cited in UNESCO 2005a)

The Experimental World Literacy Programme

The first large-scale functional literacy programme, the Experimental World Literacy Programme (EWLP), supported by UNESCO between 1965 and 1975, was based on the belief that functional literacy among workers would lead directly to increased productivity and therefore economic growth. The programme allied literacy programmes to 'third world development', stating that:

> Literacy programmes should be incorporated into and correlated with economic and social development plans.
> Literacy should preferably be linked with economic priorities and carried out in areas undergoing rapid economic expansion.
> (UNESCO 1965)

Investment in literacy was seen nationally as a way to develop a more competent and mobile workforce; a workforce both more adaptable and more open to change. In this way literacy and productivity became linked; it was assumed that the development of the first would lead to the development of the second, and 'functional approaches' began to dominate literacy programmes in the global South. While it has always been difficult to determine the time needed for someone to become 'functionally literate', it was assumed in the early days of the EWLP to be around six years.

Materials used in the EWLP included work-related information (the use of pesticides, the correct spacing of crops etc.) and the programme included elements of work-related learning alongside learning to read and write.

The EWLP was a global campaign with pilot programmes launched in 11 countries, in the hope that they would induce more widespread effects, but its impact was low and it has since been seen as a failure. This is partly due to its very rigid, work-based approach, and partly to a lack of collaboration with local people and local development agencies. The curricula, which attempted to be neutral and to set a consistent basic standard was, in reality, not functional in terms of people's different local realities, and there was little attempt to adapt literacy to local contexts. One of the key lessons of the EWLP has to be the importance of adapting literacy to local context.

There was some limited recognition of this at the time, and Malcolm S. Adiseshiah (Deputy Director-General of UNESCO from 1963 to 1970) linked the concept of functionality with that of justice: 'Functionality is a relationship between an independent variable, in this case literacy, and a dependent variable, in this case ranging from a person's environment to his fight for his rights of justice and equity' (Adiseshiah 1976). While Adiseshiah's view of literacy as an 'independent variable' suggests its neutrality and 'autonomous' nature, he does recognise the need to apply this in different environments. However there was not yet any realisation at this time that the literacy used for work-based messages and the literacy used for self-advocacy could in any way differ.

In the late 1970s, as the EWLP came to an end, literacy planners and policy makers began to question what 'functioning in a particular community' entailed, who defined that, the different functions of literacy, and the difference between economic and cultural functionality. These debates marked the beginning of a broader split between two views of literacy for 'liberation' and literacy for 'domestication' (added to by the writings of Paulo Freire; see Chapter 8 on 'literacy as critical reflection').

Freire was already beginning to draw attention to the need to see literacy in context, and to see that while it contributes to individual and community development, it is closely linked to environment:

> *Literacy does not imply the ability to remember phrases, words and syllables, out of context, things dead or half dead, but rather having creative and re-creative attitudes. It implies self-learning liable to lead an individual to intervene in his own environment.[...] Literacy cannot be dispensed from above, like a gift or a rule which is imposed, but must progress from the interior to the exterior, by means of the literate person's own efforts.*
> (Freire 1970)

The spread of the concept of functionality

In 1981 the national Adult Literacy and Basic Skills Unit in the UK (ALBSU) produced 'an approach to functional literacy' specifying the tasks needed in 'everyday situations', such as writing letters, using a telephone, skim reading a directory, or recognising street signs. It tried to outline in very specific detail what people 'need to be able to do' within each of these tasks, while nonetheless assuming a particular series of tasks that make up people's individual lives (as in the example in Figure 6.1 that shows pictures of building tools and explains their use). Another example of this is 'Read your Way to Bake a Cake' (1976). It is not difficult to recognise similarities between this type of approach and the different competency approaches described in Chapter 5.

Figure 6.1: Tools and their uses

This book is intended for craft lecturers in further education colleges who find that students on their courses have some difficulty with literacy and numeracy.

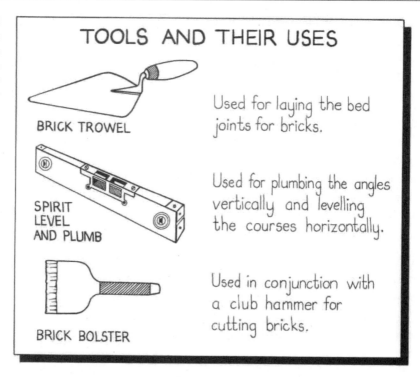

Source: © Basic Skills Agency 1983. Reproduced with permission.

The concept of functional literacy has dominated the literacy scene in many parts of the world for more than three decades. Although it is described in different ways in different places in almost all its guises it is in some way linked to either economic benefits or social benefits (health, housing, community benefit), or a mixture of both. And in most cases it is linked to the tasks people are assumed to need to undertake. Functional programmes also generally include some element of directive change or social conditioning, through messages determined by literacy providers. Economic benefits are presented in terms of either income generation or vocational skills (and income generation programmes or vocational training programmes are often run in parallel to functional literacy programmes), or linked to work-seeking skills (application letters, job searches, compiling CVs). Less commonly, programmes are integrated; they provide vocational training or income generation and literacy is embedded.

In the USA workplace literacy programmes began in the military and spread from there to other types of employment. The Egyptian national literacy programme is also run by the army, and they too have been a key proponent of functional literacy. Conscription brings together large numbers of people who are unable to read and write yet need to work as a team, and functional literacy programmes have proved to be a useful way of mobilising team work.

Although functional approaches focus attention on the needs of the society in which people live rather than on an abstract set of skills, they share with competency-based approaches a view of literacy that is not linked to the actual lived lives of learners. Tasks are usually defined before a programme starts rather than in discussion with particular learners; this implies that learners will be able to transfer learning from the programme to those situations in which they will need to use it, and this has often been seen not to be the case. Where programmes are too narrowly tied to particular sets of tasks, people are found to struggle with the use of literacy outside these specific contexts.

More recent functional literacy programmes have tried to take a holistic view of the different areas of someone's life at work and at home, and their need to develop their own potential and that of their community. The national functional literacy programme in the Philippines is one example of a programme that both defines functional literacy and provides indicators of the things all citizens should be able to do (see Box 6.1). Although these are broader and described in more general skills terms than the ability to carry out a range of tasks, they are also described as a progressive series of levels.

These levels move outwards from communication skills to critical thinking about these skills, to using skills for earning a living and personal and community development. The fifth level indicates engagement with broader issues of conflict, diversity, and the development of a more global perspective.

Box 6.1: Functional literacy in the Philippines

In the Philippines the Literacy Coordinating Council (LCC) has developed a national definition of functional literacy, linked into a national accreditation and evaluation framework. It includes a range of skills and competencies – cognitive, affective, and behavioral – which enable individuals to:

- live and work as human persons;
- develop their potential;
- make critical and informed decisions;
- function effectively in society within the context of their environment and that of the wider community (local, regional, national, global) in order to improve the quality of their life and society.

A set of major indicators of functional literacy accompanies this expanded definition of functional literacy, detailing the range of competencies an adult Filipino citizen will need to possess to function effectively in twenty-first-century society. These are:

1. Communication skills (including listening, speaking, reading, and writing in print and electronic media).

2. Problem solving and critical thinking (including numeracy, and scientific thinking).

3. Sustainable use of resources/productivity (including ability to earn a living as an employed or self-employed person, sustainable resources, and productivity).

4. Development of self and a sense of community (including self-development, a sense of personal and national history and identity, cultural pride, and recognition and understanding of civil and political rights).

5. Expanding one's world vision (including knowledge of other communities, respect and appreciation, diversity, peace and non-violent resolution of conflicts, and global awareness and solidarity).

The objectives for each of these domains describe the specific knowledge, attitudes, values and skills which must be mastered to be able to accomplish each level. The non-formal 'functional' curriculum is deliberately not a replica of the curriculum, or of grade and year levels in the formal education system. It attempts to be responsive to adult (and young adult) learners' needs and goals as they themselves see them. The Nonformal Accreditation and Equivalency Curriculum Framework aims to develop the basic skills that adult learners need to function successfully in their roles as parent, worker, and community member. The emphasis of the curriculum and learning materials is on providing learners opportunities for practical application of new knowledge and skills gained in order to facilitate immediate improvement in the quality of their lives. There is a greater emphasis on the functional relevance of skills than on core literacy learning.

Source: UNESCO 2006

Different understandings of functional literacy

Rogers (2000) suggests there are two different interpretations of functional literacy, the one leading on from the other. The first he sees as learning literacy through the everyday activities that people are engaged in, in order that they may function within that environment. This entails designing programmes for fisherfolk that enable them to learn to read and write through material that relates to fishing, and for farmers through material that is primarily agricultural. Programmes would be functional in that they would relate immediately to someone's daily tasks, concerns, and lifestyle; and literacy learning would be embedded in understanding and coming to grips with these tasks.

The second interpretation, which he suggests grows out of the first, sees the potential for expanding these task areas through literacy. Consequently someone learning to read and write through material associated with fishing can at the same time increase their knowledge of fishing. The danger of this second approach is that it has since led to a division between the learning of literacy and the learning of these additional tasks. It is therefore more common to find programmes that begin with a very generalised approach to learning literacy before learners move on to a more task-orientated post-literacy phase. In this case, rather than teaching people through the material encountered in everyday life, people are encouraged to learn literacy first and engage in task- or job-related training second. Many national literacy programmes consist of literacy and post-literacy stages.

A programme based on this concept of literacy and post-literacy stages is often easier to prepare than an integrated programme where literacy is learnt through people's everyday activities. This is beacause one set of literacy materials can be used with groups of people engaged in different activities, and a second set of task-related post-literacy materials prepared on a smaller scale for separate groups. In Senegal for example, farmers and mechanics from an irrigation scheme attended literacy classes alongside each other. Post-literacy groups for farmers focused on filling in forms associated with calculating inputs and outputs for rice growing, while mechanics worked through forms recording the fuel use and maintenance of water pumps.

In practice this approach to functional literacy reinforces a view of literacy as a neutral set of skills with little relationship to everyday life. It also indicates that people need a level of literacy before they can begin to apply it, and the development of initial literacy tends to focus on primer-based activities.

When people progress beyond this to the more task-focused activities of a post-literacy stage, these are often narrowly interpreted and can be limited to a single set of instructions or the completion of a particular set of forms. Programmes are designed by providers rather than by users, and literacy use is seen in terms of someone's role rather than their aspirations. There is a real danger that people will either lose or be unable to apply any literacy developed in the early stages of the programme, or have little sense of the use or value of reading and writing on any broader scale.

Functional literacy in context

Rogers recommends a return to the first approach, of developing the ability to read and write through using the materials that are available in everyday life (see the section on real materials in Chapter 14), and of engaging in development activities first rather than second. In this way literacy practices grow out of the things that people need and want to do rather than preceding those tasks that organisations feel they ought to undertake.

However, the term functional literacy has also been used in a more localised sense. Maria Luisa Canieso Doronila (1996), also working in the Philippines, defines functional literacy in terms of 'community activities'. She lists three types of activity: livelihood-economic (making enough money to live), socio-cultural (building friendships and spreading culture), and political-civic (understanding those procedures related to national structures). She suggests a way of defining what is necessary to function in each of these areas, and stresses their importance when designing programmes. She analyses each of these different areas in turn in terms of where and when people need literacy and where other forms of communication might be sufficient. Consequently although she uses the term functional literacy, she tries to define this by analysing the social context in which she is working. She sees reading and writing as one form of communication among others and literacy as 'communication and access to information' in very much the same way as the 'literacy for livelihoods' approach (discussed in Chapter 7). Her different 'domains' for literacy (livelihood-economic, social-cultural, or political-civic) are a useful way to look at the different ways in which literacy is used, and could be used with programme participants to help them determine their literacy needs in each of these areas.

Indonesia's functional literacy programme (see Box 6.2) is influenced by an understanding of the need for a contextually specific programme and a participatory action-learning approach. Consequently while it is referred to as functional, and is linked to the tasks of community development and income generation, it has a strong social practice focus. It is a good example of programmes that begin to merge the different understanding of 'literacy as tasks' and 'literacy as social practices'.

Box 6.2: Functional literacy in Indonesia

The new model for a functional literacy programme in Indonesia is based on a participatory action-learning approach and is a major change from the book-based, centrally-managed programme which was previously used. A comprehensive and systematic training programme was needed to prepare learning groups to take on more responsibility for their own learning, and to prepare each district to design and implement locally relevant versions.

In order to meet the needs of multilevel groups, the programme distinguishes three levels of literacy development: basic skills, guided learning, and self-learning. Basic skills activities focus on the needs of those individuals who do not have basic reading, writing, and maths skills. Guided learning activities provide an opportunity for learners to develop functional competencies for using their literacy skills in daily life. Self-learning activities focus on helping learners develop the capacity to meet their own learning needs through finding their own reading materials, joining community development programmes, planning their own income-generating activities etc.

The functional literacy programme is developed through a bottom-up strategy based on the following principles:

- Local context: the definition of 'functional' depends on what kind of reading and writing skills are commonly needed in the learners' community. People living in cities and working in factories and offices clearly need different information and literacy skills from people living in remote villages. Therefore, each group needs their own definition of functional literacy.

- Local design: each learning group makes its own learning plan based on the learners' needs and interests. The tutors receive training on how to assess the learners' literacy skills, knowledge, needs and interests; how to design their own learning activities and curriculum; how to make their own learning materials; and how to network with local organisations in order to find learning materials and resources.

- Participatory processes: the learners are involved in all aspects of the learning group. They develop their functional capabilities by making decisions and plans for their own learning activities. They also participate in finding and making their own learning materials.

- Action outcomes: results are measured in terms of the learners' ability to use their reading, writing, and maths skills for practical purposes in daily life; for learning by doing is the focus of every reading, writing, and maths activity from the very beginning of the programme.

Source: Department of National Education Indonesia, taken from ILO.org

---

A social practices approach, discussed in the next chapter, focuses on the difficulties surrounding transferability and on broader meanings of literacy that are determined by context. It also looks at possibilities for involving learners in determining some of these things for themselves.

Family literacy

Family literacy can be seen as a task-based approach to literacy in that it is linked to the tasks of bringing up children and developing in them an ability and an enthusiasm for reading. As an approach it brings together the skills and aims of those working in adult education with those involved in early childhood development. Programmes are aimed at parents, grandparents, and siblings, some of whom may find it easier to admit their willingness to help other family members than their own literacy difficulties. Sessions cover areas such as the health and welfare of children, baby massage, nutrition, behaviour management, and developmental skills as well as helping children to read and to develop their numeracy.

Some programmes, such as the one described in Box 6.3, are focused specifically on parents' associations and school involvement. They cover tasks such as registering children in school, acting as a parent governor, or marking and checking homework. Nor are they only for parents. Programmes in Africa encourage all community members to become involved in the tasks of school management, in raising awareness of the importance of primary education, and in developing the literacy skills that will enable them to do this.

Box 6.3: World Education Family Literacy Programme in Mali

A World Education* Family Literacy programme in Mali developed what they called an 'integrated approach' to adult education. While the tasks associated with learning included being able to manage and support a local parents' association and a local school, participants were encouraged to have an impact on educational access, quality, and equity in their communities. The individual literacy programme participants gained not only literacy and numeracy skills but also vital content relative to daily life, the Management of Parent Associations; and an experience of schooling, which sensitises them to their children's experiences and needs as students.

Like other functional programmes the course is divided into two phases – basic literacy and post literacy – and is taught by volunteer teachers drawn from the community and supervised by the Parent Association. The first phase, basic literacy, is a 250-hour course taught in mixed classes of around 20-30 people. In this phase, each lesson starts with analysis, by class members working in small groups, of an illustration of a social problem such as lack of water, failure to follow through on a course of vaccinations, and child labour.

The 100-hour post-literacy phase introduces the roles and responsibilities of the Parent Association. The goal of this phase is to ensure that literacy and mathematics skills become fluent, and that learners have the knowledge and capacity to participate actively in Parent Associations. The materials include text and stories that lead learners to grapple with management issues and concepts related to educational quality, and they become acquainted with Parent Association documents and accounting practices as they learn multiplication and division. Anyone who has completed the basic course in good standing has the literacy and maths skills needed to transition into the post-literacy course. In general, about two-thirds of the students continue into this phase, a few repeat the basic level, and a few discontinue participation. A small number of Parent Association Board Members who have basic literacy skills from other schooling join the literacy programme at the post-literacy level.

The literacy programme then becomes managed by the Parent Association in order that the whole model might become self-sustaining; selecting, employing, and training future teachers. With the support of World Education they design and run future training programmes for new teachers, developing among themselves the expertise to run these on their own in the future. Special literacy classes for the treasurers and secretaries of the Parent Associations are held which focus on use of the calculator and accounting for the treasurers, and note-taking for the secretaries.

* World Education Inc. is a US-based international NGO concerned with improving the lives of poor people through educational, economic, and social development programmes.

Source: UNESCO 2006

In South Africa, family literacy projects are based in pre-schools, crèches, and workplaces. Some programmes work with the children and parents together in small groups while others focus on teaching parents, and through them encouraging their children. Adults are able to improve their own levels of literacy while at the same time getting information and support on how they can help young children develop early literacy skills. The South African programmes generally start with mother tongue literacy and move on to English as children are needing to learn English in schools. The programmes, although based on the tasks of raising children, also carry a strong message that reading can be used to gain knowledge as well as being a means to relax and enjoy time alone or with others, especially children. Mothers and fathers are encouraged to read to their children and to make home literacy practices more visible. Apprenticeship reading schemes stress the importance of teaching children how and when to read by reading alongside them and allowing them to see how and where literacy has a place in everyday life.

In America and the UK many family literacy programmes focus particularly on families that do not have English, the main language of schooling, as a first or home language. Parents and other family members are encouraged to develop their own language and literacy skills by reading English texts associated with their child's development and education. Some programmes are delivered through classes that use child-focused material as learning texts; others are based in homes with tutors visiting and working alongside families. These programmes tend to be delivered directly in English and introduce parents and their children to English story books as well as to functional materials.

Work-based literacy

Work-based literacy, often categorised as work-based learning, includes literacy, numeracy, information technology (IT), and communication training delivered on an employer's premises and generally associated with the particular tasks needed within that organisation. These tasks may be related to styles of communication within or on behalf of the organisation (how to formulate particular letters, requests, or reprimands); how to complete forms or documents (time sheets, request sheets, audits etc.); or how to calculate quantities or amounts (financial auditing, stock taking). Training may be delivered by other employees of the organisation or by external groups specialising in training and subcontracted by the workplace. In some countries workplace training is government-sponsored and tied into national basic skills curricula; in others it is privately funded by an employer and focuses specifically on the tasks an employee needs to complete at work.

Work-related literacy demands tend to be repetitive and contextualised; that is, related to job-related knowledge that the worker already has. As a result, workers are often able to understand job-related material that in a functional programme would be placed at least two grade levels higher than other more general reading material that they would be able to understand. While some workplace functional literacy programmes have been limiting and limited (teaching only the vocabulary needed to work in a restaurant kitchen, for example), others have included the more generic application of reading and writing for problem solving on the job. Programmes can range from form filling to using email, to basic computing, financial accounting, or report writing for managers and supervisors.

There is a range of materials available on the Internet to help organisations undertake their own 'organisational needs analysis' in order to determine the skills and skill gaps of their employees. Employees who are new to an organisation often need to be inducted into particular work-based tasks, while others moving into more complex roles need to learn how to carry out the tasks associated with them. Though some work-based learning is instrumental and related to particular narrow tasks, other kinds of work-based learning have been found to increase an individual's earning capacity and the production and effectiveness of the organisation as a whole. Some organisations also take a more holistic view of lifelong learning by encouraging employees to continue learning above and beyond the specific tasks associated with their work. Work-based literacy has been seen as both contrasting with or supplementing family literacy programmes, by focusing on work-based rather than home-based tasks. It has also been seen as a good way of attracting men into learning programmes.

Literacy and post-literacy

A particular element of a task-based approach to literacy tends to be the separation of literacy into initial (or basic) stages and post-literacy stages. Many programmes throughout the world are based on this model, and assume that once basic, generic literacy skills have been learned, people can be taught to apply them to specific tasks.

This view has been challenged by many of the more recent approaches to understanding literacy, yet still tends to predominate. A report on post-literacy undertaken for the UK government's Department for International Development (DFID) in 1999 concluded that the separation of literacy into stages was unrealistic and not related to the way in which adults learn. Adult learning theory indicates that rather than learning and progressing in a clear sequential way, adults learn through a variety of very different experiences in different spheres of life all the time. People who come across complex writing practices in their work or daily lives are often able to undertake these because of their familiarity with them or interest in them, and it is not helpful to 'grade' texts or stages in the way that graded readers are produced for children in school. Definitions of literacy also vary greatly in different parts of the world (from decoding, recognising the alphabet, signing one's name, to reading 'simple' texts), and it is misleading to try and identify a point at which initial literacy ends. People are developing and expanding their different literacies all the time.

However, separating 'learning literacy' (in initial literacy programmes) from applying literacy to specific tasks (in post-literacy programmes) has been shown to be largely unworkable by the failure of a large number of functional literacy programmes. While people may undertake the new tasks they have been introduced to for a short period of time, it is unlikely these will continue if they are not part of their daily lives. The incidence of people successfully completing a literacy programme, but being unable to read or write a year later, is high.

Implications for planners

Key aspects of a 'literacy as tasks' approach are a strong link with economics and an attempt to define literacy needs in relation to people's lives. Task-based programmes are often planned on a regional or national scale. But, while the spread and development of literacy has been closely linked to the need to trade, the expectation that increasing literacy will increase income or production is not straightforward. There is a real danger in the rhetoric that teaching people to read will benefit them financially; the relationship between literacy and income generation is far more complex.

If people are to engage with literacy tasks in a meaningful and long-term way, the tasks need to be part of their learning from the start. Adults on the whole learn by doing, and will have become familiar with reading through the literacies that surround them on a daily basis. Large-scale functional programmes generally take their content from the activities of the dominant groups in any culture, without necessarily paying attention to the specific activities that individuals need and want to undertake in relation to their family, work, or cultural roles. They also often ignore the fact that many of these tasks can be done by different members of a family or community and that not everyone needs to do all of these for themselves. A task-based approach becomes meaningful when it is based on the particular activities that an individual feels they need to be able to do, rather than on those that are assumed to be necessary to function effectively.

Some agencies have tried to cater for the literacy needs of specific groups through a two-tiered development, with a generic basic literacy programme followed by a more specific post-literacy course. However, this ignores the cultural implications of initial literacy and suggests that people will only engage in 'functional activities' once they are literate. Because adults take on a whole range of work or social responsibilities before learning to read and write, they will already have an advanced understanding of those tasks that bear some relationship to their lives.

The rationale of a task-based approach begins with defining literacy, then identifying the tasks people need to undertake, and then teaching them how to do these. However, experience has shown that this will not work unless people are involved in identifying and specifying these tasks for themselves. Where people have coped with activities for many years without writing, they are more likely to adopt familiar strategies to continue to cope in a similar way than to begin, for instance, suddenly reading these for themselves or writing them down. The need for literacy and the way in which it is used locally needs to be fully understood before embarking on the planning of any large-scale programme.

Further reading

M. L. Canieso Doronila, *Landscapes of Literacy: An Ethnographic Study of Functional Literacy in Marginal Philippine Communities*, Hamburg: UNESCO Institute for Education, 1996.

M. S. Adiseshiah, 'Functionalities of literacy', *Prospects* 6 (1): 39–56, 1976.

UNESCO Education Sector Position Paper, 'The Plurality of Literacy and its Implications for Policies and Programmes', available at: www.unesco.cl/medios/biblioteca/documentos/plurality_literacy_ implications_policies_programmes.pdf (last accessed July 2007), nd.

7

Literacy as social practice

A social practice model of literacy directly challenges the standard concept of literacy as a set of abstract, cognitive skills that are transferable and independent of social factors. This chapter provides a brief overview of the theoretical concept of 'literacy as social practice' and gives examples of how the theory has been put into practice in Britain, Nepal, Nigeria, and Egypt. The chapter also considers the 'literacy for livelihoods' approach which links into social practice as well as the more functional approaches. The chapter concludes by indicating some of the implications for practice and how this approach can address the differing needs and aspirations of both women and men.

Different descriptors

'Literacy as social practice' is referred to in different ways as the social model, social literacies, the socio-contextual approach, the socio-cultural model, or the socio-linguistic model. All these models view literacy and literacy acquisition in slightly different ways, but whether in the global North or in the global South they all view literacy as a variety of practices dependent on specific cultural and social realities, rather than as a method of teaching people the technical skills of reading, writing, and calculating (though these are of course included).

All the models stress differences in context and meaning and the ways in which different societies use reading and writing. There are many forms of literacy, and different kinds of literacies involved in different tasks such as completing a job application form, reading the Koran, or filling in a voting paper. These demand different skills, different cultural knowledge, and different processes of selecting information. There is a long history of seeing literacy in its political, cultural, social, and economic context, and developing programmes related to these. In this chapter we will look at four aspects of 'literacy as social practice': social literacies, community literacies, literacy for livelihoods, and local materials.

Social literacies

Some of the early adult literacy programmes which began in the second half of the twentieth century might be described as 'welfare-oriented'. They were socially conscious, looking at the literacy people needed to improve and broaden their lives. The beginning of the literacy campaign in England in the 1970s was an extension and a development of this work. These programmes were learner-centred and 'the idea of a dynamic contextual basis to the curriculum was well understood' (Stock 1982). It was believed that context-related learning led to the development of learner-directed activities and locally produced materials in a pragmatic and practical way. A range of practical materials which directly addressed the current situation such as the Benefits (unemployment) and Health Packs were produced by groups of practicising tutors with funding from the Adult Literacy and Basic Skills Unit. Students' own writing on different subjects began to be used as reading texts, and the student writing movement developed out of this early work. The literacy and numeracy programme in Ireland is similarly based on these ideals, recognising the different needs of both different groups and different individual learners, and developing and adapting materials to meet their particular requirements.

New Literacy Studies

In quite a different context, Street (1984) analysed the specific social and cultural uses of literacy in a community in rural Iran. The complex and context-related uses of literacy he noted led to the development of a body of academic work referred to generally as 'New Literacy Studies' (NLS). This makes the distinction between what Street calls an 'autonomous' approach to literacy and an 'ideological' approach. The autonomous model is that used in schools and traditional literacy programmes. It views literacy as a set of technical skills, transferable from one context to another. An ideological approach sees literacy as a context-dependent series of practices, with particular social and cultural implications. An autonomous approach assumes the teaching of literacy will bring various cognitive and economic benefits;

the ideological approach challenges this, claiming it is rooted in particular western dominant conceptions of knowledge and identity. It points out that in many parts of the world people achieve many things without being literate, and suggests that there is no direct relationship between all types of literacy and increased income. As such it uses the plural form 'literacies' rather than literacy, to indicate the range of different literacies used in different spheres of life. As the NLS is primarily a way of thinking about literacy rather than thinking about literacy acquisition, it provides no single approach to teaching or learning. Rather it problematises the whole notion of teaching people to read by questioning assumptions and asking 'which literacies' should be prioritised in which programmes. However, it does have a number of important implications for planners of literacy programmes and, in certain areas, has influenced practice.

A social literacies approach is concerned with the recognition that multiple literacies exist in time and space, and that these carry different meanings for different groups of people. It differentiates between what are termed literacy events and literacy practices. A literacy event is described as 'an occasion in which a piece of writing or reading is integral to the nature of the participants' interactions and their interpretive processes' (Heath 1982) (for example writing a shopping list, sending a text message, reading a political poster). Literacy practices are described as 'a means of focusing on the social conceptions of reading and writing' (Street 2003) – that is, the use of and the meaning given to reading and writing in different cultural contexts and environments. An understanding of both the use and the meaning will enable planners to look at the different ways in which reading and writing are used in a particular society and how they relate to accessing information and power structures. For example, people learning to read and write a particular language or dialect may be prevented either from understanding, or from being taken seriously, in particular settings. Literacy educators need to be aware of the different forms of literacy that exist and the range and significance of how they are used.

It is also important to relate the experiences of learning to read and write to the reading, communication, and calculation that people engage with in their daily lives. What is 'correct' in one situation, for example writing in complete sentences and paragraphs, is not necessarily correct in another situation – writing a shopping list, notes for a course, or setting out a scientific experiment. Ideas of 'correctness' in writing are seen as context-dependent, and therefore a programme needs to be based on research into, and a full understanding of, the uses and meanings of literacy locally. Participants in literacy programmes are often involved in undertaking this research.

However, even theorists recognise the difficulties that this approach creates for planners attempting to design and run programmes appropriate for large numbers of people. If the complexity of literacy activity is taken into account, it becomes difficult to implement any one main approach. Involving participants of literacy programmes in reflective and critical research, and training them for this task, takes time and money as well as huge amounts of human resources. There are limitations to a focus on local activity as people may not only use their reading and writing locally, and may not only want to learn about events in their immediate locality. For many people, reading provides access to other societies, other parts of the world, and new information. This can be a real motivation for improving their skills.

By moving away from a view of 'literacy as skills' that are transferable between contexts, the NLS approach often minimises the length of time needed by adults to acquire the skills to read and write at all. However, the thinking behind the NLS has influenced a number of approaches discussed here, and has been specifically applied in different ways to a number of programmes.

Community literacies

Community Literacies Project Nepal

The term 'community literacies' was used to describe an approach piloted in Nepal in a project designed by Education for Development, funded by DFID, and managed by CfBT. It ran between 1998 and 2003 and drew on the work of Alan Rogers on real literacies and on the social-practices approach of New Literacy Studies (Maddox 2004). The purpose of CLPN was to 'enhance literacy practices, communication and access to information' in local communities.

CLPN was based on the idea that:

> Literacy is something that is used and learned in the community, rather than just being an activity of the literacy class, and that communication and access to information can be enhanced through oral, visual and literacy based practices.
> (Maddox 2004)

The programme was based on an ethnographic approach which began with an extensive piece of participatory action research into local literacy practices before deciding where to place resources.

Perhaps the most radical aspect of community literacies was its focus on 'communication and access to information' above merely reading and writing, and the attention given to literacy use as well as literacy acquisition in the local community. It supported activities that promoted other means of accessible communication, such as radio towers; classes and literacy teaching were only a very small part of the programme. As opposed to functional literacy which looks at the skills an individual needs in order to 'function' in society, community literacy looks at the skills needed within the community, and at who might best attain these skills on behalf of the wider group. People were therefore encouraged to 'learn what they needed' – which for the majority of people might only be signing their names – in terms of writing, as well as broader skills in terms of oracy and assertiveness. For example, rather than everyone in the community learning numeracy, the secretary of a credit group was taught to keep accounts. Individuals were taught scribing skills in order to write letters on behalf of others who could not do it for themselves.

A second important aspect of CLPN was the focus on the providers of written materials as well as the users. The project team ran workshops for publishers, newspaper editors, local government offices, and other community projects in producing 'reader friendly' materials, using simpler text, larger script, local languages, and gender-sensitive content. CLPN took a participatory 'process' approach rather than being 'centrally pre-planned'. In practice this meant working 'bottom-up' with local partners to design, implement, and evaluate literacy-support programmes to address those local issues. Research was managed locally and used to inform planning and implementation. Although time-intensive and less cost-effective than traditional centrally planned programmes, programme staff argued that it provided greater critical learning, local ownership, and sustainability.

The project was piloted in two areas of Nepal, and worked through and with organisations already engaged in the area. These organisations helped forest-user groups in the forestry programme to assess how they communicated information through the programme and who had access to it. They worked with health workers to assess their information strategies and they worked with local council offices in order to redesign and rewrite many of their official documents and forms. These programmes were designed with local partners in order to address issues identified by local people. It was clear from the baseline study that different people were looking for different types of support. Programmes were intended to be relevant to people's different expressed needs rather than being planned with the 'blanket' approach of one programme for everybody, and to reflect the diverse use of different types of 'literacies' in communities.

Political unrest in Nepal and the end of the project funding period makes it difficult to assess the impact of this as an approach. The approach still presented key challenges over 'going to scale' and long-term sustainability. Most providers do not have time to invest in intensive initial research and staff who were able to work in such a locally specific and responsive way were scarce. However, the experience provided a number of important lessons that could be taken forward in other ways. These include:

- Broadening the concept of literacy to focus also on communication and access to information – looking at the different ways in which people communicate or are able to access information, and how one might support the other. This might lead to the presentation of information in different ways, and finding means to support auditory as well as written records.

- Working with literacy providers as well as literacy learners – understanding the importance of influencing the kinds of texts that are produced, and the way they are written, in order to ensure accessibility.

- Combining literacy use with literacy learning, and helping people to develop their literacy outside the classroom and 'at the point of need'.

- Working with learners to research and question literacy use, either prior to a programme or as a group activity within it. This might include mapping local sites where literacy takes place, looking at who uses which, what kind of literacy use exists there, what it provides to those who can access it, and which kinds of literacy people want to acquire.

Learner Oriented Community Adult Literacy: Nigeria

A different and perhaps less ambitious community-based literacy programme was developed in Nigeria. The adult literacy component of the Community Education Programme (1996–2001) supported by DFID was termed 'Learner Oriented Community Adult Literacy' (LOCAL) (McCaffery 1999). The programme operated in four geographically and culturally different states. It focused on identifying the literacy people needed in daily life, and responded to this using the catchphrases:

> *People learn to read in order to read something*
> *People learn to write in order to write something*
> *People learn to calculate in order to calculate something.*
> (adapted from Barton and Ivanic 1991)

Each of the four area projects was managed at local level by a local community manager supported by a committee led by a community leader. The committees drew up their annual programme. Some of the successes of the projects were the total commitment of these committees, the leadership exercised by the local chiefs and the ardos (leaders of the nomadic pastoralists), and the way the latter encouraged their wives and the women in their communities to attend literacy groups.

In each of the four projects, PRA research methods identified the literacy practices in the community: the languages used in the public sphere, in economic activity, in sign boarding, advertising local businesses, and in the home. Developing a programme of learning demanded considerable skill from the locally recruited facilitators. Participants in the literacy groups worked with their literacy facilitators to draw up a learning programme based on the literacy and numeracy that the participants required in order to operate more effectively in their communities. Recognising the skill required, the national co-ordinators on the programme developed a nine-stage framework to enable the facilitators to put the theory into practice (see Box 7.1).

Box 7.1: A nine-stage framework

1. Establish learning aims with participants.
2. Prioritise aims with participants.
3. Conduct a survey of literacy and numeracy events with participants.
4. Assist participants to chart their economic activities and daily routine.
5. Match prioritised aims (2) with related events and activities (3 and 4) and collect real materials relevant to the aims.
6. Identify specific learning points in the materials collected.
7. Identify the teaching task required for each learning point.
8. Develop clear objectives for each lesson.
9. Develop practical and participatory learning activities to engage participants in their own learning.

Source: McCaffery et al. 1999b

It was hoped that by developing a programme that was not dependent on external expertise, materials, finance, or indeed buildings, the programme would be self-sustaining when the period of funding ended.

Recording your community's experience is one of the features of a social practices approach. This proved very popular in Nigeria in all four projects. One positive outcome was that the Fulani semi-pastoralist communities continued to write their own stories for their own communities and make these into small reading books, even though money to reproduce them was not available once the project ended.

Capacity Enhancement for Lifelong Learning (CELL): Egypt

Estimates of the number of adults in Egypt who are not literate varies between 11 and 17 million. UNESCO (2005a) calculates that 17,270,000 people over the age of 15 are not literate. Regional and national surveys tend to produce lower estimates. Since the early 1990s the government has developed a national programme to reduce this number. Technical support was provided to the General Authority for Literacy and Adult Education (GALAE) by DFID over a ten-year period. The first phase of the project operated in two governorates and was successful in introducing a more flexible approach into a hierarchical and centralised structure, which included introducing community-based activities and publishing two books of learners' writing in colloquial Arabic.

Operating on a much larger scale in six governorates and building on the first phase, the purpose of the second phase was 'to reduce illiteracy in target groups through a community participation and development approach' (Sabri and El Gindy 2003). CELL did not propose to measure its effectiveness solely on the number of people who passed the literacy test, but on the extent to which it promoted positive changes in the lives of the target groups:

> Literacy provision becomes then primarily part of a conscious raising process supporting poor and disadvantaged people's efforts to improve their relationship to the world.
> (Sabri and El Gindy 2003)

A key factor in implementing this approach was the appointment of field co-ordinators who supported the literacy facilitators in aspects of community-development work. They worked with GALAE branch staff (who work in the GALAE offices in the governorates) and community members to develop local teams committed to promoting and supporting literacy classes, and conducted a social and economic analysis of the communities using PRA methodologies:

the success…in terms of attendance and certification correlated with the strength of the community teams. Unplanned outcomes included identifying active female community members, building schools, and solving local sanitary and pollution problems.
(Ashraf *et al.* 2005)

The formal evaluation stated that what was termed an experimental literacy project 'was more effective than the existing national programme in maintaining good attendance rates, reducing drop out and achieving higher graduation rates – even in poor rural communities reputed to be 'closed' and difficult' (Oxenham and Hamed 2005). It also found the costs per successful student were twice as high, though it suggested that these could be substantially reduced to a level even below that of the national programme (*ibid.*).

The importance of this large-scale project is that it demonstrates that conducting a literacy programme on the basis of local interests, without the aid of a set syllabus and primers, is practicable and is within the competence of tutors with secondary education who have received good quality training.

Literacy for livelihoods

Literacy for livelihoods, as promoted by DFID in 2000, brings together more traditional ways of thinking about literacy as 'an effective vehicle for poverty reduction' and 'enhancing progression towards international development targets' (some of the aims associated with functional literacy) with a broadening of the concept to 'literacy, communication and access to information' and an awareness of context. In this sense it brings together some new and some traditional understandings of literacy.

The livelihoods framework has been described as follows:

A livelihood comprises the capabilities, assets (including both material and social resources) and activities required for a means of living. A livelihood is sustainable when it can cope with and recover from stresses and shocks and maintain or enhance its capabilities and assets both now and in the future, while not undermining the natural resource base.
(Chambers and Conway 1991)

One of the advantages of the livelihoods approach is that by taking a more holistic approach to the use of literacy in people's lives, it enables programmes to be evaluated with regard to their impact on participants' own development and self-confidence, and their social and communal interaction. Participants in literacy programmes often mention the outcomes as increased confidence and an increase in social activity, but such outcomes are not measurable purely in terms of skill development and have therefore been difficult to account for in the evaluation of programmes and projects. The concept of livelihoods includes not only the resources to make a living, but also the ways in which a person's assets and capabilities 'give meaning to a person's world' (Bebbington 1999: 2002). As Maddox (2005: 6) points out, Sen's (1997) concept of what people can achieve also includes the ability to avoid and escape morbidity and mortality.

In a post-conflict situation in south Sudan, project managers adapted the sustainable livelihoods framework to identify the 'vulnerability' context – the high numbers of displaced and traumatised people, the breakdown of community cohesion, the high level of inter- and intra-community tension, the destruction of the infrastructure, the neglect of agriculture, and the limited economic input from external sources. The programme, which was combined with conflict resolution and peacebuilding, initiated a range of activities including strengthening local organisations, skills training, peacebuilding activities, and mediation, as well as setting up literacy circles and training literacy facilitators. The impact of the programme was assessed in relation to all these areas, not only to literacy and numeracy acquisition and use.

Another view of literacy for livelihoods relates particularly to income generation and three types of programmes: those that offer literacy teaching prior to programmes focused on income-generation training; those that offer literacy teaching after income-generation training; and those that embed literacy within income-generation activities.

Whether focusing specifically on income generation or taking a more holistic view, a feature of the livelihoods approach is the attempt to embed literacy in other programmes such as agriculture, forestry, fishing or health, rather than to place responsibility for acquisition solely on specific literacy classes.

Local materials

The social practice approach stresses the use of locally relevant and locally produced materials. Most of us have to negotiate and deal with a range of literacy and numeracy materials every day. 'Real' or 'everyday' materials mean the literacy and numeracy materials that are part of the everyday environment.

The absence of learning materials specifically developed for adults both in the North and the global South has meant that facilitators have frequently had to draw on materials from the local environment and use these in the literacy class. Everyday material was used from the very beginning of the literacy campaign in England in 1974, largely because there were no adult primers or textbooks. Tutors at that time had no option but to identify the literacy and numeracy needs of the students and draw on those – whether these were drawing up estimates for painting and decorating, filling in child-benefit forms, or learning the names of the streets in which posters had to be put up. At the Friends Centre, Brighton, tutors made small packs of photographs of common street signs such as 'hospital', 'exit', and 'entrance', in order to ensure learning was useful. The particular circumstances of people's lives affected the materials used. Thus during the period of job losses and high unemployment, words like 'redundancy', 'unemployment benefit', and 'application' were essential and for many, easily remembered words.

This use of materials from the immediate environment was echoed in the global South. Facilitators and participants sought out the materials used in their communities, uncovering the existing literacy practices, and identifying the most important texts for people to read. The approach involves introducing these materials right from the start of initial literacy learning in order to help participants engage critically with these materials and transfer what they learn in class into practices in their daily lives.

The approach has some similarities to the 'real books' approach that surfaced in the UK and the USA during the 1980s, as a way of teaching children to read in school. A number of teachers began to question the value of using reading schemes for literacy learning, as this was an artificial way of introducing and practising new letter combinations and increasingly complex words. Their argument was that by using real books, new readers would be able to adapt to different types and styles of written texts, and get used to books of varying degrees of difficulty in word length and sentence structure. They argued that on reading schemes children appeared to progress with their reading mainly because of what they could remember and repeat. However, when they were then faced with new texts written in different styles, they had not developed the ability to anticipate meaning from the elements they were able to understand.

Those advocating a social practice model believe that adult learners do not need to learn through a previously determined sequenced order, but learn best by practising, and by incorporating the learning of the technical skills into those tasks that are central to their lives. Consequently a learning programme that is based on local social practices is more likely to have both meaning and relevance for learners and at the same time introduce using literacy into the things that people need to do anyway. Literacy is therefore not seen as a new and additional skill, but one that is bound up with existing social practices.

Rogers' (1994b) research into post-literacy separated materials into those that were specifically designed for literacy learners, and those that have a specific communication or information purpose in everyday life. He provides a useful model for introducing 'real materials' into literacy learning that shows how they can be integrated from the beginning in literacy classes, and gradually expand to form the basis of literacy programmes (see Figure 7.1).

A 'real materials' approach also advocates the importance of critiquing the materials that are used, and the assumptions that lie behind their production. By being involved in the identification and selection of texts, participants have a view as to their importance and usefulness as materials, and can also be encouraged to discuss the way they are presented and produced. They can assess their social and cultural significance, who writes them, who reads them, and the messages they contain. Consequently rather than being passive learners they are critical users of literacy texts.

Programme organisers in both the North and the South have advocated for general reading materials which are accessible to the 'new reader'. They have encouraged producers and providers of materials to consider readability and the needs of new learners in newspapers, forms, government documents, information packs and so on, to ensure that materials in the public domain are accessible to readers of different abilities (Stock 1982).

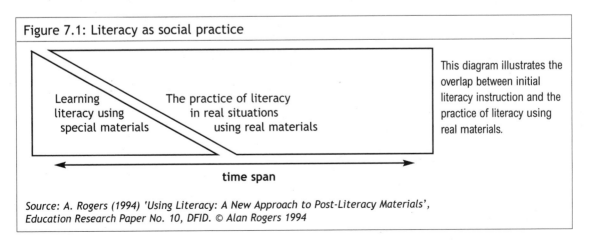

Figure 7.1: Literacy as social practice

Learning literacy using special materials

The practice of literacy in real situations using real materials

This diagram illustrates the overlap between initial literacy instruction and the practice of literacy using real materials.

time span

Source: A. Rogers (1994) 'Using Literacy: A New Approach to Post-Literacy Materials', Education Research Paper No. 10, DFID. © Alan Rogers 1994

The 'real materials' approach then does not start with the classroom but with what the participants are already doing in their daily lives. It does not start with a deficit model of what the participants lack and what they cannot do, but builds on what they are already doing. Non-literate persons receive and write letters; communicate with the school their children attend; fill in essential forms; exchange money for goods and services; travel to town; obtain ration cards; learn from election posters, signs, and other notices; understand signs over buildings and symbols on various locations such as a hospital, taxi park, or station; scan advertisements; and inspect packages in the shops they visit or on the medicines they get (ALBSU 1982; ALBSU 1985; Barton 1994; Baynham 1993; Heath 1982). Using these materials in the class ensures that the learning is utilised and practised in daily life.

Gender integration

The principle and practice of ensuring that literacy programmes are gender-integrated was discussed in Chapter 3. Here it is important to mention that one of the advantages of viewing literacy as a social practice is that by being aware of different contexts and different communities, the differing needs and aspirations of women and men can be readily addressed. The programmes can and should address these differences, which operate in a range of situations; in the public sphere and the private sphere; in employment and household production; and in decision-making processes. A social model of literacy can develop the literacy and the numeracy women and men require in different situations.

Social practice approaches will relate to both women's and men's roles and the literacy needed to carry out these roles effectively. Such approaches should address women's practical needs by developing the literacy needed to help women in their daily lives in the communities in which they live. One of the advantages of socially orientated literacy programmes is the opportunity they provide for reflection, and there is considerable evidence that participating changes women's view of themselves and of society. The programmes do not necessarily seek to change women's roles in society but the increase in confidence women experience on becoming literate 'so that I can respect myself' is a step towards this (this statement is from a woman in Pakistan, cited by Bown 2004).

However, women's roles are not always obvious. When literacy facilitators attending a training course interviewed a dozen women in Gedaref, eastern Sudan in order to discover their literacy needs and aspirations, their findings surprised them. They had assumed women were dependants and their literacy needs would be related to the domestic sphere. Instead, the survey revealed that three-quarters of the women interviewed were heads of households. They were divorced or their husbands had died, were absent working overseas, or were incapacitated. This situation meant that a considerable conceptual shift on the part of the facilitators was required. The women were not dependants; they were breadwinners and required literacy and numeracy for the public as well as the private sphere (Abuzeid and McCaffery 2000b).

In Canada, researchers discovered that in Spanish-speaking immigrant communities, women rather than men attended literacy classes in English as it was their role to deal with officialdom and bureaucracy (Barton and Ivanic 1991).

Implications for planners

Social models of literacy constitute a real opportunity to provide a programme that addresses the *real* needs the learners, not the *supposed* needs. This requires the tutors or facilitators to have considerable skills in analysing the environment, working with the participants to determine their literacy and numeracy requirements, translating these into learning objectives, and developing sessions for learners to acquire the technical skills to achieve these. It is therefore essential that tutors and facilitators receive good training and continuing support. The social model not only addresses the technical aspects of literacy and numeracy; it goes further and locates these, as the name suggests, in the social context. It is an active model of learning in which dialogue and discussion are an essential part of the learning experience.

Those that implement the programme will therefore need to:

- understand the social practice model and realise that while progress in reading and writing is the purpose of the programme, so also is the development of the individual and the community;
- have a knowledge of basic research processes or PRA;
- have a good understanding of the economic and social context;
- have a knowledge of and preferably an ability to speak the local languages;

- be aware of culture and gender issues;
- appreciate the skills and knowledge that learners bring to the programme, and the importance of working with them to identify their goals.

In addition to these skills and knowledge, a social practice programme will also require a level of budget decentralisation in order to provide the support that tutors in different localities and different contexts might need.

Tutors for the social practices model also have to be skilled facilitators able to address both the needs of individuals and the needs of the whole group simultaneously. They have to be able to encourage participation and build trust and confidence among group members. The tutor crucially has to know how to work with group members to identify their goals and aspirations, and how to develop learning strategies and activities which over a period of time will enable individuals and the group to achieve their learning goals. This is no easy task. An effective system of recruiting, selecting, training, and supporting tutors is essential.

While all social practice models provide the opportunity for critical reflection, some models place more emphasis on critical reflection and the possibility of change than others. These are discussed in the next chapter.

Further reading

B. V. Street, *Literacy in Theory and Practice*, Cambridge: Cambridge University Press, 1984. This is Brian Street's important seminal work.

D. Barton and R. Ivanic, *Writing in the Community*, Thousand Oaks, CA: Sage,1991. This book provides a very interesting account of the ways different communities use literacy.

P. Fordham, D. Holland, and J. Millican, *Adult Literacy: a Handbook for Development Workers*, Oxford: Oxfam, 1998. This is a very practical and useful book on aspects of implementing literacy programmes.

8

Literacy as critical reflection

The social model of literacy discussed in the previous chapter challenges the dominant technical model. By recognising the complexity and richness of literacy practice it also challenges the idea of deficit and the correlation of 'illiterate' with 'ignorance'. 'Literacy as critical reflection' goes one step further. By focusing on what participants both require and aspire to, but also on what they can do, it opens up the space for critical reflection at the communal and individual level and also for reflection on society and its organisation.

This chapter provides examples of how 'literacy as critical reflection' can change individuals and societies. It shows how literacy can be used as a tool for liberation or as a tool for oppression. It describes Paulo Freire's psycho-social model of literacy, PRA research methods, and how these are used to analyse the social and economic environment to ensure that a programme is relevant to the context. The chapter shows how ActionAid merged the methodology and methods of PRA and Freire to develop REFLECT. It outlines the development of the student writing movement in the UK and demonstrates how writing and producing local literacy materials encourages individual and communal critical reflection, addresses strategic gender needs, and becomes a stimulus for change.

Literacy for change

Testimonies from across the world demonstrate that acquiring literacy as an adult has a profound impact. It changes people in many ways – what they can do, their perception of themselves, their social interaction, and sometimes their economic situation (what Charnley and Jones (1979) call enactive, personal, social, and socio-economic achievements). Individual changes can be comparatively small but have a considerable impact on a person's life.

'I understand the television now' was a comment made in both Egypt and the UK; more personal was 'I can now talk to my mother-in-law'. Acquiring the ability to read and write can also go beyond individual change. Learning to read can change and transform societies at the macro level (as in Nicaragua after the Sandinista revolution) and at the micro level of community and household.

Observers and community leaders have commented on these changes. During the evaluation of the Community Education Programme in Nigeria, Ardo Umuru, one of the Nomadic leaders, commented on the changes in his clan: 'They know how to live with people now. The main thing is co-operation between people' (British Council 2002).

At one level this is adaptive literacy; on another it indicates a significant change within a community. A community able to reflect on the processes it is involved in is better able to analyse and effect those changes. Nomadic communities are frequently marginalised. Introducing literacy learning with these communities can enable them to take far greater control of their situation. In one example, they were able, after literacy learning, to challenge officials and police who continually harassed them over tax returns and identity papers.

The ability to access information beyond the immediate environment can have a powerful and transformative effect. An ex-member of the Ulster Defence Force participated in the truth and reconciliation process in Northern Ireland facilitated by Archbishop Tutu. Speaking on a BBC television programme in April 2006, he said that 30 years earlier he had killed a Catholic youth 'simply because he was a Catholic', but in prison 'I learnt to read and began to understand more'. Reading gave him information and understandings he had never had as a youth. It transformed his world view, and consequently changed his actions.

In this example the access to information resulted in critical reflection, which transformed the individual's view of himself and his society. While social models of literacy can be used in different ways, including enabling people to function better in the existing social order, a more critical approach to literacy can challenge the existing social order.

Underpinning the idea of literacy as contributing to critical reflection is Gramsci's (1968) idea that everyone is a philosopher. He argued that everyone could develop critical awareness, not simply to question dominant ideas, but also to envisage alternatives (Mayo 1997).

Literacy and power

Without the skills to access and interpret information for themselves, people are dependent on others; often on those who hold power. The issue of power and who holds it is conceptualised in the ideological model of literacy. This recognises that literacy not only varies with social and cultural norms and concepts 'but its uses and meanings are always embedded in relations of power...it always involves struggles for control of the literacy agenda' (Street 2006). Becoming literate can involve:

> Learning to be critical readers and writers in order to detect and handle the inherently ideological dimension of literacy and the role of literacy in the enactment and production of power.
> (Lankshear et al. 1997)

This ability to access information and to communicate can change the dynamics of power in the religious, political, and domestic spheres. When viewed in this light it is easy to see why improving access to information has not always been popular with dominant groups in society, whether these are ruling classes or ethnic groups, governments or religious bodies. Translating the Bible from Latin to enable people to read the word of God for themselves threatened the power of the Church. Governments both past and present have feared that increased access to information would increase discontent and lead to unrest. In the eighteenth century a few months before the French Revolution, the Attorney General of France said: 'They are pursuing a fatal policy, they are teaching people to read and write' (quoted by Oxenham 1980:11).

Critical literacy can assist in making power visible. Many participants in literacy groups who speak minority languages want to learn the dominant language of the region or country as they perceive, probably correctly, that this will provide them with more work opportunities and an increase in income. They do not necessarily relate this dominance in language to the subordinate position of their own ethnic group or tribe. Nor do they see their lack of education as a result of decisions made by the dominant group. Those on the margins, the least powerful, are frequently left out of the education system and out of literacy programmes.

It is no accident that indigenous women, oppressed because of both ethnicity and gender, have the lowest literacy rates of all. In Rajasthan, India, the literacy rate among indigenous men was 39 per cent and among women eight per cent (Rao and Robinson-Pant 2003). Until as recently as the middle of the twentieth century, countries in the global North prioritised the education of boys over that of girls, and in many countries still do. Despite the growing recognition of the importance of education for women, there is still a significant disparity in the levels of literacy of women and men in most countries, apart from the few exceptions. In many countries in South Asia, the Middle East, and North Africa twice as many men as women are literate.

An amusing cartoon by Australian cartoonist Judy Horacek recognises the impact that teaching women to read can have on domestic relations (see Figure 8.1). This perceived threat to male power is now challenged by research, which shows that educating women improves the health and welfare of the whole family.

Figure 8.1: Domestic relations cartoon

Source: Judy Horacek 1994, reprinted with permission

However, even though the importance of literacy for women is recognised, in most societies attending literacy classes is not always easy for the individual woman. Attendance can be seen as challenging her husband's power. Nor is it always easy for women to become involved as literacy facilitators, even in places where there are no apparent physical restrictions on women. A woman in south Sudan was locked up by her husband for wanting to attend a facilitators' training course and another in Nigeria was threatened with divorce (information gained from personal communications).

The objectives, the materials, and teaching methods of programmes designed to promote economic development and up-skill the workforce are different from those that aim to promote critical enquiry, justice, and social change. Functional literacy and programmes that are related solely to educating the workforce have one agenda; programmes relating to social change have another. The extremes of these positions are demonstrated by materials produced in the mid 1980s by two very different schemes in South Africa during the period of apartheid. A 'Practical Course for Housewives and Domestics' (1983) taught black maids how to use the electricity in white households: 'To cook, bake or fry food, to boil water in the kitchen, to wash dishes'. At the same time, a magazine for literacy students took a very different approach and described the police raids: 'They came at four o'clock in the morning…They had big guns…And then they took my husband away'(*Learn and Teach* 1983, volume 9). *Learn and Teach* was a radical magazine published for literacy students which constantly and cleverly attacked the apartheid segregation laws. It ran a cartoon strip in which a loveable character named Sloppy gets into various scrapes, yet always manages to find a way round the laws. One amusing cartoon strip shows how Sloppy and his family were not defeated by a 'Whites Only' sign (see Figure 8.2).

Figure 8.2: Sloppy cartoon strip

Sloppy and his wife and four-year-old son, Lucky, go shopping for a bicycle for Lucky. Lucky prefers roller skates and zooms off, with the salesman, Sloppy, and his wife in hot pursuit. The salesman collapses on the ground exhausted. Lucky's parents catch up with Lucky and reprimand him. By now they are all tired and thirsty but the only place to get a drink is a 'Whites Only' restaurant. The owner will not even let them have a glass of water. To overcome this, Lucky skates into the restaurant and comes out with a plate of food and drink, knocking the white owner over in the process.

Source: Sloppy Cartoon Strip, Learn and Teach 1983, Volume 9

The cartoon represents a win for black people over the oppressive white government – a small victory over extreme racism. The contrast in these two examples of reading materials from South Africa could not be greater – literacy as a tool of oppression or literacy as a tool for liberation.

Certain approaches to literacy and certain methodologies encourage participants to think critically, to analyse their surroundings and their situation, and to take action to improve them. Probably the most important influence on 'literacy as critical reflection' and an agenda for change was Paolo Freire. His influence informed the literacy campaigns in South America, most notably the literacy campaign by the Sandinistas in Nicaragua, and contributed to the 'radical pragmatism' of the English literacy campaign in the 1970s. His ideas, combined with PRA, led to the development of REFLECT. These 'literacies for change' are described below.

Paolo Freire

Paulo Freire's ideas and methods, sometimes called the psycho-social method, had a profound influence on literacy programmes in both the global North and global South. In a poor oppressed agricultural context, Freire aimed to enable poor peasants and workers to recognise the nature of their oppression. He saw literacy as enabling them to explore and understand the root causes of their situation in order to challenge it. He described traditional education as an 'act of depositing, in which the students are the depositories and the teacher is the depositor' (Freire 1992: 58). Freire believed that: 'we can transform a reality we did not make, and we can transform the reality we make'.

Freire identified three stages of learning – task-related activities, activities concerned with personal relationships, and 'consciencisation activities' (activities to perceive the reality of oppression but to believe in the possibility of change). He advocated a learning cycle which starts with experience, leads to action, then to further reflection and action again (Freire 1970: 68).

Learning to read, according to Freire, is a process through which we can begin to perceive the world as it really is, 'to read the world' and through this reading and consequent understanding, take action to change it. Freire believed that dialogue was intrinsic to the learning process:

> Dialogue is the encounter between men, mediated by the world, in order to name the world. It must not be a situation where some name on behalf of others. It is an act of creation; it must not serve as a crafty instrument for the domination of one person over another. It is a conquest of the world for the liberation of humankind.
> (Freire 1970: 69–70)

In order for those learning literacy to see the reality of their oppression, the realities are 'codified' into images, pictures, photographs, or key generative words. Representation of reality can also be through drama and video. Images or words are used to present some aspect of the world around, the society or the situation in which the people attending the literacy group live and work.

> *Since…the coding is representative of an existing situation, the decoder*
> *tends to take the step from the representation to the very concrete situation,*
> *in which and with which he finds himself.*
> (*ibid.*)

By discussing the word or picture, the learners move towards discussing the
situation it represents – work or land, for example. The primer in the
Sandinista literacy programme in Nicaragua started with the word 'revolution'.
In programmes combining conflict resolution and literacy in Sierra Leone and
south Sudan, two of the generative words used were 'anger' and 'conflict'
(McCaffery 2005). Paolo Freire's concept and approach drew on Christian
liberation theology and was adopted by Catholic activists and used in Nigeria
and other countries. One critique is that discussion is not always easy to
generate and after cursory attempts, literacy facilitators may move quickly on
to the 'meat' of the lesson – that of learning the letters or syllables as 're-vo-lu-
tion' and using these to make new words.

Participatory rural appraisal

Participatory rural appraisal, and its successors rapid rural appraisal and
participatory needs assessment, were not developed in relation to literacy
programmes or to education. Initially PRA was a research methodology for
development, which aimed to seek the views of poor and marginalised people,
not only the views of the rich, the powerful, and the male leaders of communities.

PRA was developed by Robert Chambers (1983) and altered the way many
development and research programmes operated. Much greater consideration
was given to working at community level and hearing the previously unheard
voices of those who would be directly affected by potential change. This
coincided with the idea of 'responsibilisation' – encouraging local
communities to take more control over local services and a greater share of the
costs. PRA developed tools to identify local issues as they affected the whole
community in order to identify action that communities could undertake to
improve their situation. These tools included drawing maps of villages, of
households, and of land ownership and usage, drawing calendars to identify
different diseases and their impact on the community, creating personal and
historical timelines, seasonal calendars of agricultural production, matrices of
commercial activity, profit and loss, and Venn diagrams analysing local power
structures. These are now used extensively in development programmes (see
Figure 8.3 for an example of a timeline).

Figure 8.3: Timeline

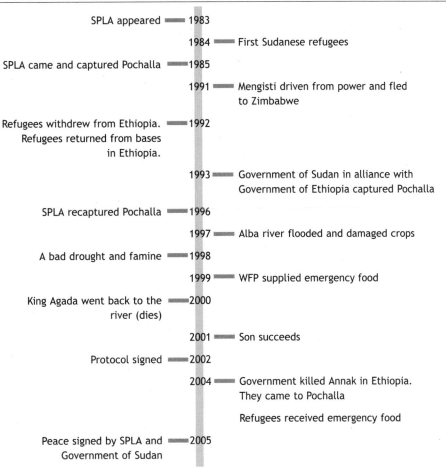

SPLA appeared	1983
	1984 First Sudanese refugees
SPLA came and captured Pochalla	1985
	1991 Mengisti driven from power and fled to Zimbabwe
Refugees withdrew from Ethiopia. Refugees returned from bases in Ethiopia.	1992
	1993 Government of Sudan in alliance with Government of Ethiopia captured Pochalla
SPLA recaptured Pochalla	1996
	1997 Alba river flooded and damaged crops
A bad drought and famine	1998
	1999 WFP supplied emergency food
King Agada went back to the river (dies)	2000
	2001 Son succeeds
Protocol signed	2002
	2004 Government killed Annak in Ethiopia. They came to Pochalla
	Refugees received emergency food
Peace signed by SPLA and Government of Sudan	2005

On the day peace was signed in January 2005, this timeline was constructed by facilitators from a village in south Sudan on the Sudanese Ethiopian border during a training course for literacy facilitators. Three other timelines were constructed by other groups, one of which told the story of the civil war from the time of independence from Britain in 1956. After each group of facilitators had explained their timeline in turn to the others (and the author) they then wrote the four stories down, read them out, and compared their different experiences. Not only was important history recorded but it provided highly motivational material to read and discuss in a context where reading materials were minimal.

Source: Training course for literacy facilitators, 'Rebuilding Communities in South Sudan 2000-2005', McCaffery (unpublished 2005)

PRA methodology has proved useful to literacy programmes adopting a social practice approach as outlined in Chapter 7, as well as the more radical programmes. It provides an ethnographic research tool to analyse the social, economic, and cultural environment. In the Community Education Programme in Nigeria, PRA research methods were used in designing the programme. The involvement of communities in this initial design and the feeling of ownership it generated were key factors in its successful implementation. PRA was also used to mobilise communities in CELL (Capacity Enhancement for Lifelong Learning) in Egypt (see Chapter 7).

A very different project developed by SOLO (Sudan Open Learning Organisation) in Sudan used PRA in developing post-literacy materials (see Chapter 14). They mapped the community, drew a 'visions' tree of the future, and interviewed community members.

In the post-conflict literacy programmes in south Sudan and Sierra Leone (2000–2005), PRA tools were used to identify potential conflict 'flash points';

Figure 8.4: Book about conflict near Bo

Timeline showing the impact of a rebel attack on a community near Bo, Sierre Leone, with pictures showing before, during, and after the war.

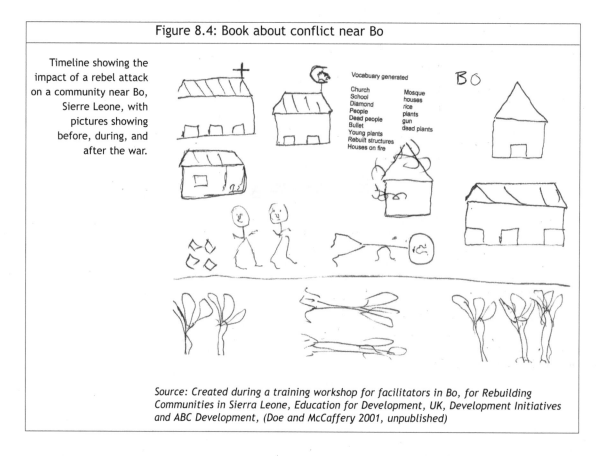

Source: Created during a training workshop for facilitators in Bo, for Rebuilding Communities in Sierra Leone, Education for Development, UK, Development Initiatives and ABC Development, (Doe and McCaffery 2001, unpublished)

the bore hole, disputed land, the taxi park and voter registration. Analysis of the economic situation and the impact of the war enabled participants to reflect on the past and plan for the future (see Figure 8.4).

REFLECT

In the early 1990s the international NGO ActionAid saw the possibility of merging the techniques of PRA and the concepts of Freire to create local literacy programmes with the potential to radically change immediate circumstances (REFLECT). Using the analytical techniques of PRA, the maps, diagrams, and matrices produced are used to generate the vocabulary, reading text, and writing themes from which to develop and improve reading, writing, and calculating skills. The REFLECT Mother Manual (Archer and Cottingham 1996) provides the theoretical background, clear advice, and ideas on how to develop and implement a REFLECT programme. It gives ideas for different maps, matrices, and diagrams that can be developed with the literacy participants. The concept is not one of instructing the participants but of facilitating their learning.

A REFLECT programme often begins by drawing a 'map' of the community on the ground using sticks, stones, twigs, leaves, or whatever is at hand (see Figure 8.5).

Figure 8.5: PRA map (twigs and leaves)

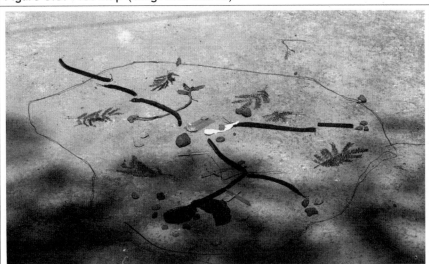

Source: Training workshop on 'Integrating Literacy and Conflict Resolution' in Kampala for facilitators from south Sudan for Rebuilding Communities in South Sudan (Doe et al. 2004: 87).

This inevitably generates dialogue and discussion; it is rare for the whole group not to get involved in this representation of their community. The use of moveable materials enables changes to be made as different people add their voices and ideas. Drawings are made on small cards to show certain aspects of the 'map'. These may be the houses, school, church, or mosque. When the 'map' is finally agreed, it is transferred to a large piece of paper and some additional words added such as 'road' or 'river'. A selection of these words is then chosen to develop reading and writing skills. At this stage individual words and letters are selected to identify and learn the sound–symbol relationship, or to learn individual words. As the maps, calendar, and matrices develop so does the vocabulary, the ability to write short sentences, and the themes for writing. Any calendar for example will contain the months of the year and provide practice in writing the date. A calendar of annual festivities will provide the opportunity to talk and write about local festivals.

Evaluations of the RELECT approach demonstrate that these programmes do lead to community action (Archer and Cottingham 1996; Millican 2006). A report on REFLECT in Bangladesh encapsulates both the aims and outcomes of REFLECT programmes:

> As well as sustaining their new found literacy skills, the Loko Kendra (People's Centre) provides their members with a space in which to develop and sustain their problem analysis capacity and to take action to bring about positive and empowering change in their lives.
> (Hassan 2005)

One good example of REFLECT leading to action can be seen in Figure 8.6, which shows a drawing that a community in Kambia (Sierra Leone) produced, to calculate the materials needed to repair buildings destroyed during the civil war. Practical and locally relevant numeracy was also used to calculate the size of vegetable plots and the crops they would produce.

Figure 8.6: Calculating the building materials required

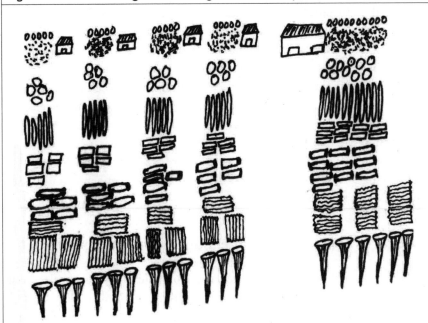

Diagram of reconstruction from a training workshop on numeracy in Sierra Leone. Symbols represent the different building materials including stones, bricks, poles, and zinc sheets needed for roofing.

Source: (Doe et al. 2004: 25)

Rao and Robinson-Pant (2003) point out that literacy provides a social space for women to discuss ideas and issues. An example from a Burundi REFLECT project working on peace and reconciliation between Hutu and Tutsi shows the power of writing:

'It is important that we have learned to read and write. It means that we have been able to write letters. We have written letters to some of our community who are still in Tanzania, asking them to come back. We want to encourage them to come home. We encourage them to come home by our personal testimonies of peace and by telling them about REFLECT. We write and tell them that they should not listen to the rumours and radio propaganda, life really has changed here. Three people came back last week because of the letters we were able to write.' Juvenal Ndikumagenge (age 24)
(Rao and Robinson-Pant 2003)

Critics of REFLECT maintain that progress in reading, writing, and calculating is no better than in traditional primer-based programmes (Carr-Hill *et al.* 2001). It is possibly for this reason that ActionAid has begun to focus more on the developmental aspects of the approach and the importance of communication in its many forms, not only on the acquisition of literacy skills.

REFLECT was also the primary methodology used in programmes in Sierra Leone and south Sudan. These programmes combined literacy with conflict-resolution and peacebuilding. Using PRA tools to explore the post-conflict environment to identify tensions and disputes, participants were able to use mapping techniques to identify post-conflict areas of tension such as disputed land, destroyed buildings, changes in economic production before, during, and after the conflict; and seasonal calendars to show how community tension rises during festival periods. This was combined with the Freirean technique of 'codification' to explore post-conflict trauma. The techniques used in conflict and peacebuilding combined well with the Freirean and REFLECT literacy methodologies. A particular important component was that of recounting the experience, or 'telling the story'.

Radical pragmatism and the student writing movement

Freirean ideas had a great influence on programmes in the global North as well as economically developing countries. In the UK the combination of social and political movements and the need to respond quickly to demand, coupled with the dearth of materials, led to the development of what has been termed radical pragmatism (Mace *et al.* 2006). The school-based language experience (as described in the introduction) gave the children control over their own learning and their own vocabulary. A similar approach was used with adults. They generated their own short sentences, for example:

My name is Arthur.

I am unemployed.

I have four children.

This became the reading text which invited critical reflection on a range of issues including the reasons for his unemployment, the number of children he had to support, and the prospects of finding another job.

Using student experience as text resonated with the 'worker writer movement' of the time. This was challenging the master narrative and seeking to move the history and language of workers from the sidelines to the mainstream. Working-class people were writing their life stories and their experiences and publishing the results. The idea of publishing experiences transferred to the adult literacy scene and gave rise to the development of materials written by literacy participants. Life stories, experiences, and observations were then used as the text from which to develop reading and writing skills. The movement was led by voluntary organisations in Manchester, London, and Brighton which had the time and commitment to work with students to publish these writings as short books or collections of writing. Not only were the texts of intrinsic interest but the language used in many was closer to that of the learners than standard or national languages and therefore easier to read, at least in the initial stages. One of the very first was *Father's Cap* (1976) by students at the Cambridge House Literacy Scheme, London, followed by *Brighton Writing* (1976) produced by the Friends Centre, a voluntary adult education centre in Brighton. Gatehouse in Manchester produced a range of small books written by students over a 30-year period. At the same time a group of tutors and students produced a newspaper of student writing, *Write First Time*, and published it quarterly.

Whether or not those involved in the literacy schemes considered their methods to be radical and politically contentious, the government of the time became concerned and intervened. After complaints from a Member of Parliament in 1976, investigations were carried out into the materials used in the adult literacy programme at the Friends Centre, Brighton, and the writing in *Write First Time*. The Centre was charged with 'filling empty minds' and exonerated, but the students were outraged and politicised as a result. *Write First Time* was ordered to make changes. Despite agreeing to these, two years later funding for the paper was not renewed.

In the development context the texts produced became known as learner-generated materials (LGMs), though in rural communities they were often also produced by the facilitators who had equally important stories to tell. The telling of the story is a key component in peacebuilding and it became an important part of the programmes in Sierra Leone and south Sudan. In east Sudan where a community facilitator with little education beyond primary school adopted the idea with enthusiasm, the people in his literacy groups produced 140 stories in six months. In the whole programme 204 small books and 85 pieces of writing in five languages Arabic, English, Dinka, Nuba, and Tigre were produced by 40 literacy circles (Abuzeid and McCaffery 2000b). This provided a wide choice of learner-generated writing appropriate for a wider audience and publication.

Participants in the Community Education Programme in Nigeria responded with similar enthusiasm and 72 small books were published in six languages: Bura, Hausa, Ibibio, Ibio, Fulfulde, and English. When the programme ended, the process continued; stories were told, written, typed, and used at local level

(Ezeomah *et al.* 2006). In Nigeria and Sudan the writing was about personal experiences, communal histories, and folk tales, often with a moral twist. In Egypt women took the opportunity to write about their lives. Two books of stories and experiences were written by women attending literacy classes, often in colloquial rather than standard or classical Arabic, and many told of the hardship and sadness of their lives (GALAE and British Council 1997).

However, some literacy educators consider learner-produced materials as much more of a supplementary or follow-up resource, used to develop confidence in reading and in writing. Individual life stories, class newsletters, and journals may be important for developing confidence in writing, but they are supplementary to the learning agenda. There are also debates about whether or not these are the best materials for new readers. Language purists become concerned about non-standard language. Others believe that LGMs are written without consideration for readability, produced with limited resources, and may be more relevant to the writer than the reader. What is often forgotten is that if any writing goes beyond the immediate literacy group there is an editing process – which is itself part of learning about writing clearly for different audiences. The process of publishing learners' writing also demystifies the authority of the printed word. It is worth remembering that writing is part of a process of learning that one is not invisible. Writing can confirm the existence of both the individual and the community.

Cultural literacy

Literacy programmes concerned with individual and communal development and change recognised the importance of facilitating these normally unheard voices and encouraged the writing. In Nigeria, Sierra Leone, and Sudan, the 'student writing' methodology resonated with the storytelling and poetry endemic to the cultural context, and the writing produced became part of the community resources. Cultural literacy is a term used by a programme in Yemen to 'link literacy programmes to the rich local culture' (personal communication with Zein Mohamed Fouad). The 'outpouring' of writing by participants on literacy programmes testifies to the importance of this link.

The concept of culture in terms of values and beliefs, and the expressions of those beliefs in daily life also link to the modalities of peacebuilding. While differences in values and beliefs can cause immense schisms in communities, culture confirms identity and a sense of community and continuation.

The strengthening of cultural expression in the process of rebuilding communities is important in providing a sense of belonging and emphasising the continuity of life, linking the present to the past, despite recent or ongoing disruption. Accepting and validating the culture and beliefs of others (especially of refugees and internally displaced people, for example) is one of the many challenges for adult education and peacebuilding.

A striking example of sharing communal history was provided on a training course for local facilitators in south Sudan. After the peace agreement between the Government of Sudan and the Sudanese Peoples Liberation Army of the South was signed in January 2004, the organising NGOs combined PRA techniques and student writing methodologies, and used timelines to recount and reflect on the decades of civil war. They were working ' to co-investigate their reality, to test the validity of existing knowledge and create new knowledge in the process' (Allman 1988: 97).

The difference between traditional, adaptive models of literacy and more radical and transformative ones is in the control of the learning. Even the most radical primer such as that produced in Nicaragua contains messages decided by those in power. In radical and transformative models, what is learnt and the materials used are not prescribed by others, but by the participants who, while improving their literacy and numeracy skills, develop tools for critical analysis and ultimately action.

Critical reflection and strategic gender needs

The model of 'literacy as critical reflection' includes critically reflecting on the organisation of society and the patriarchal system in which men dominate and women often have little control over their lives. Programmes aimed at reflection and transformation include addressing the subordinate position of women and taking action to address this, both at the personal and community level, thus directly addressing the strategic gender needs of women and men referred to in Chapter 3. They specifically aim to improve women's control over their own lives, to help them think about the structures of society, to participate in decision-making processes in the family and in the community, and to take action to improve their own situation.

Thus women in India decided to stop the men drinking so heavily, and poured the drink into the road. In south Sudan women became involved in mediating in community disputes (Newell-Jones 2004). In Akwa Ibom, Nigerian women reported that they were able to challenge what they termed 'negative' practices: 'fattening houses' for women to gain the desired weight before marriage; very early marriage; or rape of adolescent girls resulting in vesicovaginal fistula and the ostracisation of the girls from society (McCaffery 1999).

Radical literacies in which critical reflection is an integral part of the programme can lead to significant change. Such change can occur through national government programmes as part of the construction of a new society, as in Nicaragua. More often these kinds of programmes are run by NGOs which have experience in community development. The importance of literacy programmes in initiating change should not be underestimated.

Implications for planners

'Literacy as critical reflection' enables participants to move beyond thinking, to recording and communicating their reflections to others. By consciously engaging in debate and discussion, 'literacy as critical reflection' opens up new avenues for thinking and reflection. As such it is a powerful tool for change. Not only does it seek to give participants control over their learning, what they learn, and how they learn, it also provides the space for women and men to reflect critically on their society and their place within it.

'Literacy as critical reflection' is important for women. Though a programme may be focused around practical needs, discussion and debate are major components which often lead to critical reflection on the ways their lives are circumscribed. Critical analysis and reflection within a literacy programme can also assist men to review women's position in their own households, the community, and society, and to modify their own behaviour towards women.

Those operating such programmes should be aware of the implications and possible impact at all levels, on those around the participants as well as the participants themselves. They should have strategies for addressing any impacts whether positive or negative. They should be aware that:

- change can be frightening;
- change can upset the dynamics of a household and create difficult and sometime irresolvable tensions;
- change can threaten established power structures at local as well as national level;

- writing by participants can be seen as critical of the existing political and social order, and tutors should be aware of possible ramifications if critical writing is widely distributed.

However, organising and supporting programmes that lead to change and improvements in the community can be exciting and very rewarding.

Further reading

D. Archer and S. Cottingham, *The Reflect Mother Manual: a New Approach to Adult Literacy*, London: ActionAid, 1996. This is an absolutely essential manual for those working in critical literacies, full of ideas for PRA exercises.

J. Crowther, M. Hamilton, and L. Tett, 'Powerful literacies: an introduction', in *Powerful Literacies*, Leicester: NIACE, 2001. This is a useful collection of literacy in different contexts including several which challenge bases of power.

J. McCaffery, 'Using transformative models of adult literacy in conflict resolution and peacebuilding processes at community level: examples from Guinea, Sierra Leone and Sudan', in *Compare* 35 (4): 443–62, 2005. This provides a description of the methods of literacy as critical reflection, as used in literacy programmes following conflicts in Sierra Leone and south Sudan.

M. Mayo, *Imaging Tomorrow: Adult Education for Transformation*, Leicester: NIACE, 1997. This is an excellent general book on how literacy and literacy programmes contribute to the transformation of society.

S. Doe, J. McCaffery, and K. Newell Jones, *Integrating Literacy and Peacebuilding: A Guide for Trainers and Facilitators*, Reading: Education for Development, 2004. This is a practical guide with a range of exercises for combining literacy with processes for conflict resolution.

UNESCO, Education for All Global Monitoring Report 'Literacy for Life', Paris: UNESCO, 2005. Basic reading for all involved in literacy work.

Part III
Understanding the Preparation Process

9

Planning for literacy

This chapter begins to set out the things that need to be considered when planning a literacy programme. It raises a whole series of questions that planners will need to think through before deciding which approach to literacy might work best in their area. Most of these questions can only be answered in relation to local context, so this chapter presents a pre-planning agenda, indicating what information may need to be researched or compiled before real planning can get under way. After explaining why and how to conduct a needs assessment involving the whole community, the chapter sets out implications for planners in the form of pre-planning questions organised under five headings: purposes, outcomes, context, resources, and scale.

Conducting a needs assessment

Whether the decision to embark on a literacy programme has come from above or below, an early needs-assessment exercise will help to indicate the priorities of local people in respect to literacy and numeracy, and the shape and scale of a programme that is likely to succeed. An initial needs assessment should aim to provide planners with:

- an understanding of different literacies and their use within the area, and who needs to read and write what;
- a clear picture of local levels of education, how many girls and boys are in school, how many have dropped out or never attended school, the range of possible male and female participants and facilitators for a new literacy programme;
- a baseline measure of literacy use, particularly for those programmes that need to formally measure impact;

- an understanding of women's and men's availability for learning, who wants to attend, and what time and space in their day is available for this;
- an understanding of who is prepared to learn with whom (ethnic, age, or gender differences may make it difficult for people to learn together in the same class or to be taught by people from other groups).

How to conduct a needs assessment

Some programmes have begun with extensive ethnographic research to help understand the language, cultural, and gender issues associated with literacy use and literacy learning. Local researchers have been trained to carry out focus-group discussions or individual interviews in order to draw up a full picture of existing literacy practices. While this is broadly in line with a social practices approach, proper ethnographic research takes time and money. It may yield useful results but it is important to keep this in perspective in relation to what a programme is logistically able to offer and the objectives and funding restrictions of providers. Other programmes have involved representatives from local groups or potential tutors, and used PRA tools to gain an overview of the existing literacy context. Activities have included mapping literacy use, drawing up calendars of seasonal and daily work, and holding discussions on barriers to learning in mixed groups. This is an important awareness-raising exercise for anyone who will later act as a facilitator, and even if potential facilitators originate from within the community it is likely to provide them with new insights into what people want from literacy.

Whether local people or trained researchers are used to carry out an initial needs assessment, people are unlikely to be honest about their views unless their trust has been gained. It is therefore important to consider who should be consulted and who might best consult with them. The first stage in any needs-assessment process is to identify the stakeholders, or those people who ought to be consulted.

Identifying stakeholders and getting the community on board

'Stakeholders' is a term used by planners and development workers to indicate those people who may have a stake in the outcomes of a programme or a particular intervention. These include not only the funders and potential participants but anyone who is likely to be affected either positively or

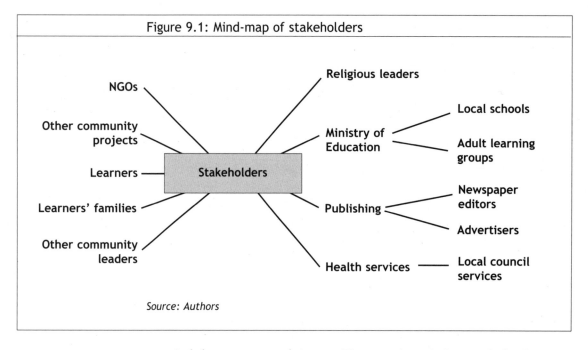

Figure 9.1: Mind-map of stakeholders

Source: Authors

negatively by a programme's impact. Figure 9.1 is a mind-map of who the stakeholders in a literacy programme could include.

Some kind of early consultation with all identified stakeholders is important both to anticipate any resistance to a new programme and to ensure that it meets the greatest need and fits in with other local initiatives.

Once stakeholders have been identified and consulted it is important also to feed back on information that has been gathered and decisions that have been made. People are more likely to accept changes if they can understand the reasons behind them and can see how the information they have offered has been used. As a group they may also form a useful support to the implementation process and provide advice or practical help throughout the duration of a programme.

With any new initiative it is important to get the local community on board and encourage them to take some ownership of the programme. In a rural context this is often done through village meetings or discussions; in an urban context by working through specific interest groups. It is important to ensure that opportunities are provided to hear women's voices and those from religious or ethnic minorities. It is often best to meet any resistance head on and deal with this through discussion. Groups which are not broadly in favour of a particular initiative are likely to demonstrate greater resistance if not consulted from the outset. Gaining the support of the broader community is important in encouraging and sustaining the participation of individuals, and it is useful to consider the broader community needs for literacy as well as individual ones. The density of people in urban areas means that more classes can be run for different groups, so people with mixed abilities or varied needs are not obliged to learn together. A rural programme on the other hand may bring together a more cohesive social group, be led by community rather than individual needs, and be linked in to other development initiatives in that area.

It may be possible to ask the community to take responsibility for identifying or constructing a building to learn in, or for recommending potential facilitators. The more ownership the community feels, the more support they are likely to provide. Community responsibility is important for the sustainability of a programme, particularly if it has been initiated through a time-bound grant.

Understanding learners' needs and motivations

It is important to build a profile of potential learners early on in the planning process and to start to understand women's and men's learning needs and motivations. There is a huge difference between programmes run in response to an outside or top-down directive and those requested locally by people wanting literacy for themselves. Programme managers and facilitators often ask how to 'motivate people' to want to learn to read and write, but if this motivation is lacking there may be little point in trying to create it.

While it has been claimed that literacy leads to change, conversely familial or local change is often a factor that propels people into literacy programmes. Lalage Bown (1991) suggests that change in personal or economic situations – such as the loss of a spouse or a job – often precedes the need for literacy learning. In other communities the introduction of pension rights or a threat to local land ownership has mobilised communities to demand literacy in order for them to understand their position better.

Talking with larger groups or interviewing individuals will begin to indicate people's needs and expectations from literacy. This might best be done informally through extended semi-structured interviews rather than using questionnaires or surveys, in order that any particular issues raised can be followed up. It might be necessary to identify a representative sample of people to interview (ensuring a gender balance, an age balance, people from different castes or classes) to get a rounded picture of common needs. Think through the kinds of questions that could be covered, and take time to brief interviewers on how they might respond. Asking who, what, when, and why questions (e.g. who do you know who can read and write? when do you feel that writing down numbers would be useful to you?) usually generates a fuller response than 'yes or no questions' (e.g. do you need to keep accounts?), but the responses generated from such in-depth interviews are harder to record and to compare.

Some programmes have also consulted learners about a choice of tutor; for example, whether or not they want to be taught by a male or female, a familiar local person or a more qualified teacher from elsewhere. But it is important to bear in mind that asking people what they want raises expectations. While planners need to understand why people might want to read or write, it is also important during a needs-assessment exercise to communicate the boundaries or limitations of provision. If for example people ask to learn to read mail-order catalogues (as was the case in a programme in South Africa), would this fit with the intentions and policies of providers? If they ask for a fully qualified female teacher, is there someone who would fill this role?

It is also important to be honest with participants what completion of a literacy programme is likely to enable them to achieve. Often people have unrealistic expectations of literacy, fuelled by the rhetoric of providers who over-promise. Factors affecting improved health or increased income are complex, and do not hinge on the ability to read and write alone.

The expectations of participants and the policies of funders are both factors that will influence the approach to literacy that is taken. If the purpose of the programme is linked with economic development, a task-based or functional literacy approach may be most relevant (see Chapter 6), while if it is in response to a social justice or change agenda, then the literacies described in Chapter 8 may provide a better model.

Mapping literacy use

Even if the programme is in response to an outside directive, it is important to understand local context and local literacy needs before continuing with planning. Mapping literacy use in the local area will help to identify the different literacies that already exist and their uses. It will also help in deciding the language for initial literacy classes. Language issues are dealt with in depth in Chapter 10.

The realisation that literacy is a series of diverse practices and not a single autonomous skill is now widely appreciated. The formal literacy used in classrooms or government documents may not be appropriate for people's immediate purposes, and if it is not useful it is unlikely that people will either learn it or sustain their use of it.

A needs assessment should aim to identify the different locations in which literacy is used in a local environment (school, health centre, home, market, shop, government office, tea house etc.) and the range of literacies that are used there (see Figure 9.2). This exercise can be carried out in discussion with a focus group, by visually representing the different buildings in a particular area and listing the different practices that go on there. It is likely that different groups (women, men, older and younger people, people from different trades and backgrounds) will mention different practices, according to their priorities and lifestyles. Capturing these and comparing them will provide a lot of information about the range of potential learners and the different literacies they might use. It also provides a comprehensive picture of the literacy environment, and of the range of practices that individuals might encounter.

Figure 9.2: Kambia PRA map

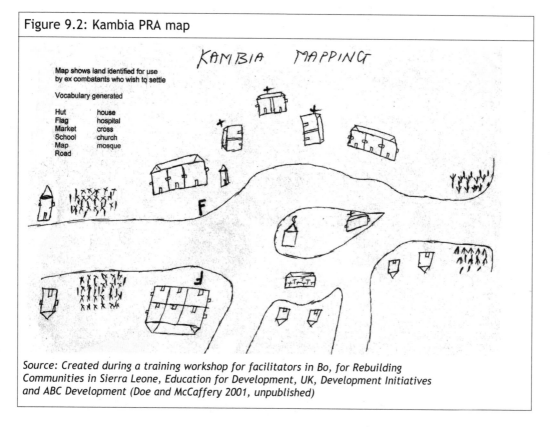

Source: Created during a training workshop for facilitators in Bo, for Rebuilding Communities in Sierra Leone, Education for Development, UK, Development Initiatives and ABC Development (Doe and McCaffery 2001, unpublished)

Agreeing scope and considering sustainability

A needs-assessment exercise should also seek to answer questions about the best venue for a programme to take place in, and people's availability for learning. PRA tools can be used to prioritise between different buildings available, or to map relative distances between meeting places and participants' homes. Seasonal or weekly calendars can indicate months or days when people are more available for learning than others, and when created with groups of potential learners can give them some say in where and when their classes are organised (see Figure 9.3).

Figure 9.3: PRA seasonal calendar

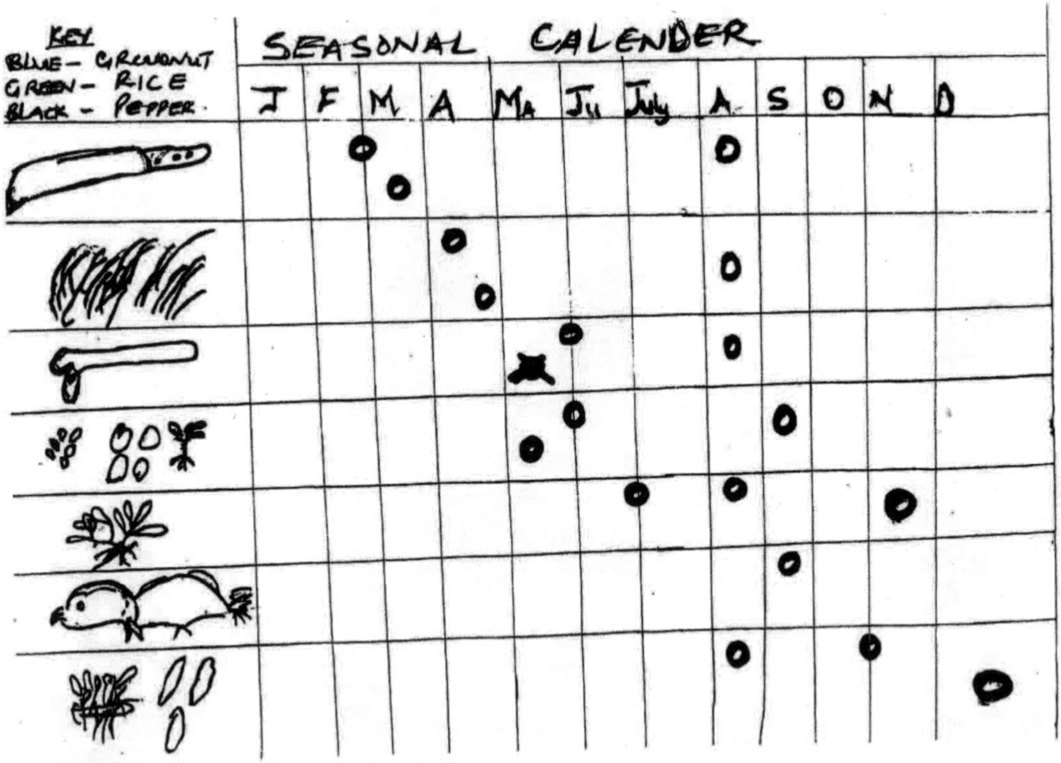

Seasonal calendar showing agricultural activities involved in the cultivation of ground-nuts, rice, and peppers. Activities include ground clearing, sowing seeds, weeding, and harvesting.

Source: Doe et al. 2004: 27.

The broad range of definitions for literacy makes it impossible to generalise about the length of time and the number of hours needed to sustain literacy, and claims vary from 26 hours (for recognising the alphabet and signing a name) to three years (for an equivalent primary education certificate). The scale of a programme, the finances available, and the time given to a project will all affect the programme approach and the frequency of classes. While meeting only once a week may be too little and learners may find they forget what they have learned between classes, meeting four days a week is probably too much to keep up for very long.

Adult literacy programmes are never self-sustaining, and a project with short-term funding should take into account the longer-term avenues of support open beyond that period. Too many projects absorb time and money in developing training materials for a programme that lasts at most five years; the issue of long-term sustainability needs to be addressed at the outset. Stakeholders can be involved in developing possible strategies for continuing the programme even at the initial planning stages. If there are no structures in place to support people's learning beyond an initial period, it is possible that they will not sustain what they have learnt. It is important to link people's learning right from the beginning with literacy they will actively use.

It may be possible to identify other avenues for individual students to continue with their learning through ongoing vocational or other school-based programmes: gaining some understanding of what these might be should form part of the planning process. It is not financially viable to keep one student on the same programme beyond the period in which they can usefully learn from it. If a group of learners has met the goals set by planners but is still benefiting from learning together it may be more economical for them to run their own learning group without a facilitator and to free up space for new people to attend a funded class.

Whether or not your programme is taking a 'real materials' approach, there is limited point in teaching people to read when they have nothing available for reading. Some programmes include specific activities to build the literacy environment. This might mean working with the providers of materials (newspapers, local government etc.) in order to help them improve their distribution and adapt their language and format to make texts more accessible to new readers. Other programmes have included activities such as the creation of mobile libraries or book boxes, or provided support for the production of learner-generated materials. However, the advantage of working within existing structures is that they are far more likely to be sustained beyond the life of a particular project or intervention. The danger of creating specialist book boxes or setting up newsletters written by other learners is that these are likely to disappear again once funding for the initiative stops.

Planning for gender-integrated programmes

The Gender and Development (GAD) framework described in Chapter 3 is useful for ensuring that women's and men's specific needs are not omitted from literacy programmes.

Moser and Levy (1986) developed a useful gender planning methodology which has been adopted by DFID and used extensively since the 1990s. It helps planners to focus on the different needs of women and men. Despite the fact that women predominate in most programmes, according to Lind (2004) we still 'need to pay more attention to women's needs and conditions, in design, contents and organisation'. However, we also need to look more closely at the needs of men and why men are not coming to classes. This is known to be the case in many parts of the world. Mwiria, writing in Kenya, cites the reason as a combination of lower levels of literacy among women, and women's need to socialise, but there are a range of cultural norms that, both in the global South and North, prevent men from coming to classes (Mwiria 1993). The danger of a programme design that does not specifically look at the needs of both women and men is that basic needs – such as the timing of the literacy group, or the availability of a teacher of the appropriate sex – can be ignored. GAD methodology identifies key concepts and introduces specific planning tools to develop an understanding of gender issues – in order to assist people in the implementation of gender-aware interventions. The starting points for any gender-aware programme are:

1. Recognising the various roles of women (see Chapter 3)
2. Identifying the programme's policy approach towards women – welfare, equity, anti-poverty, efficiency, empowerment (see Chapter 3)
3. Recognising practical and strategic gender needs
4. Analysing the economic, social, cultural, and political context from a gender perspective (see Box 9.1).

Box 9.1: Framework for analysing context

The political framework	Does the government subscribe to international policy statements on women's equality? Is there national legislation safeguarding women's rights?
The economic situation	What is women's level of participation in the labour market? What sectors are they employed in? What opportunities do women have for gaining credit and opening small businesses?
The cultural and social context	What is the dominant religious practice in the area? What are the minority religions? What is the legal age of marriage and what is the socially accepted age of marriage? What are the limits on women's freedom of movement?
The organisational frameworks	Are the implementing agencies, donors, governments, NGOs, and community-based organisations gender-aware themselves? At what level are women recruited and employed in the organisation?

Source: McCaffery 1999, adapted from Moser 1989

Though the questions in Box 9.1 relate predominantly to women, they also relate to men. Using these tools helps planners to focus on gender issues. There are also a few key principles which, if followed, will minimise the risk of a gender-neutral programme finding it had missed a key issue:

- programme targets, objectives, outputs, and outcomes should be gender-specific;
- statistics should be gender-disaggregated in order to know the impact of the programme on both sexes;
- the implementing organisation should be gender-aware and gender-sensitive and employ both women and men at all levels.

If gender issues are not considered at the very beginning of the planning stage, the particular needs of women and men can be overlooked and the programme may fail to meet its objectives.

Implications for planners

The questions outlined below cover key considerations in the planning process. Some of these might be built into the needs-assessment exercise, others need to be answered by planners in collaboration with other stakeholder groups. They form a general checklist of areas to be covered prior to developing a programme.

Purposes

What are the crucial factors leading up to a literacy intervention at this time? Do people need to read and write for a particular reason? Do women and men want to write for different purposes? Is there a particular kind of literacy that different groups will need? Are there other changes happening locally, politically or economically, that mean people's existing methods of communication will no longer be sufficient? Answers to these questions will help to determine the kind of approach (skills, tasks, social practice, or critical reflection) that is needed.

Outcomes

What are desirable outcomes for planners? For participants, for women, and for men? It is important to be aware of the priorities of planners and funders for literacy (school involvement for parents, improved health, or a more qualified local population?) and those of participants (income generation or improved employment prospects?).

Is the literacy initiative tied in with national or organisational targets? To EFA goals? National or organisational targets often determine the amount of funding available for a programme, but rarely reflect the needs or wants of local people. If a programme is target-driven, there is a danger that achievement of targets overrides the priorities of a local community. Local interests must be taken into account and woven into curriculum design.

What literacy interventions have taken place in this area before and how will this affect how people view this one? It is important not only to look at the current picture, but also the historical one when designing a programme. People are likely to be suspicious of a programme if it is felt unlikely to deliver, or contains elements of programmes that have not worked in the past.

Context

What is the context for the programme? Urban? Rural? The context in which a programme is to be based will have a huge impact on both its content and its mode of delivery. The literacy needs of people in urban areas and the literacy environment in which they live, is often vastly different from those in the surrounding countryside. This can create huge problems for national programmes or national qualifications frameworks. Similarly the process through which learning programmes are delivered is closely tied in to local infrastructure. An urban programme, where there is a regular supply of electricity, can be delivered at a different time from those in rural areas dependent on gas lamps after dark. The quality of natural or artificial light makes a huge difference to what adults are able to see, and most people's eyesight begins to deteriorate after the age of 40. While older people blame a failing memory on not being able to read well, it is as likely to be their eyesight and poor lighting that gets in the way.

What other organisations are working in the area? What are the options for collaboration? While networking and collaborating with other organisations takes time, there are real advantages to thinking through in advance how any new initiative fits within a bigger local picture. Although individual NGOs may have specific aims for their literacy programmes, there may be possibilities to integrate these within national literacy programmes or broader qualifications frameworks.

Some funders encourage cross-sectoral working, and literacy can often be used as a vehicle for improving communication processes in other development initiatives. An approach that seeks to embed literacy in other development practices can work well for example with an organisation delivering primary health care, or improved forestry practices, or an AIDS-awareness campaign.

Where literacy environments are sparse, it is important to capitalise on the different materials that are available, and programmes will have a better chance of success if they are tied in to existing support structures.

Resources: human, financial, and material

What are the human resources available? Who might you employ or use as volunteers? The selection and training of facilitators is a crucial issue (see Chapter 15).

Some programmes (in Egypt, Israel, and China) are utilising university students as teachers, and require them to work on a literacy programme as part of their degree studies. However, university campuses tend to be situated in cities and students are based here for a large part of the year. Those who return to their villages during vacations may not have long enough there to get a proper programme off the ground. In some countries literacy programmes grew up in the armed forces and have extended outwards from there. In Egypt for example, the national literacy programme is managed by soldiers and ex-soldiers. However, their own training, to follow and respond to orders, may not make them best suited to working with adults in supportive groups.

Will people be paid or work as volunteers? There are arguments for and against paying facilitators, and a decision on this will depend on the size of the programme and the available budget. Literacy campaigns that are large-scale, government-led, and fuelled by a particular ideology often very successfully use volunteers as tutors. The 1980 Sandinista campaign in Nicaragua claimed to have reduced the overall illiteracy rate from 50.3 per cent to 12.9 per cent within only five months. It was run entirely by volunteers and produced a lasting impact on a whole generation of young people. However, acting as a tutor or facilitator is a skilled job and people get better at it over time. Tutors are more likely to stay in a programme if they are paid a realistic wage and have opportunities for career development.

Who is available to act as trainers or support staff? Who can provide back-up? Can you find both women and men for these roles? The difficulties of setting up a new programme include finding sufficiently skilled people to act as trainers for facilitators and to provide ongoing support. Buying in literacy trainers from existing programmes inevitably means they bring with them an existing philosophy and may find it hard to adapt to the particular approach you want to use. They are also less likely to be easily available for ongoing support once initial training is over. New facilitators will always benefit from a trainer visiting and observing them in the area in which they are working, and transport and time will be needed for this. It is often best to get a team of trainers on board in the early stages of programme development, rather than bringing them in later on. If they are involved in planning meetings they are more likely to share and fully understand the ethos of the programme, and more able to develop a team approach.

Some programmes have recruited trainers from a range of different external organisations. Others have recruited trainers who are familiar with the local area and community needs. If outside consultants are used to plan a programme, it is important that they are also involved in training the trainers. They must spend sufficient time with them to ensure that they understand all aspects of the work. If there is confusion at the level of training and support, this will filter down through all aspects of a programme.

What are the financial resources at your disposal? Is there a set budget? How many years will it be available for? How much per learner per year? Any programme will need to be planned in accordance with the finance available to support it, and it is important to try to gauge a realistic idea of the period of time for which funds are likely to be available. A calculation of costs per individual per year can indicate whether or not it is financially viable. Students who are gaining other benefits beyond literacy from weekly meetings might be encouraged to set up their own study or discussion groups that don't require the same level of funding.

What material resources are there? As well as assessing the literacy environment, it is important to take account of material resources that might support learning. Are there any facilities to copy materials (photocopiers, stencil machines) or to enlarge real texts (newspaper articles, labels, prescriptions) in order to make them easier to read? If these facilities are easily available to tutors it will be much easier for them to work with a flexible and responsive curriculum. If these are not available, tutors will be far more dependent on set texts.

If it is possible to access computers (in local organisations, schools, or government offices), facilitators can learn to produce their own materials and will need training in how to do this. Where there is access to television or radio these might also be integrated into the learning programme.

Are formal classes with teachers and learners the best way to work? What about more informal learning groups in people's houses, scribing, support at the point of need, distance learning, family literacy groups, mentoring models etc.? How and where people will learn is an early consideration for the programme and it is important to remember that there are alternatives to traditional groups meeting in classes. Former literacy programmes have included 'each one teach one' where individuals met in pairs in people's homes, and apprenticeship or work-based programmes where people learnt in their work environment. There have been examples in Nepal of working through scribes who helped people to learn while they acted as mediators, writing or interpreting texts for them. In Sierra Leone there were 'literacy shops' where people dropped in for support. Mentoring can include a colleague or family member informally helping someone with their specific literacy needs.

Many classes in Africa are run in school buildings at evenings and weekends, and while these tend already to be equipped with blackboards and desks, they can carry both bad and good associations for people. Those who have never been to school often find it a privilege to be going into school for the first time and like to have their lessons as similar to a school curriculum as possible. Other adults are intimidated by a school environment and feel they will be laughed at if the programme is run in a school building.

Some classes are held in rural areas under trees, but writing while sitting on the ground is often difficult and there can be disturbances from stray animals or curious observers. People's voices carry less well out of doors, and it can be difficult for participants to hear.

Scale

What is the scale of the programme you are envisaging? Is it a pilot? If so, what are the possibilities of upscaling? Most programmes begin as pilots but it is important to keep in mind possibilities for upscaling right from the start. Having a sense of what resources might be available if it were to be extended to other areas, and the difficulties of managing and supervising the approach you choose should all inform the planning process. Programmes designed for rural areas are rarely transferable to urban contexts, but might be adaptable to regions where the literacy needs of participants are similar.

Further reading

Community mapping at: www.unu.edu/unupress/food2/UIN11E/uin11e)c.htm
This a web-based resource derived from PRA that provides useful tools for gathering information about a local community.

Department for International Development, *Gender Manual: A Practical Guide for Development Policy Makers and Practitioners*, London: DFID, 2002. This a practical guide that will be helpful with the gender elements of literacy programmes.

PRA Tool Box at: www.fao.org/docrep/003 This an online introduction to PRA and its uses.

10

The language of literacy

This chapter considers the debates about the language of initial literacy and the relative economics of teaching people first in their mother tongue rather than going straight for the languages of power. It also looks at the impact of written literacy on minority spoken languages and at possibilities for dual-language programmes.

The choice of language for a literacy programme is a complex one. It relates both to how adults learn to read and to issues of power, culture, and identity. It will need careful consideration at the planning stage of a programme and will eventually be determined by the purposes for literacy, the things people want to read, the budget available for a programme, and the local literacy environment. However, a decision on which language or languages to use will also need to take into account the desires of local people to participate in a global economy and a global environment, and their need to protect their own identity and indigenous minority languages.

Different theorists have tried to provide perspectives on language choice. Michael Omolewa (2000) outlines the language debate as being between those who argue that people should learn in the language in which they dream, and those who see language as an instrument which reflects the goals and purposes of literacy, often defined in terms of national unity and prosperity. Skutnabb-Kangas (2000) is concerned about linguacide, or the 'killing off' or 'letting die' of minority languages. She suggests that countries need a multilingual education policy to protect minority languages and cultures, and argues that linguistic diversity encourages respect for other views. The huge rush for English and other dominant languages as the only languages of modernity, science, and technology may distort possibilities for regional language development. Professor Omelowa also indicates that the preservation of indigenous languages is critical to a country's growth and development when this has been adversely affected by the imposition of colonial languages (Omelowa 2000).

Language use

Over 5,000 languages are spoken in the world (Crystal 2000) and almost all countries in the world are multilingual. However, 97 per cent of the world's population speak only four per cent of the world's languages, with only three per cent of people speaking the remaining 96 per cent. The imbalance between dominant and minority languages is huge. It has also been predicted that, if languages continued to disappear at current rates, 90 per cent of the world's living languages will be gone within the next hundred years. Already around 50 per cent of existing languages are no longer being taught to/learned by the children born into that language group, and another 40 per cent have noticeably fewer speakers with each generation. This leaves only ten per cent of the world's total languages with reasonably large numbers of speakers and official state support. Linguistic diversity, like cultural and biological diversity, is under serious threat around the world.

Language standardisation has been part of building national unity for a long time, from the French revolution in the late eighteenth century to the creation of the state of Israel and the choice of a national language in post-colonial countries. Over half of the world's states are officially monolingual and the decision to prioritise English as a national language in the Republic of South Africa (in spite of a formal recognition of 11 official languages, and the fact that English only ranks as joint fifth out of the 11 as a language used in the home), has political as well as social significance. But despite the fact that many countries have a national or official language and a number of regional and local oral and written languages, many do not have a language policy for education.

Language and power

The use of majority and minority languages has strong implications for access to power. Language is often seen as a tool of the nation state and associated with colonialism and the imposition of national boundaries in areas that were previously ethnically divided. Disparate groups that fell within state frontiers needed to be persuaded or coerced into identifying with state priorities. Ruling powers erected state frontiers that often divided linguistic groups and, in needing to assimilate them, different languages have at times been promoted or forbidden. Over a hundred years ago parents in Wales in Great Britain did not teach their children Welsh, and it was forbidden in schools. People felt that children who grew up using it would be disadvantaged and not have the same opportunities as those who spoke English. Recently it has had a revival and is now compulsory learning in all local Welsh schools.

Linguistic and ethnic groups have been supported or silenced accordingly, and the issue of 'language rights' is now associated with the ethos of human rights. Those groups that can access and interact with the language of the powerful can play an active part within the nation that uses that language, while those who cannot are in danger of being marginalised or unrepresented. Where state business, access to education, employment, or financial resources are only conducted in one language, that language quickly becomes the language of power.

Literacy practitioners remain divided on the best way to work with languages of power. Freire felt that access to power could only come through developing critical awareness and reflection and that people had to do this through their own language. 'Literacy can only be emancipatory and critical to the extent that it is conducted in the language of the people' (Freire and Macedo 1987). By seeing themselves in relation to the powerful, people would be able to confront the language of power and decide themselves how they wanted to work with it. This is in line with an approach to 'literacy as critical reflection'. Rather than seeing language as a means of communication it focuses first on the role of language in making meaning, and a programme conceptualising literacy as critical reflection is likely to start with the first language of its participants.

It is important to be able to actively engage with the language of power through voting, application, or legal procedures at a national and international level as well as a local level. Some practitioners feel that denying people access to this language, or making them wait until they are proficient in literacy in their first language, is to act as gatekeepers to a broader political domain. A skills-based or task-based approach to literacy would favour the use of the language in which those tasks are carried out. However, this is likely to promote the language of the public sphere for men who work within it, and the local language of the home for women who operate predominately in the domestic sphere. This kind of approach could exacerbate power inequalities in gender relationships rather than address them.

From mother-tongue literacy to national languages

Many educational programmes start with mother-tongue literacy. Primary schools often use local languages as both a medium for education and the language of initial literacy before moving on to the use of dominant languages in secondary education. Research has indicated that learning an indigenous language helps with the learning of a second language, and enriches the quality of that learning. Students often feel more at ease with a local language, which they know well, than with a language they know little about and may be reluctant to use for fear of being laughed at.

At the University of Ibadan in Nigeria, two groups of students attended English classes for 12 months. One group was literate in Yoruba and the other had no written language. Unsurprisingly the literate group – who were used to formal learning – did far better than the other group. While this has been taken as evidence that 'literacy in the vernacular has a positive transfer effect on literacy in a second language' (Omelowa 2000), it also indicates that once familiar with the culture and practice of learning, students will fare better in a second round of classes.

Similar research conducted with adults in the USA also showed that learning to read in a first language aids the acquisition of and reading ability in a second language. Studies with adult learners from a range of language backgrounds including Spanish, Cambodian, and Korean suggested that there is a transfer in basic reading skills from the first to the second language irrespective of the scripts involved (Carlo and Skilton-Sylvester 1994; Wagner *et al.* 1999). These all indicate that first-language literacy development is strongly related to successful second-language learning and academic achievement, and that literacy skills developed in the native language transfer to the second language.

While it can be argued that bilingualism and bi-literacy provide intellectual, economic, and social benefits to learners, they also have an economic cost for programme designers and time implications for learners. The use of first-language literacy helps learners to make sense of what they read and to read for meaning rather than decoding. People start by reading words they may have a deeper attachment to, and are more able to remember what they read, to use sentences properly, and to correct themselves. But it is difficult to sustain mother-tongue literacy if there is limited use for it, and if primary school children or adult literacy groups move on to learning dominant languages the literacy of their first language may soon be forgotten. Teaching initial literacy in a first language may help the learning process but may do little to sustain a minority language. In areas where resources are limited and local languages are predominantly oral, it may be difficult to justify the time and money needed to prepare people to teach groups in their mother tongue.

Resistance to the promotion of minority languages in education has been mainly economic. It is argued that it is wasteful to use several languages in communities that have a common language, and that resources do not exist to develop parallel materials simultaneously. In Nigeria, the National Language Policy has been to adopt the three major languages of Hausa, Yoruba, and Igbo, the three official languages in which the network news is broadcast. However, a local project (described in Box 10.1 and supported by the European Union) worked with primers in eight indigenous languages. A second programme, designed with learners in South Africa, experimented with teaching literacy in two languages as these shared a similar script and were used in parallel by learners (Box 10.2).

Box 10.1: Indigenous languages in Nigeria

The Federal Government, in cooperation with the European Community, supported a project to prepare literacy primers in eight of the indigenous languages of two of the States in Nigeria. The response to this development from the people was enthusiastic, as many adult learners who would otherwise have stayed away from literacy classes began to enrol and remain in the classes. They joined in the process of rewriting their history and in documenting songs, idioms and proverbs in the area. The experience of the University Village Association (UNVA) is instructive. At the beginning of its literacy project, there was considerable reluctance by the people to learn the local language. The European languages were preferred because jobs could be secured among the expatriate population and more readily in Government offices. UNVA, however, encouraged the people to begin to use the local language. Materials were prepared for first learners and post-literacy learners. The project recorded considerable success as more people turned up for classes. The community felt comfortable with owning the project, which respected the culture and language, and there was increased community participation. Soon, the community, which began to sing local songs and take pride in wearing traditional attire, began to contribute to the project by building community centres and literacy classes.

Source: Omolewa 2000

Box 10.2: Multilanguage - South Africa

A project in South Africa based literacy learning around the language of use.
In practice this meant a programme that integrated elements of Zulu and English according to the particular documents people wanted access to. Multilanguage use is much more part of African life than it is in other parts of the world, and Zulu, where it is used colloquially, integrates many English terms. Consequently people in the townships where this project took place were used to speaking Zulu with each other, bits of English when communicating with officials, and a mixture of both when discussing one with the other. In this instance where both used the same script, it was not difficult to teach letter use and letter signs and apply this to both languages. Consequently names were written in Zulu, as was personal information, but transferred to English in formats used for form filling. People wrote letters and read Bible texts in Zulu but looked at ordering from shopping catalogues in English. In some cases learners did not themselves distinguish between what was a Zulu and what was an English word, and in most cases they knew the words and the terminology they wanted to learn to write.

Source: case study from author's experience

Regional language variations

Even the decision to use a dominant language is not simple, and learners are likely to be challenged by the differences between the ways in which language is spoken and written. English for example has many variations, including transatlantic and post-colonial differences in words, spelling, and regional accents. Regional vocabulary differences and varied grammatical patterns have been added to by the language patterns of large immigrant groups. Literacy students have to reconcile the way they speak a home or second language with the way they are required to write it. This might entail learning the standard form of the language, as well as learning to decode the spoken language from the script and encode the oral language.

Over 200 million people speak Arabic, but the speakers of the different dialects do not necessarily understand each other. There are also many forms of the language; classical Arabic found in the Koran and religious texts, Modern Standard Arabic (MSA) used by many countries as the national or official language, and over thirty modern or colloquial varieties (UNESCO 2005a). In the national Egyptian literacy programme, MSA was taught but participants also wanted to write in colloquial Arabic and record oral stories in the way in which they were spoken (GALAE and British Council 1997). In a literacy programme in south Sudan, three national languages (English, Arabic, and

Amharic) and three African languages were spoken by facilitators and participants. There were three different scripts and two different directions, right to left for Arabic and left to right for English, Amharic, and the African languages.

Box 10.3 illustrates the use of text language on mobile phones to develop written literacy among deaf users of sign language.

Box 10.3: Multi-modal literacies, Gambia

There have been recent debates about the impact of new technologies on literacy learning and literacy use, and experiments with email messages, MSN, and mobile phones as motivators for people to learn to read. A literacy and sign-language programme in the Gambia gives a good example. Deaf tutors were trained to teach deaf people sign language and literacy alongside each other. By beginning with people's names, they introduced sign names as a concept – relating an aspect of the person to a way of denoting them, and then linking this to their written name. The sign-language alphabet and the written alphabet were introduced alongside each other, and, in helping participants to learn to communicate in sign, they highlighted those words that also might need to be written down. These might include elements of personal information to be written on official documents, or street signs and shop signs that people might want to read. They took a thematic approach and looked at hospital language (how to communicate health problems, how to read health information), transport language (how to communicate where you want to go, where you come from, how to read direction signs), restaurant language and so on. The explosion of mobile-phone technology – crucial to deaf people if they are to communicate across distances, meant that suddenly everyone wanted to text each other, and the need to understand and to send texts had an immediate impact on a particular form of literacy. How and whether to use this as part of formal literacy learning, and the transferability of text literacy to other forms of literacy use is rich material for future research and development.

Source: case study from author's experience

Creating an orthography for oral languages

While there is a strong case for the preservation of minority languages, it is less clear as to the best way to do this. Some projects (including those run by SIL International, a faith-based organisation that studies, documents, and assists in developing the world's lesser-known languages) have gone to great lengths to create an orthography for a previously unwritten language, analysing systems and grammar patterns, and developing a literature. Linguistic ecologists warn against the random introduction of writing and literacy into previously oral languages and claim that 'reducing' languages to writing can diminish rather than preserve a rich oral heritage. They argue that the process of developing a writing system requires the selection of a dominant dialect which then leads to the denigration of other less powerful varieties of the language, and reduces rather than preserves linguistic diversity.

Others disagree and point out that dialects and varieties of language have demonstrated an amazing resistance to the effects of literacy standardisation, as is the case with English and Arabic. Literacy practitioners argue that literacy has been brought into the linguistic and cultural lives of many minority communities and that it has been shaped and used by them for their own purposes, rather than shaping and determining the way that language is used. While producing curriculum, literature, and learning materials is resource-intensive, some governments have chosen to do this in order to preserve and promote home languages. Instructional materials, literature, and training materials have been produced successfully by members of minority-language communities around the world: South America (Aikman 2001), North America (Watahomigie and McCarty 1994), Asia (Geary 2001), and Africa (Dutcher 1998), in collaboration with institutes, universities, and NGOs which have provided technical assistance where needed (Malone 2003). Educators in Papua New Guinea are experimenting with mother-tongue literacy in almost half of indigenous languages (Box 10.4).

Box 10.4: Mother-tongue education in Papua New Guinea

Papua New Guinea, with a total of some 800 languages, have set educational goals for mother tongue pre-primary level education and are now supporting 3-year programs of elementary education in over 300 community languages. They are using a bottom-up approach to materials development by helping the local community to produce their own elementary-level, culturally appropriate curriculum and instructional materials. While this is a task that many government education departments cannot perform on their own, with adequate training education departments are well positioned to support and assist the local efforts.

In PNG, local community writers and educators collaborated with an international NGO and bilateral donor to produce the 17-volume Kaugel Reading Series containing 96 Kaugel stories which, in addition to numerous teacher-student generated stories, are currently in use in 15 elementary-level mother-tongue classrooms serving some 600 children.

Source: S. Premsrirat and D. Malone (2003) 'Language Development and Language Revitalization in Asia', paper presented at the Bangkok conference on Language Development, Language Revitalization and Multilingual Education in Minority Communities in Asia, available at: www.sil.org/asia/ldc/plenary_papers/ suwila_and_dennis_malone.pdf, last accessed July 2007.

If minority languages are to be used, training in language development and language revitalisation is crucial. It is likely that people working in education or those with sufficient schooling to become literacy facilitators may not themselves be able to write their local language. Learning how to do this fluently cannot be done with academics alone. Developing a community language and training people to use it needs the expertise of people who are proficient users of it as well as specialists who can help with technical linguistic support. The community who currently use this language need to be fully on board and development work should be done *with* them, not *for* them. Participatory research into attitudes towards and uses of the local language and how it interfaces with other languages in the area is essential if the intervention is to promote the use of that language rather than its historical preservation.

Gender-specific language

Over the last 30 years feminists all over the world have analysed the gender implications of how language is used and the effects of these on people's perceptions of gender roles. In some cases this has led to the change in a particular term or the phasing out of certain language elements. In English, for example, the term for a person presiding over a meeting has changed from 'chairman' (which assumes that person to be male) to 'chair' (which can apply equally to a male or a female). Similarly, terms for trades formerly undertaken by men (such as postman) have adopted the suffix 'person' (to become post-person), or changed altogether (such as labourer rather than workman).

However, the gender neutrality of many English words can be problematic – terms used in this text, such as teachers, facilitators, instructors, students, learners can all refer to either women or men. When translated into other languages these words frequently have to be put in either the feminine or masculine form, and traditionally are often given the masculine form. This can lead to the women involved becoming either invisible or having their particular concerns overlooked. Box 10.5 describes one example of this (the lack of female facilitators recruited for a literacy programme in Nigeria). In Egypt, even in a programme that employed principally female facilitators, the male form of the word was generally used (Box 10.6).

Box 10.5: The language of gender in Nigeria

In north-east Nigeria a monitoring report halfway through the project stated that the targets which were gender-specific would not be met. It was not clear why, as there was great enthusiasm for the programme. A gender analysis was undertaken. One of the main reasons for the project not being on target was that the local male project manager had asked the male village chiefs to select people to be trained as literacy facilitators. 'Literacy facilitators' was, naturally, in the masculine form. So quite properly the chiefs had chosen men. As almost no women were trained as facilitators, women could not attend the literacy groups because of cultural stipulations that women had to be taught by women. Once realised, the situation was remedied; women were trained as facilitators and women joined the programme.

Source: McCaffery 2004

Box 10.6: The language of gender in Egypt

In a programme in Egypt, two-thirds of the classes were for women, and women facilitators had been recruited and trained, yet the masculine form was used when referring to women facilitators or literacy participants – even when only women were present. The female interpreter challenged this on the grounds that if women are not kept consistently in mind, the literacy needs and aspirations of male learners would dominate and the programme would become inappropriately male-orientated. Even then the interpreters refused to use the female form as it 'sounded wrong'.

Source: McCaffery 2004

Gender difference in language usage

There are also differences in the way women and men use language. While there may be a number of languages in use in a particular region, it is likely that women and men will make use of them in different situations. As men operate more frequently in the public sphere and travel more frequently out of their community, they are more likely to have more knowledge of regional or national languages (if these differ). Women may be more familiar with local languages but may want access to the languages of power, as in a programme run by Nirantur in India, described in Box 10.7.

> **Box 10.7: Local languages and gender in India**
>
> In a programme in India the planners felt strongly that the local language should be taught and learned, as this was the language used predominantly by women. They tried to show groups how local language embodies the culture of a people, and marginalising it results in making that culture invisible. However, the women felt strongly that the language of power, Hindi, should be given priority as it was this that enabled them to access the mainstream. They argued that they already knew their own language, but underlying these arguments were notions that their own language was also inferior. They resolved this through looking together at words that existed in Hindi and their equivalent in the local language. The women soon began to realise that a lot of the elements that made up their day did not have a direct equivalent in Hindi. Items of jewellery for instance, that had a particular significance for them, had one common Hindi word. They also realised that English, which was seen as a more powerful language than Hindi, lacked many of the kinship terms that their own language captured.
>
> Eventually the group agreed to work through the medium of their local language, to undertake written tasks in Hindi, and to continue to incorporate idioms and particular expressions in their own languages. This echoes some of the work undertaken in South Africa where two languages with the same script were used alongside each other, and written tasks undertaken in the language of use.
>
> *Source: Nirantur 1997*

Implications for planners

There is no one simple answer to the question of which language should be used in a literacy programme. While research in some areas suggests that people who learn in their mother tongue transfer more easily to second-language literacy, this is not systematic, and there are no firm conclusions on the relative time and cost of the two approaches. Where there is no clear language policy, decisions on the language to use should be made in collaboration with participants, funders, and those who have a clear understanding of the process used in the formal education system. Adult learners themselves often express a demand for literacy in a regional and/or national language and in Tanzania, literacy programmes in Swahili proved far more popular than ones in local languages.

Balancing these factors is not easy and the key features of an inclusive multilingual policy should be based on:

- studies of the linguistic and socio-linguistic situation, including attitudes of communities towards the languages they use and towards official languages;

- consultations with local communities as an input to learning and to the governance of adult programmes;
- locally written and produced teaching materials;
- the addition of second (and third) languages that take account of learners' competence and knowledge;
- a consideration of the extra cost of training teachers and developing materials in multiple languages which must be weighed against the inefficiency of teaching in languages that learners do not understand so well.

Further reading

J. Millican, 'I will stay here until I die: a critical analysis of the Muthande Literacy Programme', in A. Robinson Pant (ed.) *Women Literacy and Development*, London/New York: Routledge, 2004. Millican provides an analysis of a particular programme in South Africa that used a dual language approach with older people.

M. Omolewa, 'The Language of Literacy', final remarks delivered at a strategy session on 'Literacy for All: A Renewed Vision for a Ten-Year Global Action Plan', organised on behalf of the EFA Forum by the UNESCO Institute for Education (UIE), the International Literacy Institute (ILI), ISESCO, ActionAid, and SIDA, available at: www.iiz-dvv.de/englisch/Publikationen/ Ewb_ausgaben/55_2001/eng_Omolewa.html, 2000. Omelowa's speech discusses the role of language in the definition of identity.

UNESCO Bangkok, 'Manual for Developing Literacy and Adult Education Programmes in Minority Language Communities', available at: http://unesdoc.unesco.org/images/0013/001351/135164e.pdf, 2004. This is a useful online manual for designing and implementing literacy programmes in minority languages.

'First Language First: Community Based Literacy Programmes for Minority Language Contexts in Asia', www2.unescobkk.org/elib/publications/ first_language/first_language.pdf. This is an online resource documenting the outcomes of a workshop in China in 2004 on the use of minority languages in literacy programmes. It provides a good overview of facts and figures as well as advice on taking minority programmes forward.

Monitoring and evaluating literacy programmes

This chapter suggests that monitoring and evaluation of literacy programmes is an essential element in the planning process. It describes the main elements of monitoring, formative evaluation, and summative evaluation, and how to make these fit for purpose. It outlines some key elements in planning monitoring and evaluation: deciding on who, what, how, and when. The chapter then discusses the kinds of questions to think about in monitoring and evaluation, not as an exhaustive list but as a stimulus to the planning process.

Monitoring and evaluation provide different kinds of insights into programmes. Monitoring is a systematic way of checking and reporting on day-to-day operations. Evaluation is a way to ask (and answer) 'value' questions about how well the project is working and what its outcomes are. Its purpose may be 'formative' (to form and improve the project as it continues) or 'summative' (to sum up how well the project achieved its goals).

Why monitor and evaluate?

Monitoring and evaluating programmes and projects gives opportunities to:

- learn from experience;
- change and improve;
- be accountable to others (whether these are external to the programme, like funders and governments, or stakeholders like learners and partners).

Yoland Wadsworth in her book on 'everyday evaluation on the run', points out that all of us evaluate all the time in our daily lives: 'We decide whether things are valuable or not important, worthwhile or not 'worth it'; whether things are good or bad, right or wrong, are going OK or 'off the rails' … every time we choose, decide, accept or reject we have made an evaluation' (Wadsworth 1997: 5).

Monitoring

Monitoring is about recording and reviewing day-to-day activities in a systematic way – for example how many people are involved in the project, how often they come and for how long, whether certain kinds of people are involved (e.g. women, indigenous peoples), and what their learning involves. Monitoring can help keep track of operations by recording answers to questions like:

- What kinds of learners are taking part in the programme (and are these the people who were expected to take part)?
- Who is participating at different times of day, and in different locations – are there patterns and does anything suggest changes to be made in order to attract key groups of learners?
- Are participants continuing to come to learn, and if there are high levels of drop-out is there an indication why?
- Are participants making progress with their learning?

Evaluation

Formative evaluation

Formative evaluation gives insights while a project is operating that can help it improve. It looks at how the project is carrying out the original design and intent. It may reveal flaws in the original design, or changes that require action. Formative evaluation will include reviews of monitoring data. It may also involve gathering other kinds of data from participants, staff, and others to answer questions like:

- Are participants satisfied with the programme?
- Do participants have suggestions about how it might be improved?
- Are staff satisfied with the way the programme is going, and do they have suggestions for improvement?
- Is the programme reaching the people intended (and if not, why not)?
- What would make the programme more effective (e.g. resources, training of facilitators, changes in time and place of classes)?

Summative (or impact or outcomes) evaluation

Summative evaluation is conducted at the end of a project (or a major stage of the project). The main focus is often on the outcomes or impacts achieved, but it will also try to distil lessons learned that could inform future work. It may analyse many kinds of data, including day-to-day monitoring data, input from participants and from others in the community, as well as staff reviews. It can help answer questions like:

- What were the outcomes for learners?
- Were there impacts on learners' lives and those of their families and communities?
- What lessons were learned from a project?
- What would be done differently, if the project were to be run again?

It is not easy to identify the outcomes and impacts of literacy programmes, although there are a variety of ways of trying to do so. Developing better ways of demonstrating outcomes is a priority of international agencies like UNESCO (see Box 11.1).

Box 11.1: UNESCO priorities for monitoring and evaluation

UNESCO regards the most urgent actions in monitoring and evaluating international literacy programmes as the following:

- refining literacy indicators and emphasizing those measuring the qualitative impact of literacy;
- promoting widespread and better use of census and population data;
- developing improved methods for assessing the literacy levels of individuals as well as for evaluating learning outcomes at the programme level;
- working out and utilizing a common yet locally acceptable framework for assessing progress towards achieving 50% improvement of levels of literacy by 2015;
- building management information systems in support of literacy policies and programmes;
- studying the specific impact of literacy on the quality of life.

Source: UNESCO nd

The LABE project in Uganda constructed a summary for monitoring and evaluating literacy programmes (Box 11.2). This clearly links the aspect of the programme being evaluated (for example access and quality), the specific data collected for monitoring and evaluation (for example number of learners enrolled and number demonstrating competence), and the purpose for which collected data will be used (for example accountability to the local community or to funder, improving teaching and learning, making decisions about future programmes).

Box 11.2: Monitoring and evaluation in LABE, Uganda		
Aspects of evaluation	**What specifically is evaluated**	**For what purpose**
Access	Number of learners enrolled (as an estimate of potential attendees)	Largely accountability to communities, local authorities and donors
	Number of functional literacy classes	Planning distribution of literacy services
Quality	Learning and instructional materials	Relevance of instructional and learning materials
	Number of trained and active instructors	Access to relevant materials
	Methods of evaluating attainment	Capacity building for instructors where needed
	Adult literacy policy formulation and planning	Attainment levels of learners in reading, writing and numeracy
	Number of learners demonstrating competence in basic literacy skills	Determine progression of learners
Efficiency	Resources used both financial and material	Financial management and accountability
		Management of literacy classes and programmes
Effectiveness	Partnership strategy	Investigating multiplier effects working with and through partners
	Approaches employed in adult literacy instruction	
Relevance	Instructional materials	Making decisions on design of future programmes
	Literacy services offered	Curriculum reform
		Development of the right instruction and materials
Equity	Participation of all learners in the programme	Levels of participation of females: learners, instructors, managers
	Focus given to female learners, ethnic minorities, learners in conflict areas, refugees	
Impact	Utilization of literacy skills attained	Determine the effect of our intervention for future planning purposes
	Changes in lives of learners, instructors	

Source: Okech and the Country Project Team 2005

Making monitoring and evaluation fit for purpose

Monitoring and evaluation must be clearly linked to the goals and approaches of the programme. They also must meet the need for accountability of the programme to a potentially wide range of other organisations and individuals. If monitoring and evaluation are to be useful rather than a burden, it is essential to make them fit for purpose, perhaps a challenge when there are often multiple purposes.

Consistency with programme focus and goals

The underlying concept of literacy upon which the programme is based (skills, tasks, social practice, critical reflection), will lead to particular questions and methods. For example:

- A skills-based programme may place a priority on measuring improvement in the literacy and numeracy skills of participants in the programme. Other kinds of outcomes (for example, changes in application of skills in daily life) may be less significant.

- A task-based programme may put a priority on documenting learners' ability to accomplish tasks, whether these are everyday literacy, work-related, or community-related tasks. An abstract view of skills may be less important than whether learners can do things.

- A social practice programme is likely to place a priority on how learners engage in their own communities of practice, and what changes are taking place in their lives.

- A critical reflection programme is likely to place a priority on how groups use literacy to analyse and act on issues.

Accountability

Accountability is an important reason for doing monitoring and evaluation. Accountability means being 'responsible for the effects of your actions and willing to explain them or be criticised for them' (Longman's Web Dictionary – www.ldoconline.com). It has four key elements:

- responsibility for actions
- reporting – giving an account
- entitlement to receive an account
- consequences (simply reporting does not constitute accountability).

Different models of accountability set out different ways of answering key questions: Who is held accountable? For what? To whom? What are the consequences of failing to meet goals?

In any literacy programme there will be accountability relationships involving different stakeholders. These might include:

- accountability to international agencies which are funding the project
- accountability to national or local government departments which may be funding or have other responsibilities for the programme
- accountability within the programme to partners, staff, and community organisations
- accountability within the programme to participants or learners.

Sometimes these accountability relationships cause tensions, as different ones pull in different directions – for example, responsibility to funders may conflict with what learners want and expect. Developing a framework for monitoring and evaluation as part of the planning process will include clarifying the different accountability relationships and how they might work together rather than in conflict.

Programme improvement

Monitoring and evaluation can be crucial tools to improve the current programme or to lay a stronger basis for future ones. To improve their programmes, managers must understand what has worked well for particular groups of learners in specific contexts. Monitoring and evaluation needs to make links between aspects of the programme (for example tutors and tutor training, recruitment of learners, resources and materials, teaching and learning processes) and the impacts and outcomes on participants and communities.

Planning monitoring and evaluation

Programmes funded by international agencies may be required to monitor certain kinds of data and to evaluate particular aspects of the work. They may be required to employ an external evaluator. Sometimes an external evaluator can be a useful means of getting a fresh perspective and may bring useful knowledge of similar programmes elsewhere. They may have useful methods and tips to offer. But evaluation can be and often is done by insiders, by members of a project's own staff, participants, and other community members. These insiders are not only the ones with the critical knowledge about the programme's work, but they are also the ones who can bring about change.

Whether or not an external evaluator is involved in some or all of the evaluation, programme planners need to think about the 'why, who, what, when, and how' of evaluation:

- *Why* is monitoring and evaluation being done?
- *Who* will be the main audience for the evaluation report and who will be key participants in the evaluation (providing and gathering information, reviewing and analysing it)?
- *What* aspects of the work need to be monitored or evaluated?
- *When* will monitoring and evaluation activities take place?
- *How* will the monitoring and evaluation be done?

Evaluation plans will of course be affected by the available budget and resources: it is important to be realistic about what can be achieved with limited resources, and better to answer a few questions well than to have many questions that cannot be satisfactorily answered.

Why is monitoring and evaluation being done?

Different purposes will often require different monitoring and evaluation methods. Whatever the purpose for evaluation, it should be consistent with the purposes of the programme itself, and with the capacity of the staff and resources available. The purpose may be to learn from the work in order to improve the programme; there may be outside funders or agencies who want to know whether the programme is effective and represents a good investment; it may be a pilot project with the need to decide whether it should be continued and expanded.

Who will be the main audience and who will be key participants?

The main audience for the evaluation report may be participants and their communities or outside agencies. It will be important to find out what they need and want to know – their purposes for evaluation.

Different people may be involved in aspects of monitoring and evaluation:

- What will be the roles of learners and staff?
- Will there be roles for other community members (including leaders)?
- Are outsiders to play a role (e.g. evaluation experts, government officials)?
- How will these people be prepared to take part in the evaluation (especially participants and community members, who may not be familiar with evaluation activities)?

What aspects of the work will need to be monitored or evaluated?

Both monitoring and evaluation may collect information about many different aspects of the programme's operations. Broadly, these may include inputs, processes, and outcomes or impacts.

Inputs may include information such as:

- characteristics of participants
- needs and resources of the communities
- experience, training, and qualifications of facilitators
- curriculum resources available
- links with other agencies.

Processes may include information such as:

- where learning groups are operating
- who is attending and how often
- what teaching methods are used
- how long participants stay engaged with learning
- feedback from staff, participants, and those who have left the programme.

Outcomes and impacts may include information such as:

- *reaction* – what participants and community members think about the project and how it is going
- *learning* – how much participants learned and whether it was what they planned to learn
- *behaviour* – whether participants changed what they do in their lives
- *results* – whether the project made a difference and achieved the outcomes desired (it is better to be realistic about what outcomes the programme might achieve, given the constraints in its environment and capacity).

When will monitoring and evaluation activities take place?

To provide the most useful insights, monitoring and evaluation may need to take place at different time points during the project:

- Monitoring will be ongoing, but it is important to be clear about specific points of time when data needs to be gathered, and to ensure that the record-keeping is not so onerous that it interferes with the effectiveness of the project.
- Formative evaluation takes place while the project is operating – there should be enough time for the project to have had some results but it should still be early enough to use the evaluation in modifying the project activities.
- Summative evaluation usually takes place at the end of a project, or the end of a key stage of a longer project or programme. But the information it reviews may need to be gathered at different times, including establishing a baseline (perhaps from a needs analysis) at the beginning.

In the initial planning process it is important to plan what kinds of monitoring and evaluation activities will be conducted when. Tutors may need to collect initial information from learners on their needs (including literacy levels on entering the programme), their learning goals and purposes, and how they use reading and writing in their daily lives. These create baseline data for evaluation purposes. A programme in Indonesia (Box 11.3) illustrates the planning for evaluation activities at different stages: before the learning process, during the learning process, and at the end or after the learning process is completed.

Box 11.3: Evaluation in the Functional Literacy Programme, Indonesia

Evaluation before the learning process begins

The evaluation was designed to gather information about the learners' interests, technical skills and literacy skills. This information was used for planning the initial group activities. The tutor helped the group produce a learning contract and learning plan. The organization collected copies of the evaluation forms to document the learners' starting points. Copies of the learning contracts and learning plans enabled supervisors to keep track of what type of learning activities each group is doing.

Evaluation during the learning process

In contrast to traditional programme planning where needs are assessed only at the beginning, the Indonesian literacy programme incorporated ongoing needs identification, planning and evaluation. The reason for this is that the learners don't know all of their needs and interests from the beginning. In fact, the ability to identify learning interests and needs is a skill which is developed during the learning process. The tutors and learners fill out monthly reports, identify new learning needs and make new learning plans on a regular basis. Supervisors use the monthly reports to monitor the progress of the groups.

Each month, the tutor is also expected to review each learner's progress and record their achievement on progress checklists. The tutor uses two different types of checklists. The first checklist (Basic Skills) is designed for learners who do not yet have basic literacy skills such as knowledge of the alphabet, or the ability to sound words, or read sentences fluently. The second checklist (Functional Competencies) includes a list of functional literacy applications generally arranged in order from most simple to most difficult. The tutors use these lists to get ideas for teaching activities as well as to document when the learners have the capacity to use their literacy skill for daily life activities. The tutors are also encouraged to supplement the checklists with their qualitative observations of the learners' progress by writing notes in a teachers' log or diary. In addition to helping the tutors plan and evaluate, these checklists provide a valuable source of data about the learners' progress.

Evaluation after the learning process

At the end of each funded learning period, an achievement test is given to the learners. This test is being used to gather comparative data, but many learners and tutors want some sort of certification. Although the main purpose of the evaluation process is to provide information and feedback to the tutors and learners, tests are also designed so that the organization can use the same information for certification and for research and monitoring purposes.

Source: Indonesia Directorate General of Out-of-school Education, Youth and Sports, Department of National Education 1999

How will the monitoring and evaluation be done?

Planning will include the methods for collecting information, the process for analysis, and how conclusions will be drawn and communicated.

Planning the ways of gathering information includes thinking about:

- whether information will be gathered from all learning groups and all learners, or from a sample of learning groups and learners. If a sample approach is used, the sample needs to represent the range of contexts, levels, gender, and other components of the programme;
- whether information will be gathered from documents (e.g. course records), interviews (individual or group), artefacts (e.g. learning materials, PRA matrices, and maps), or tests;
- how to document participation in learning (how many and who), drop-out, learning achievements, other outcomes achieved.

Planning analysis and drawing conclusions includes thinking about:

- who will be involved in analysing data, when this will happen, what the process will be (there are effective participatory methods for group analysis using matrices, drawings, and charts);
- what benchmarking can be done – comparing results with those of other similar projects (if there are similar projects to benchmark against and if they are willing to share data) or from a single project over time;
- when tentative conclusions are drawn, how to check these with participants, staff, and community members.

The evaluation plan from a literacy programme in Uganda (Box 11.4) may illustrate the kinds of decisions that have to be made in planning evaluation. This evaluation is extensive, in part because the literacy programme is explicitly linked with other areas such as health. The evaluation plan gives a broad view of the social and other impacts of literacy, not simply the question of whether the learners gained skills. A search for wider social impacts is common in literacy programmes, especially in the South.

Box 11.4: ADRA Uganda: What is evaluated and for what purpose?

Learners

In ADRA, a humanitarian and development implementing agency in Uganda, evaluations focus on whether learners in the target groups are being reached and whether the project objectives are being achieved. Evaluations will usually include:

- the participation and contribution of learners in project activities
- the knowledge and skills they develop, especially how they are applied
- the relevance of the topics and skills to learners' needs and daily activities
- the extent to which the programme has influenced traditional gender roles
- changes in attitudes of the learners in relation to human rights issues, HIV/AIDS awareness and conserving the environment.

Curriculum

All evaluations normally look at the curriculum used in classes including:

- the relevance of the curriculum to the interest and priorities of learners
- the applicability and adoptability of the contents
- the gender sensitivity of the contents
- the contribution and relevance of the contents in relation to other poverty reduction strategies
- the possibility of replication and integration of the curriculum with other social, civic and development issues such as human rights, environment, gender and HIV/AIDS among others
- the user friendliness of the curriculum for the instructors
- the methodologies and approaches encouraged in the curriculum.

Impact

Impact evaluation is normally done during end of phase and post implementation evaluations. The impact is normally looked at in relation to:

- the direct beneficiaries (the learners)
- indirect impact on others such as learners' families and the community.

The guiding principle is normally to assess the extent to which the programme has been able to add quality to the lives of the beneficiaries by looking at their income levels, capacity to access the basic needs, capacity to participate in both personal and community development and the general change in attitudes and outlooks to life. Impact evaluations also look at sustainability of the impact and the extent to which the programme has contributed to national goals and priorities, institutional strengthening and capacities of Community Based Organisations.

Other areas

Normally evaluations also take into consideration the cost effectiveness of the project, quality of the services provided, institutional capacity to implement such programmes and linkages with other national players. Since most programmes are integrated, the synergy between these (e.g. health, HIV/AIDS, micro finance, environmental protection, food security, school construction and training of school managers and teachers) is also evaluated.

Source: Okech and the Country Project Team 2005

In another example of the questions that evaluation might ask, a literacy project in Afghanistan carried out an internal formative evaluation to identify whether the project was on track in terms of the original design, and whether any adjustments needed to be made. The evaluation identified a series of questions to be answered (Box 11.5).

Box 11.5: Afghanistan Literacy and Community Empowerment Program

Purposes of the formative evaluation were to:

- assess the relevance, appropriateness and sustainability of the project design as described in the project appraisal report, proposal, USAID Cooperative Agreement, training materials and protocols, and work plans;
- assess the extent to which ongoing literacy [and to the degree that it is feasible, governance and economic empowerment] activities are consistent with project design, and are meeting project indicators and expected outcomes at this point in project implementation cycle;
- assess the degree of efficacy of literacy (and to the extent possible, governance and economic empowerment) materials and training.

In addition, a set of evaluation questions was formulated for the literacy component:

- To what extent, and in what ways is (or isn't) the design of the LCEP literacy component relevant, appropriate for and sustainable within its targeted constituency?
- To what extent, in what ways, and with what result is (or isn't) the LCEP literacy component consistent with project design?
- To what extent, in what ways, and with what result is (or isn't) the LCEP literacy component meeting project indicators and expected outcomes at this point in project implementation cycle?
- With what degree of skill, understanding and efficacy are targeted trainers implementing the LCEP training approach and materials? What are possible reasons for these outcomes?
- How are LCEP literacy activities viewed and understood among trainers, learners, and the community as a whole?
- Given project design parameters, what is the degree of quality and efficacy of LCEP literacy materials?
- What things is the LCEP literacy component doing right? How can these things be built upon and expanded?
- What things is the LCEP literacy component doing wrong? How can these things be corrected?
- To what extent, in what ways, and with what result do operational synergies exist between the LCEP literacy, governance and economic empowerment components? How might synergies be maximized for the benefit of the project as a whole?
- What are some promising non-LCEP approaches to literacy instruction that are currently being implemented in Afghanistan? How can LCEP learn from and/or adapt some elements of these into its programming?

Source: Bell et al. 2005

There are many general guides to evaluation available, and some of these are listed at the end of this chapter. The section below will focus on particular questions to consider in monitoring and evaluating literacy programmes.

Questions in monitoring and evaluation

Monitoring literacy programmes

What kinds of learners are taking part in the programme (and are these the people who were expected to participate)?

Who is participating when and where? Are different people coming to learn at different times of day, and in different locations? Does anything suggest changes are needed in order to attract key groups of learners?

What do participants express as their own learning goals? Do these reflect the programme goals?

How many hours are participants involved in learning each week, and is this enough time to make progress with their literacy?

Are participants staying engaged in learning long enough to have an impact? If there are high levels of drop-out are there any patterns (e.g. certain locations or times of day, certain kinds of learners)? What is known about their reasons for dropping out? Can any changes in the programme be made to keep key learners engaged?

Evaluating literacy programmes

What literacy (and other) outcomes are planned and how will you know they have been achieved? What kinds of literacies are participants expected to learn? Are participants expected to do other things in their lives differently as a result, not just reading and writing? Which other people in the community might have a stake in the programme (e.g. community leaders, family members, employers)?

How are learners recruited into learning programmes? Are intermediaries involved in this (e.g. community-development workers)? Are recruitment strategies successful in attracting key groups of learners?

How are tutors/facilitators and other project staff recruited? What training are they expected to have before they join the project? What is expected of them?

What training is provided for facilitators as part of the project? What further mentoring and support is provided for tutors following the initial training? How do tutors evaluate their training and support? Is there evidence about how training has affected teaching and learning processes?

How is the learning curriculum planned, and what is it expected to include? How are learning materials produced? Is there evidence about how these have affected teaching and learning?

In a situational analysis to explore how literacy programmes in Kenya conduct evaluation, nine programmes were asked questions as to what they evaluated in terms of learners, curriculum, and impact. The results are summarised in Box 11.6.

Box 11.6: Evaluation practices in literacy programmes in Kenya

Learners

All nine programmes focused on whether learners had acquired skills, six on behavioural changes among learners and two on learners' appreciation of the programme. Learners are expected to have undergone some transformation at the end of the learning process: not only to acquire both academic and life skills but also to utilize them in improving their lifestyles. Some expectations were that learners would be able to change behaviours, such as reduce domestic problems, engage in conflict resolution, attain better health and improve their standards of living.

Curriculum

The curriculum is a key ingredient in the teaching-learning process as it to a large extent determines what will be taught. Seven of the programmes evaluate the relevance of the curriculum to learners' needs. For instance, those leading a pastoralist lifestyle require an adult education curriculum which differs from those whose occupation is farming. Thus, an adult education curriculum must be culturally sensitive. Three programmes assessed weaknesses or gaps in the curriculum and its effectiveness as a teachers' guide.

Impacts

Six programmes evaluated learners' increased literacy and numeracy skills and seven evaluated changes in attitudes and behaviour in terms of gender and other issues.

Source: Department of Adult Education, Kenya 2005

Implications for planners

If an evaluation report is filed away or sits on a shelf, the effort in preparing it will have been wasted. Evaluations are a tool to enable organisations to build on their strengths and address their weaknesses. Assuming the programme is ongoing, or that other programmes are being developed to make use of the lessons learned, an action plan can be developed. This would translate the findings of the evaluation into action steps. As the action plan is implemented, ongoing evaluation can help track whether it is making a difference and achieving improvements.

Evaluation can be built into the work of the programme, involving staff and participants. Embedding an evaluation approach into the activities of the programme can help assure the sustainability of the literacy programme by reassuring funders about programme quality and effectiveness. Engaging learners and staff in participatory evaluation has double impact. It means that the experiences of the programme at all levels can be part of the evaluation and learning. But it also helps learners and staff become reflective and critical evaluators of their own experience, increasing the professionalism of staff and the autonomy of learners.

No matter how small- or large-scale a programme is, monitoring and evaluation need to be part of the planning and implementation so that there are ways of learning from experience, improving programme practice, and being accountable to others.

Further reading

ELDIS website, available at: www.eldis.org/participation/pme/index.htm
This has many resources to support participatory monitoring and evaluation.

M. Estrella and J. Gaventa, 'Who Counts Reality? Participatory Monitoring and Evaluation: A Literature Review', IDS Working Papers 70, available at: www.ids.ac.uk/ids/bookshop/wp/wp70.pdf, 1998. This resource introduces the key principles of participatory monitoring and evaluation, its applications for differing purposes, and a number of tools and methods used, including participatory learning methodologies as well as more conventional approaches.

Y. Wadsworth, *Everyday Evaluation on the Run*, St Leonards NSW, Australia: Allen and Unwin, 1997. This is a hands-on guide to programme evaluation, focusing on building the capacity for thoughtful, reflective, evaluative practice in the day-to-day work of service providers, community groups, and agencies.

Part IV
Understanding the Learning Process

12

How people learn to read and write

This section provides detailed analysis of the process of learning literacy (Chapter 12), and goes on to suggest how knowledge of this process should influence curriculum design, choice of resources, training of facilitators, and assessment of learning.

Reading and writing require technical skills and knowledge including sound–symbol associations, alphabet, vocabulary, and grammar rules. Literacy also requires cultural and social knowledge, including the application of skills in carrying out particular literacy tasks and practices. While skills are important aspects of literacy, they are not enough on their own without an understanding of how to apply them appropriately within different social and cultural contexts.

Learning literacy involves the same general processes people use for learning throughout their lives: observing and copying, listening to explanations from others, practising and repeating, trial and error, working alongside others, and learning from experience. Some people learn to read and write on their own but most people learn in school or other educational settings. Literacy skills and knowledge develop further as people take part in life activities that include reading and writing, as well as speaking and listening. Most people 'learn by doing'.

The first part of this chapter briefly outlines some of the research about how people learn in general that has particular significance for literacy learning. This includes the recognition of people's own purposes for learning, the role of experience in active learning, and the ways in which the brain organises and acquires knowledge.

The second part of the chapter reviews some research on how people learn the particular skills and knowledge involved in reading and writing. The research has some useful suggestions for the range of different teaching and learning methods that can be effective in literacy programmes.

Understanding learning

Psychologists of learning have taken two broad theoretical approaches. In earlier psychological models (behavioural, cognitive, and constructivist) learning was seen as something that takes place within individuals (Tusting and Barton 2003). Behaviourism saw learning as changed behaviour patterns, while cognitive and constructivist learning saw it as altered mental models or ways of thinking. More recent social models of psychology (social constructivism, activity theory, and situated cognition) see learning as socially situated, a feature of people's participation in their social contexts. Social psychological research on learning in everyday life, and neurological research on how the brain works have both contributed to socially situated models of learning. This part of the chapter reviews three key points from research on learning that have particular relevance to literacy learning: the importance of the purpose and context for learning; the role of experience and action in learning; and how knowledge is acquired and organised.

The importance of the purpose and context for learning

Learning is purposeful. People learn in order to accomplish purposes that are important to them. Because humans are social beings, these purposes are defined socially and culturally. People may want to read the Bible or Koran. They may want to write letters to family members or official letters to government agencies. Women and men may want to learn skills that help with work or income generation. They may also want to learn the words of popular songs or traditional ones, play an instrument, look after children, or take care of the sick. Being aware of the purposes people want to accomplish in their learning is an important foundation for good teaching.

Although learning happens within an individual, it takes place in a social context that shapes what is learned, by whom, and in what ways. We learn within the groups we are members of – work groups, voluntary groups, families, and informal networks. Social psychologists like Wenger (1998) call these 'communities of practice': that is, a group of individuals who do things together, create what is meaningful for them, and gain their identity. People's learning through life experiences in different communities of practice gives them assumptions about how things work and beliefs about what is important and who they are. They use these assumptions and beliefs to interpret new experiences.

A community of practice might be a group of traders at a market, where there are established ways of organising space, conventions about buying and selling, and unwritten rules about who can do what. New traders might start as assistants to existing ones (perhaps a family member) and learn the rules as they go along. They might have to apply to a government office or traders' association for permission to set up a new stall, or the process might be completely informal. Along the way the individual gains an 'identity' as a market trader and as a member of a particular market group, at the same time as he or she learns the practical knowledge and skills. Within a community of practice, members learn things through copying and trial and error.

Understanding and consciousness about what has been learned often comes later. The role of the teacher, whether in formal education or as a peer, is to support the learning process and provide a safe space for learning. As people learn, there is a gap between what they are able do on their own and what they can achieve with the support of a teacher or more capable peer. Leon Vygotsky, a Russian psychologist, called this gap the 'zone of proximal development' (ZPD) and it is a very useful concept for learning (Vygotsky 1978). Teachers are often looking for what might be called the 'next do-able step' for learners. This is a step that challenges them and takes them further on their learning journey without being so difficult that they will fail or give up. Two learning processes that help people through their ZPD are scaffolding and apprenticeship.

Scaffolding

A scaffold is a temporary framework put around a building to support workers and materials during building work. Scaffolding in a learning process is a similar temporary structure to support learners as they accomplish increasingly more challenging activities. A step-by-step guide is a kind of scaffold. Parents often use scaffolding with their children by showing them how to do things and helping them the first few times (Bruner 1983 gives some good examples). Scaffolding is also valuable for adults as they move into new situations. Someone learning to be a wood carver observes a master craftsman and is gradually given simple tasks to undertake alone. Tutors using a scaffolding approach may ask supportive questions, and give clues to help the learner. They may point out familiar words in a text while explaining unfamiliar ones. They may write a learner's own words and use these for reading exercises (the 'language experience' approach).

Apprenticeship

An apprentice is a novice who works alongside skilled workers over a long period of time and learns from them. Apprenticeship is a process through which newcomers to a social or work group slowly develop knowledge and skills as they take part in the group's activities, alongside other members. Apprentices learn the particular skills needed to complete tasks and at the same time they learn how to operate within a field of work or social life. Apprenticeship may involve many different ways of learning: observing, copying, asking questions, trial and error, practising. Other members of the group take on roles as informal teachers, both directly (through scaffolding and direct instruction) and indirectly (by being observed). The experience of being part of the group as a junior member is a learning experience.

The implications for learning literacy are that:

- Learners bring their own purposes to the learning process, and good teachers will help learners identify these and use them as part of the learning plan. Learners usually want to acquire literacy to accomplish tasks in their lives. The literacy curriculum needs to be flexible enough to respond to these learning purposes. Literacy programmes could include a process for identifying these and agreeing a learning plan.

- The learning group itself can become a community of practice, with more experienced members supporting newer members.

- The 'zone of proximal development' or next do-able step is a useful idea for tutors to use in identifying ways of challenging learners to move forward without their being discouraged by failure.

- Scaffolding offers a variety of ways to support the learning process, from use of primers and worksheets that offer structured support, to pairing two learners to work together on a task.

- Apprenticeship within the literacy group provides ways for newer learners to learn from those who have been part of the group.

The role of experience and action in learning

The American educator John Dewey, an early pioneer in experiential education, believed that the most important learning happens through undergoing and interpreting experience (Dewey 1938). Not all experiences are educational: mis-educative experiences stop or distort the potential for further growth and experience. Dewey believed that traditional school classrooms were mainly mis-educative, and he was an influential and passionate advocate for more democratic education. He did not imply that children do not learn at all in traditional classrooms, but that instead of opening up children's potential they close down creativity, innovation, critical thinking, and understanding.

Dewey had a different idea about the kinds of learning that could be more effective, and these involved encouraging learning from experience. He used a spiral to represent the process of learning, starting with experience, moving into a quest for new ideas and information to solve the problems that experiences generate, which in turn become the ground for further experience in which new problems arise. Kolb proposed an experiential learning cycle (Kolb 1984, with many variations from other authors since) with four stages:

- starting with an experience
- observing and reflecting on the experience
- making generalisations
- experimenting and putting those ideas into practice.

Putting ideas into practice then generates further experiences, continuing the learning process and turning it into a spiral as Dewey suggested earlier. Prior experience shapes how we perceive our environment and therefore new experiences. Each new experience shapes how we will experience things in the future. Reflection is the process of thinking about experiences and the problems they may create.

Most adults do most of their learning through life experience. The work of Dewey and Kolb emphasises the importance of real-life experiences for learning. But experience alone is not enough: in order to extract the most learning from experiences, we need to reflect on them. Reflection happens in different ways. We might simply stop what we are doing for a quick reflection – am I doing this right? How does this look? Or we might reconsider the assumptions on which we based our original action.

The relationship between reflection and action or experience is complex. Reflection is the process of interpreting experience but also lays the groundwork for future action. Freire uses the term 'praxis' to show the relationship between thought and action and argues that it is through praxis (action and reflection) that transformation occurs:

The insistence that the oppressed engage in reflection on their concrete situation is not a call to armchair revolution. On the contrary, reflection – true reflection – leads to action. On the other hand, when a situation calls for action, that action will constitute an authentic praxis only if its consequences become the object of critical reflection.
(Freire 1992: 52)

Literacy learning gives opportunities to reframe our understanding of the world. The more we learn to read the more we may see the world differently. Freire reminds us of the importance of linking reflection and action. Not only does literacy enable us to get information from outside our own experience but also it gives us the chance to reassess power and authority. Literacy is not the only source of transformation in how we see the world and interpret our experiences, but it can offer an important tool for such a process.

The implications for learning literacy are that:

- Experiential education offers experiences through which people can learn: for example, teaching democracy by providing democratic experiences. People can learn literacy through experiencing literacy – through language experience stories, reading and discussing texts together, using literacy and numeracy to accomplish a group activity.

- Experiences from learners' lives outside the learning group can become part of the process of active learning and reflection.

- The learning group can offer a 'safe space' to learners in which they can experiment and learn from mistakes.

- Reflection is an important part of learning and can take place at levels from a quick 'check' on what has been learned to in-depth critical reflection.

- Reflecting on real-life experiences can provide opportunities for learners to change their understanding of themselves and the world. Learning can be transformative.

Acquiring and organising knowledge

The old notion of learners' minds as blank slates to be filled with knowledge by teachers or parents has been overturned by research on how the brain works and how learning takes place within it. Now we understand that even babies are active learners trying to make sense of the world. A summary of recent research on learning says:

> *Humans are … goal-directed agents who actively seek information.*
> *They come to formal education with a range of prior knowledge, skills,*
> *beliefs, and concepts that significantly influence what they notice about the*
> *environment and how they organize and interpret it. This in turn affects*
> *their abilities to remember, reason, solve problems, and acquire new knowledge.*
> (Bransford *et al.* 1999: 10)

Literacy programmes may find particularly useful the research on memory and how the brain structures knowledge; on problem solving and reasoning; and on 'metacognition' (self-monitoring of one's performance and learning).

Memory and structuring knowledge

The brain is not a passive recorder of facts and ideas: the mind creates categories for processing information. Without this way of structuring information we would be overwhelmed. People perceive things selectively, make links to other information, make assumptions about gaps and unstated ideas, and reframe what they see to fit with what they already know. In some experiments people consistently 'remember' words that are implied but not stated. 'False' memories can be as convincing as events that actually happened.

Each individual makes knowledge coherent by creating patterns and clusters, linked around core concepts or meanings. These patterns of existing knowledge underpin understanding and thinking. New knowledge has to be linked with existing knowledge and core concepts to make sense – people tie it into the pattern of what they already know and believe.

But women and men are not locked forever into existing patterns of knowledge: creativity depends on being able to think beyond existing patterns and concepts, to create new links and associations. People can think 'outside the box' or beyond it. Their life experiences and their reflection on them provide the impetus and means for rearranging knowledge patterns.

Problem solving and reasoning

Research on problem solving and reasoning shows how people apply their knowledge to solve problems and accomplish tasks. In order to solve problems individuals must understand the problem, retrieve useful knowledge, apply it, and monitor the impact. Research has looked at the differences between 'novices' (beginners) and 'experts' (people who are proficient in a particular area, not because of their formal education but because of their experience). In tasks as diverse as playing chess, building electronic circuits, packing dairy products for delivery, programming computers, and piloting aeroplanes, it has become clear that it is not just the amount of knowledge that makes a difference, but how it is organised (Bransford *et al.* 1999: 19ff). Experts recognise patterns in a situation that novices don't notice. Pattern recognition is the key difference between experts and novices. Experts begin problem solving at a higher level than novices because they recognise important features, know what to pay attention to, and understand how to represent the problem in a way that helps the solution. They comprehend a problem in terms of core concepts and are able to retrieve the important and useful knowledge from memory quickly in order to solve the problem.

Metacognition or self-monitoring

Metacognition is the ability to monitor one's own thinking and reasoning. This ability is an important part of developing expertise through learning: the ability to step back from an initial over-simplistic definition of a problem and rethink it. This self-consciousness allows everyone to recognise their limitations and to go beyond what they already know.

Adults have the advantage over children in having a wealth of experiences that can be analysed to form the basis of new learning. By understanding how they learn best, learners can gain control over their learning and become more effective learners. Some educators suggest there are four stages in learning any skill, which allow us to progress from *incompetence* to *competence*. These are:

1. Unconscious incompetence: the individual neither understands nor knows how to do something, and neither recognises the deficit nor has a desire to address it.

2. Conscious incompetence: though the individual does not understand or know how to do something, he or she does recognise the deficit, without yet addressing it.

3. Conscious competence: the individual understands or knows how to do something. However, demonstrating the skill or knowledge requires a great deal of consciousness or concentration.

4. Unconscious competence: the individual has had so much practice with a skill that it becomes 'second nature' and can be performed easily (often without concentrating too deeply). He or she can also teach it to others.

While no-one is quite sure of the origin of this as a model, and it has been attributed to both Confucius and Socrates, it is a good way of presenting the move from unawareness to tacit knowledge of a skill. The model has been used in the training of new tutors and facilitators to help them understand the learning process of their learners and themselves.

Some implications for learning literacy include:

- Understanding how memory works, tutors can link new knowledge to existing knowledge through questions and discussion.
- 'Novices' become 'experts' in any task through practice: literacy programmes can offer many different opportunities to practise skills, especially by linking with everyday tasks in learners' lives.
- Problem solving can be a powerful learning tool and if well-supported can be an approach in the literacy learning group.
- Becoming a reflective learner includes becoming more conscious about what one has learned and how one learned it, and monitoring one's own thinking processes.

Learning to read

Most researchers who study reading have looked at the process of learning to read among children. Two recent reports provide a detailed summary of research on teaching reading in American schools (NICHD 2000; Snow 2002). (Of course, this research may not reflect other contexts and languages, and may not be fully applicable to adults.) In the UK an exploratory study looked at adult learners' difficulties in reading and identified a range of strategies being used to address these (Besser *et al.* 2004).

Two areas of reading research have practical applications for adult literacy programmes: reading for understanding and the technical skills of reading.

Reading for understanding

Comprehension, or reading for understanding, is not just extracting meaning from a text, but is an active process of constructing meaning. There are three elements in any reading task:

- *the reader*, who brings a particular set of capacities, abilities, knowledge, and experiences to the act of reading
- *the text*, which may include any written, printed, or electronic text
- *the activity* of which reading is a part, which has its purposes, processes, and consequences (Snow 2002: 10).

The reading task also occurs within a larger socio-cultural context. While there are features of a text itself that make it easier or harder to understand (including how familiar the form and vocabulary are to the reader), comprehension is affected by all the elements of the task and varies over time as well as in different contexts. The reader will change as he or she gains new knowledge or insights. This changes how he or she views the text, and affects the purpose for the next reading activity.

Snow's report acknowledges the crucial role that good teaching plays in developing students' comprehension strategies and skills, and recognises that we know less than we should about how effective teachers select instructional strategies to work with particular groups of students. Snow suggests that effective teachers:

- manage their classrooms to ensure minimal disruption and the maximum amount of time on tasks;
- provide an atmosphere of support and encouragement (students feel comfortable taking risks and are expected to achieve);
- use a variety of instructional practices that relate specifically to reading comprehension;
- help readers make connections between texts they read and their personal lives and experiences;
- use small-group instruction to meet the individual needs of their readers;
- provide their readers with practice reading materials at their appropriate reading level (Snow 2002: 42–3).

Teaching and learning approaches likely to increase reading for understanding also draw on some of the general approaches discussed earlier: linking new knowledge (including vocabulary) to established patterns, using problem-solving techniques to construct meaning, and providing scaffolding support to the learning process.

Technical skills of reading

American research has identified three key elements in learning to read that may be relevant to anyone learning to read for the first time, whether child or adult (NICHD 2000):

- *alphabetics* – the correspondence between letter/symbol and sound that is the basis for text
- *fluency* – the process of reading with speed and accuracy, necessary to remember what has been read and to relate to the reader's own knowledge and ideas
- *comprehension* – the active process of constructing and extracting meaning from text.

Reading and writing require an understanding of the relationship between sound and symbol. Readers need to be able to 'decode': turn a symbol into its equivalent sound (a phoneme, the smallest unit of spoken speech). Writers need to 'encode': turn a sound (phoneme) into a symbol. Alphabetics is the process through which people understand and manipulate the system in their language for linking letter or symbol with sound. It includes both phoneme awareness and phonics.

Phoneme awareness

The first step in reading is phoneme awareness, being able to 'hear' how speech is made up of separate sound units. Although children acquire phoneme awareness as they learn to speak, there is evidence that deliberate phoneme-awareness training is valuable in learning to read. This reinforces the importance of oral language (speaking and listening) for reading.

There are obvious problems for deaf learners who have limited or no awareness of the sounds in spoken words. Those who have been through formal education and have been taught speech will have some phoneme awareness but in countries of the South, where specialised education is limited, deaf adult learners depend more on memory and visual links between signs and written words.

Phonics

Phonics is the system for associating sounds and symbols within any language. Phonics instruction helps beginner readers understand letter–sound links and how to apply these in reading and writing. There is evidence that systematic phonics teaching enhances children's success in learning to read (NICHD 2000: 10). There are two main approaches to phonics instruction: synthetic and analytic. Synthetic phonics starts with teaching learners to convert letters into sounds and then blend the sounds to form words. It has been shown to have a positive effect on beginner readers with learning disabilities. Analytic phonics starts with a whole word set in context (a sentence, a picture) and works with the learner to break it down and identify the phonemes within it.

Fluency

Fluency is the ease, accuracy, and speed of reading. Reading fluency helps the reader to remember the words and relate the ideas to existing knowledge. 'Practice makes master' when it comes to reading fluency, but research suggests that some kinds of practice are more effective than others (NICHD 2000: 12). Independent silent reading with little or no feedback from a teacher does not appear to be effective in improving reading (however, research with beginner English language students at the University of Portland, USA, suggested that modified sustained silent reading was effective in modelling reading behaviours and in helping students think about reading as an activity for getting meaning). Guided oral reading, with a teacher, peer, or parent offering guidance and feedback in a scaffolding approach, does appear to improve reading fluency.

Features of a text itself affect the ease and fluency with which someone can read it, and in turn their understanding. The vocabulary of a text may be familiar to the reader or strange. The content may be related to the reader's previous knowledge and experience, or it may be new. The style may be common or unusual. In fluency, as in most aspects of reading, the three key elements are the reader (and what they bring), the text itself, and the activity of which reading is a part.

Comprehension

Comprehension is the active process of interacting with a text in order to interpret or make sense of it. As with fluency, features of the text and their degree of familiarity to the reader affect the process of understanding. The vocabulary, content, structure, and style of the text may be familiar or unfamiliar to the reader, and unfamiliar texts are harder to comprehend.

Teaching comprehension explicitly can help students with skills to use when they come up against barriers to understanding what they are reading. According to the US National Institute of Child Health and Human Development, 'explicit or formal instruction in the application of comprehension strategies has been shown to be highly effective in enhancing understanding' (NICHD 2000: 15). This American research review identified comprehension-teaching strategies that appear to have a solid research basis:

- comprehension monitoring: where readers learn how to be aware of their understanding of the material
- co-operative learning: where students learn reading strategies together
- use of graphic or semantic organisers (including story maps)
- question answering: with immediate feedback from the teacher
- question generation: where readers ask themselves questions about various aspects of the story
- story structure: where students use the structure to help them recall content to answer questions
- summarisation: where students are taught to integrate ideas and generalise from the text information.

This understanding of the technical skills of reading implies that literacy facilitators should:

- promote reading for understanding by linking new knowledge to prior knowledge and experience, using problem-solving techniques to construct meaning, and providing scaffolding to support the learning process;
- teach the basic structures of language – especially phonemes (the smallest units of oral language), phonetics (letter–sound links), and vocabulary;
- support developing fluency – through providing opportunities for practice, scaffolding, feedback, and support;
- support comprehension through first modelling and then encouraging learners to use strategies to increase their understanding.

Learning to write

Much less research has been conducted into how people learn to write than into how they learn to read. Three key ideas from the research are reviewed here: the idea of writing as a process, the link between writing and thinking, and the link between writing and reading (drawing on an NRDC research review by Kelly *et al.* 2004).

Writing as process

Early ideas of writing as a 'product' gave way in the 1970s to understanding writing as a 'process' of planning, writing, and revising. These three main elements in the writing process are not necessarily carried out in order: writers often go back and forth between one stage and another (they may start writing, go back and plan a structure, write more and then reorganise, continue writing, revise, and re-plan).

The process view has been applied to learning to write, and the research has generated some suggestions for practical applications in literacy teaching:

- Novice writers tend to focus on themselves as writers while more proficient writers think about the reader – literacy teachers can help writers think about readers and how they might see the text.

- The inexperienced writer may find it very difficult to come up with ideas and at the same time carry out the mechanics of writing (handwriting and spelling) – extensive practice of mechanical skills may lead to their becoming more automatic, and free up beginner writers to pay more attention to composition.

- Beginner writers do less revision of their text and focus mainly on surface changes while experienced writers do more revision focusing on more substantial changes – tutors can demonstrate and support learners through the process of revising their text, and reading aloud during revision is a useful way of picking up problems.

- Errors provide insights into the writing process – both tutors and students can learn from these although tutors need to discuss errors sensitively so as not to discourage learners.

- Giving students an insight into the process of writing helps them write more effectively.

(Drawn from Kelly *et al.* 2004)

Writing and thinking

Writing and thinking are closely linked. While the research is limited, there are a number of practical suggestions for helping learners generate and organise ideas for writing:

- Brainstorming discussions and mind-mapping techniques encourage free-thinking ideas as a starting point for writing.

- Information-gap activities are used widely in teaching English for Speakers of Other Languages (ESOL) in the USA and UK: learners work in pairs and at the most basic level, one of the learners is in possession of all the information and the other one has to ask them questions (e.g. one learner gives directions to a location and the other plots the route on a map). In two-way gap activities both learners have information to share to complete the activity, and both write something as well.

- Conversation-grid activities work well for learners with limited writing skills: they might be asked to complete a table giving information about all the learners in the group, such as name, birthplace, whether or not they have children, etc.

- Ordering and sorting activities include classification, ranking, and sequencing: for example, learners might be given cards with statements to sort into 'true', 'false', or 'not sure'. They can write a list of all the true statements or a table sorting the different statements into columns for true, false, and not sure.

- Problem-solving activities might start with a real problem of one or more people in the learning group or with picture prompts about everyday problems. Either individually or in a group, learners talk about what is happening in the picture, and a learner or teacher writes down what they say. Learners can then make suggestions for how the problem could be resolved, giving rise to more writing.

(Drawn from Kelly *et al.* 2004)

Writing and reading

Writing and reading are so interconnected that some researchers argue they cannot be viewed apart. Many everyday activities involve both writing and reading (for example, filling in a form). Mace argues that authorship (especially through publishing student writing) is the central principle in adult literacy education (Mace 1992). She argues that it strengthens reading as well as writing and increases the learners' confidence.

'Language experience' is a long-standing teaching method that uses writing to teach reading. The learner dictates to a scribe (usually the teacher) and the resulting text is then used for reading practice by the learner. Because the ideas and vocabulary are familiar, the learner can more easily make the connection between spoken and written language.

Writing journals can be a way for learners to record information and reflect on their learning or on their lives. These can in turn be a source of reading as learners look back over their past writing, and also a form of assessment as they see how much they have developed and learned.

Publishing the writing of learners also has a long history among literacy programmes, especially in the UK, although there are also many examples of learner publishing from Nigeria, South Africa, and elsewhere (see Chapter 8).

Implications for planners

This brief review of the research about learning in general and learning to read and write in particular suggests some practical principles for adult literacy programmes:

- Purpose and context of learning: learners bring their own purposes and intentions to any learning activity, and the more closely and actively learners are engaged in developing the learning the better.

- The role of experience: learners do not come empty-handed to the learning activity, and will use their prior experience and knowledge to interpret and make sense of new knowledge. The process can be supported and encouraged through scaffolding.

- Knowledge is already organised in patterns: new knowledge will be linked to these existing patterns. Making the connection with existing knowledge can be a valuable part of the teaching and learning process.

- Readers and text interact to create meaning: reading is not simply an attempt to recreate what the writer intended but is newly formed each time from the interaction between reader, text, and activity. The social context within which this interaction happens is crucial and leads to what Freire called reading the word and the world.

- The role of technical skills: reading requires particular skills including recognising letters or symbols, associating them with spoken language, developing vocabulary, and fluency. While some readers are self-taught and master these skills on their own, such skills can usefully be taught, so long as we recognise that the technical skills alone do not make a reader.

- Reading and writing interact and are part of the same process. A variety of teaching and learning activities use both reading and writing, as well as discussion and interaction among learners, to advance skills in both.

- Training teachers: research is consistent in identifying the importance of skilled teaching, the value of responding flexibly to learner needs, and being able to draw on a range of possible strategies. Teachers learn from the experience of teaching if they have the opportunity to approach it as a learning experience.

Further reading

J. D. Bransford, A. L. Brown, and R. R. Cocking, *How People Learn: Brain, Mind, Experience, and School,* Washington DC: National Academy Press, 1999. This is a fascinating and readable overview of research on learning.

The UK's National Research and Development Centre on Adult Literacy and Numeracy has published a series of research reviews for practitioners. These are available on their website, including research on learning to read and write: www.nrdc.org.uk

13
Approaches to curriculum

An understanding of how people learn to read and write will influence how a programme of learning is devised. This chapter presents four models of curriculum and discusses how a curriculum can best be developed.

What is curriculum?

The word curriculum refers to what is taught, or learned, within a particular course of pre-planned learning. It has been interpreted differently in different fields of education, and so can cause misunderstanding. It sometimes implies a list of topics or subjects to be included over the course of a programme. (In formal education the school curriculum might include language, maths, geography, history, and science.) It can refer to a range of learning organised at a particular level, such as for year one primary or initial literacy. A curriculum can be expressed in terms of what it is intended a group will do during a learning session (i.e. activities; the things the group will be engaged in). It can also be expressed in terms of outcomes (the things the learners will be able to do by the end of the course or programme). Curricula can be produced as a table (with lists of topics and the order in which people will cover them) or a framework (which might outline the skills, knowledge, and attitudes that a programme of learning will contain). However, it is difficult to consider curricula without referring to materials (discussed more fully in the next chapter) as the two are closely associated. In some places the term 'curriculum' is used to describe a primer or teacher's book that contains all the material (including texts and exercises) that is to be delivered to a particular class.

Many people also use the terms curriculum and syllabus interchangeably. Curriculum comes from the Latin, and indicates a course of study. The word syllabus originates from the Greek and means a concise statement, or table of topics, or the subjects of a series of lectures. A syllabus will not generally indicate the relative importance of its topics or the order in which they are to be studied. However, both terms originate within formal schooling and discussions about curriculum tend to make sense when considered alongside notions like class, teacher, course, lesson, and so on. The concept of curriculum was developed in relation to teaching and within particular organisational relationships and expectations, and when curricula are introduced into more informal programmes such as literacy groups or community work, they tend to formalise certain aspects of that work. In almost all cases a curriculum outlines the content (and occasionally the process) of learning, and has been planned or decided upon before the programme begins.

Who designs a curriculum, who uses it, how it is presented, and what is expected from it are all important issues to consider before beginning to plan one. Curricula can be planned in advance without any consultation with tutors, facilitators, or learners; or they can be produced as a framework that leaves room for negotiation at local levels. While this chapter includes a section on participatory curriculum development as one specific approach, the rigidity or flexibility of any curriculum is part of a broader discussion. Such a discussion ranges between the need for clarity or equivalency between different courses for standardised programmes, and the need for flexibility and individual responsiveness for learner-centred programmes.

Many countries now have a national curriculum which specifies what each child should learn in each subject area in each year of schooling. This has sometimes been used as the basis for an adult literacy curriculum. While it has the advantages of providing learners with a roughly similar experience of education wherever they live in a country, and the possibility to return to school through equivalency programmes, a national programme designed for children rarely meets the needs of adults. A fixed curriculum has the disadvantage of determining the range of learning and the speed with which it is undertaken without reference to the needs of the particular locality or ability of the individuals in the class.

Adults come into literacy programmes with a range of previous experience, needing different things and knowing different things, and it may be difficult to determine in advance a list or an order of relevant content. Rigid, pre-set literacy curricula have been criticised for not allowing sufficient flexibility for learners or tutors, or for preventing people from changing their ideas about what they want to learn as a programme develops. Loosely specified, open curricula have been criticised for being unprofessional, giving too little guidance to tutors and learners, and making it difficult to measure a student's progress. Students often feel they don't want to 'miss out' on elements of learning that their children or those on more traditional programmes might cover, and that they need access to knowledge they may have been denied by not going to school.

The challenge to those developing curricula is to provide sufficient structure to make the key elements of a programme clear, with the flexibility to respond to local context and changing learner needs. It is to provide an experience that is relevant to the lives of those involved in it, while at the same time taking them beyond the things they already know. While this presents some difficulties in areas where materials can be adapted or reproduced on the spot (through photocopiers or computers), it is even more difficult in areas where this technology is not readily available.

Four ways of looking at curriculum

Within literacy work, a curriculum can be broadly specified in four different ways:

1. *The content model*: a body of knowledge to be transmitted.
2. *The product model*: an attempt to achieve certain ends.
3. *The process model*: a series of activites to engage in.
4. *The praxis model*: an approach committed to radical change.

Content

In a content-based approach to curriculum, knowledge is often determined by history, or seen as a more classical or uniform series of topics which are understood to be 'valuable knowledge', regardless of the context in which they are taught. In literacy this might be learning the alphabet, punctuation, and certain grammar rules. Tutors who follow curricula designed in this way see their task as merely delivering what they have been asked to in the right order. It has much in common with a primer-based approach to literacy that sees literacy as a mixture of skills (what you need to do) and facts (what you need to know). As such it fits within a 'literacy as skills' approach.

Product

In the product approach, priorities are determined according to the product or the outcome of learning. Objectives are set, a plan drawn up, then applied, and the outcomes (products) measured. Franklin Bobbitt, writing as long ago as 1918, says:

> The central theory [of curriculum] is simple. Human life, however varied, consists in the performance of specific activities. Education that prepares for life is one that prepares definitely and adequately for these specific activities. However numerous and diverse they may be for any social class they can be discovered. This requires only that one go out into the world of affairs and discover the particulars of which their affairs consist. These will show the abilities, attitudes, habits, appreciations and forms of knowledge that men need. These will be the objectives of the curriculum. They will be numerous, definite and particularized. The curriculum will then be that series of experiences which children and youth must have by way of obtaining those objectives.
> (Bobbitt 1918: 42)

What Bobbitt is suggesting is that curriculum is determined by studying what people actually do, and then deciding what they need to learn in order to do this better. This approach is not dissimilar to a competency or functional literacy approach used in an understanding of 'literacy as tasks'. It takes context into account (in terms of studying the context in which people live) and looks at the functions for which that knowledge will be used.

Tyler was one of the first people to talk about the outcomes of learning:

> Since the real purpose of education is not to have the instructor perform certain activities but to bring about significant changes in the students' pattern of behaviour, it becomes important to recognize that any statements of objectives of the school should be a statement of changes to take place in the students.
> (Tyler 1949: 44)

This is an early indication of a competency-based approach to learning that seeks to specify what students need to be able to do.

Content and product approaches

Both of the above approaches fix knowledge and pre-determine what is to be achieved in advance, without any consultation with potential learners. The programme and the completion of it become more important than the aspirations or achievements of the learners or the sensitivities of the tutor in understanding these. Content and product approaches set the time within which a topic should be covered or an outcome achieved, and suggest that groups should stick to this regardless of whether or not it has been successful. In the content approach this is determined in terms of content (knowledge of facts) and in the product approach in terms of outcomes (what students can now do). While such approaches seek to be relevant to learners' lives, they do not take into account people's aspirations. They specify required knowledge and behaviour rather than understanding. Curricula designed in this way will be easier for a tutor to follow, more uniform in the experience they offer learners, and may prove easier to implement on a large scale. They do allow for some kind of measurement of learning, even if this is mechanistic (has what has intended to be taught been learned?); but unless specific consideration is given to this, content and product approaches can easily miss some of the incidental learning that happens during a programme. (Many such programmes only measure the outcomes specified.)

Process

A process model on the other hand sees learning as active and dynamic, including critical questioning or exploration, and is less concerned with determining the content of that learning. It is an approach that can be implemented with a view of 'literacy as social practice', in that literacy is not defined as a single set of skills to be acquired, and the model provides scope for exploring the social and cultural implications of different literacies.

However, working in this way is very dependent on the quality of the teaching and the ability of a tutor to be properly responsive to their group. Two groups participating in a process-focused curriculum may achieve very different outcomes and these outcomes may be difficult to measure or to accredit. A process curriculum needs to be clear and defendable, but also practical and easy to apply, as it describes the processes through which learning will take place.

A curriculum provides a way of helping educators to think about their work before, during, and after interventions, and to make judgments about the direction their work is taking. A process curriculum encourages reflection on the practice of teaching. It is not a package of materials or a syllabus of topics designed to be delivered almost anywhere. Outcomes are not the central and defining feature. Rather than tightly specifying behavioural objectives and methods in advance, these develop as teachers and students work together. Learners are not objects to be acted upon, but have a clear voice in the way that the sessions evolve. The focus is on interactions; so attention shifts from teaching to learning.

This means there may be little uniformity between the experiences of learners in different settings and with different tutors, and any central assessment or measurement of learning becomes very difficult. A successful group is also very much determined by the abilities and creativities of its tutor. Some programmes have tried to overcome this by producing teacher handbooks with a choice of activities to be undertaken at different times, or packages for students to work through as they choose, but both of these depend on tutors interpreting and using them properly.

Praxis

The fourth approach to curriculum design sees curriculum as praxis, or a process of reflection leading to action. It has similarities with the process model, but brings together the experience of the facilitator and the learner in negotiating and deciding on what the groups will learn. As such it has more in common with a Freirean philosophy, leading facilitator and learners to question and reflect on both their values and their practice. It has strong links with the concept of 'literacy as critical reflection' or 'literacy for social change'. It focuses not only on what teachers and groups decide they want to learn, but also on how that learning relates to questions of action and empowerment to act. It is primarily an approach concerned with facilitating change. Success is measured in terms of attitudinal and value change, but also in the actions that groups of learners decide to take forward.

The REFLECT programme is a key example of a praxis approach to curriculum development and it is discussed more fully in Chapter 8. Box 13.1 gives an overview of how REFLECT curricula are developed.

Box 13.1: REFLECT curricula

The curriculum for a REFLECT literacy circle is created through the use of graphics and mapping tools (calendars, matrices, diagrams etc.). It also incorporates other participatory activities, such as dance, role play, and songs. Facilitators are trained to work with communities to identify aspects of their daily life that they want to interrogate or projects they wish to develop. The group, with the facilitator, constructs maps or matrices in order to look at this together.

For example, the group may decide to look at food supplies, times of plenty and scarcity, and at what can be done about this. This can be plotted as a matrix on the ground. They may then go on to discuss a matrix looking at the advantages and disadvantages of creating a vegetable garden and the relative costs of this. Further diagrams could be constructed around where to place the vegetable garden, and the relative nutritional and market values of different crops. The group members keep copies of all maps, diagrams, and matrices, and these form the basis of their learning materials. They learn skills of mapping and representation, of discussion and communication, and of writing and calculating different amounts.

The programme is supported by a mother manual of units that show facilitators how to adapt different stages in the REFLECT process to the local context. The mother manual gives the theory behind the REFLECT approach, guidance on how to set up a REFLECT circle, and sample units of activities that can be used. However, the curriculum itself is produced through facilitators working directly with groups, and the activities are determined according to the actions that people want to under-take. Consequently it is led by action rather than by knowledge, skills, or activities.

Source: www.reflect-action.org

Process and praxis approaches

There are many similarities between both process and praxis approaches in terms of their flexibility, intention to be relevant to the local context, and the extent to which those involved can help to determine what is learned and when. Both consider the needs of learners and the literacy of the local context, as well as the action that will follow from literacy learning, and the way that literacy might be integrated into people's lives. However, because both approaches aim to work responsively, they place huge responsibility on tutors to be able to assess the learning needs of their students and in many cases to source materials to meet these needs.

Approaches to curriculum development

Alan Rogers, in his book *Teaching Adults* (1986), suggests a series of questions that need to be addressed in the early stages of curriculum development. These are:

- What is the aim of our programme and the purpose for literacy? What approach to literacy will we use?
- What educational outcomes should the programme seek to achieve?
- What educational experiences can be provided that will support these outcomes?
- How can these educational experiences be effectively organised?
- How can we determine whether these purposes have been achieved?

These questions begin to frame the steps that curriculum developers need to work through.

Step 1: Clarifying the purpose of the programme

Questions such as 'why literacy?' and 'why now?' should help to clarify a programme's aims and purposes. These are discussed in Chapter 9. They should also help to determine the approach to be used both in planning a curriculum and in the programme itself. If the programme is driven by top-down criteria (such as a national directive) and there is specific content that needs to be included, there may be little point in conducting a consultation on what people want from literacy. Similarly if the content is pre-determined by such a directive there may be limited involvement of other stakeholders in the curriculum development process. If the programme has radical or revolutionary aims it may need more of a 'critical reflection' focus and to be planned on a large scale with input from those groups who will be involved in the campaign, but there is less scope for individual consultation with learners in the planning process. However, a small curriculum-planning team could, with little consultation, design a very open process-driven programme that learners might then find difficult to comprehend.

Step 2: Diagnosing need

Conducting a needs assessment has already been discussed in Chapter 9. The results of a needs assessment should help to inform the design of a curriculum. A programme hoping to adopt a participatory design process should aim to involve a range of stakeholders in the needs-assessment process. It is often a good way for potential tutors to increase their understanding of the local context and for potential learners to share their perceptions of literacy.

Step 3: Formulating objectives

Formulating objectives for a programme and deciding what learners will achieve as a result of it is the next step in designing a curriculum. These learning objectives might be specified as generic or specific, depending on the model of the programme to be adopted. Getting these objectives right – both those that will be achieved by the end of the programme (such as being able to cope with a range of numerical or textual material) and those that will be achieved by learners in the earlier stages (such as an awareness of their own literacy needs and some sense of how they best learn) – will provide a clearer guide to the range of content needed.

Step 4: Selecting content

The amount of content to be specified in a programme will differ according to the curriculum model used. However, even in process-driven programmes the range of topics to be discussed will be broadly specified according to the learning objectives set. Process and praxis programmes will seek to take these topics from the local environment. Content may be specified in terms of the skills to be included in the programme, the range of contexts to which these skills should be applied, and/or the particular texts that these need to be applied to.

Step 5: Organising content

Content needs to be organised in a way that will make sense to tutors and learners, allowing them to build new ideas and skills onto existing ones. An experienced curriculum designer will have some sense of the speed at which people can grasp new material, and what constitutes a manageable learning session. However, this varies hugely between individuals, and any curriculum needs to leave some scope for the different paces at which people learn.

Step 6: Selecting and organising learning experiences

Where a curriculum specifies the experiences and activities that will make up the learning programme, these will need to be designed once the content has been determined. They might range from copying from a board to small-group discussions or games, and will be organised to provide variety in individual sessions and to reflect the content of the programme.

Step 7: Selecting or producing materials

All programmes require some materials, whether these are tutor manuals, learner workbooks, or a series of written or electronic texts. The selection and design of these will be determined by the content and learning experiences indicated in the curriculum. The following chapter looks at this in more detail.

Step 8: Deciding what to evaluate and the ways and means of doing it

Deciding what and when to evaluate is part of curriculum design and will be determined by a programme's approach, objectives, content, and learning experiences. Monitoring and evaluation are discussed more fully in Chapter 11.

Participatory curriculum development

Although the degree of flexibility and the scope for tutor and learner involvement varies within different programmes, some curriculum-design teams set out to consult different stakeholders during the planning stage. These might be learners themselves, local school staff (in order to tie in new curriculum with existing school curricula), community representatives, and/or people who have an understanding of the different areas in which literacy will be used. This more inclusive approach has been referred to as 'participatory curriculum development'. Taylor (2000) has described this as:

> Rather than belonging to a small select group of experts, PCD involves a wide range of stakeholders in a meaningful way, drawing upon their experience and insights in a structured approach to curriculum planning, implementation and evaluation. They may help identify needs for training, set aims and learning objectives, contribute to the development of the subject matter to be taught, and participate in delivery and evaluation of the curriculum.

Participation as a term can be used to cover a broad spectrum of involvement and is often clarified in reference to a ladder of participation with a sequence of rungs (see Figure 13.1). These range from participation as providing information to users, to participation as consultation with users, to partnership working, or handing over the power of decision making. The extent to which different stakeholders are involved in a curriculum-design process, and the amount of power accorded to them varies, but it is generally agreed that curriculum design cannot happen in isolation and that some level of consultation or participation is essential. Stakeholders from different social backgrounds will bring with them different patterns of language use and cultural preferences and these will impact on the decisions they make. As a result the curriculum they design is likely to be more inclusive and more relevant to a broader range of learners.

Figure 13.1: Arnstein Ladder

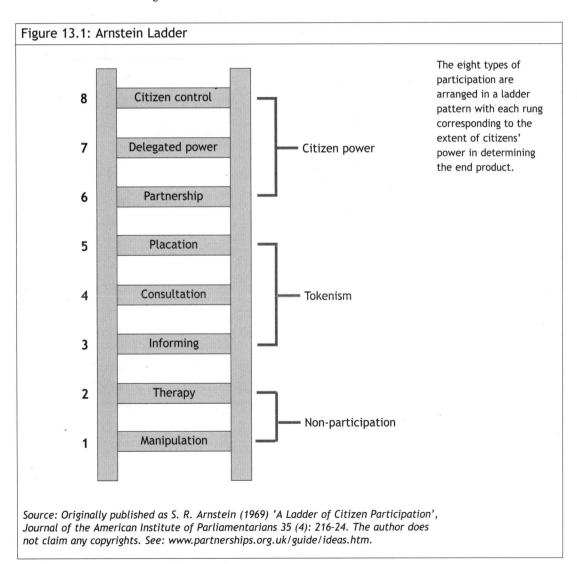

The eight types of participation are arranged in a ladder pattern with each rung corresponding to the extent of citizens' power in determining the end product.

Source: Originally published as S. R. Arnstein (1969) 'A Ladder of Citizen Participation', Journal of the American Institute of Parliamentarians 35 (4): 216-24. The author does not claim any copyrights. See: www.partnerships.org.uk/guide/ideas.htm.

The aim of PCD is to develop a curriculum from the exchange of experiences and information between the various stakeholders in the education and training programme; but identifying who these stakeholders are and finding ways to work with them on an equal basis needs careful thought. Community representatives, school teachers, and potential learners may all have an important contribution to make to the whole curriculum-design process, not just concerning the subject matter being taught but also the experiences and activities that the learners will engage in during the course. Some development teams have organised exchange through individual or small-group consultations, others through bringing together stakeholders in a series of workshops. Potential learners or facilitators might be asked to get involved in conducting a needs assessment to help them gain a fuller picture of the needs of the wider group. However, the relationships between different stakeholders and their ability to speak in front of each other needs to be taken into account. Potential learners may be intimidated and reluctant to express their views in front of education professionals or powerful community leaders, and a process may need to be put in place to deal with this.

While a PCD approach is flexible, it still sees as important a structured means of planning, implementation, and evaluation, involving different stakeholders in appropriate ways in each activity. Rogers and Taylor (1998) suggest that curricula developed in this way can be more appropriate to a range of learning, outside teacher-led classes:

> *Curriculum describes all the ways in which a training or teaching organisation plans and guides learning. This learning can take place in groups or with individual learners. It can take place inside or outside a classroom. It can take place in an institutional setting like a school, college or training centre, or in a village or a field. Curriculum development is central to the teaching and learning process.*

As such, curriculum takes the process away from its school-based roots and opens up the importance of planning for learning that can be delivered in a range of different ways and provides a means of ensuring quality in any learning programme.

Gender considerations in curriculum development

Whatever the nature of the literacy programme, the student, male or female, is at the heart of the learning process. Whether the curriculum is designed to promote economic efficiency, to improve the general education of the population, or to be a factor in a process of change, what is learnt in the literacy session must relate to the skills women or men need for the different work they undertake in the home and in the community. While a radical model of literacy might seek to change these roles, the activities, the reading material, the topics for writing, and the numerical calculations learnt must be gender-appropriate. In some contexts women will be restricted to their home, compound, or community and will need the literacy and numeracy associated with this situation. This does not necessarily limit them. With the help of the Internet, women in Saudi Arabia are able to run businesses from home. While in some contexts women are not allowed in public spaces, in others they will dominate market trading. In some situations men do all the farming, in others it is women. The curriculum must relate to the context of each programme and be gender-specific.

Examples of different approaches to curricula that consider the needs of women are given in Boxes 13.2 and 13.3 below.

Box 13.2: The Capacity Enhancement for Lifelong Learning (CELL) programme in Egypt

A British Council-funded literacy programme in Egypt set out to redesign the traditional literacy curriculum in order to make it more context-specific and to reflect the issues and concerns of people's daily lives. A Basic Curriculum Framework (that covered initial literacy) was produced, leading to a programme with alternative curriculum pathways that learners could choose to join, according to their future aspirations. The programme was developed using a curriculum-design team that included external literacy consultants, national academics, and planners and managers from the existing literacy programme.

Stakeholders were consulted at different stages of the planning process, culminating in a two-day workshop designed to bring together different ideas on the structure of the framework and the content of some of the materials.

The team attempted to revise a 'content-driven' curriculum that took a skills approach and introduce a more 'process-driven' approach that took account of the different literacies in people's lives.

The programme was to be delivered in an area of low infrastructure and where tutors had received limited education. Consequently the revised curriculum needed to combine sufficient structure to enable tutors to follow it easily and to understand what they should teach during each session, with sufficient flexibility to respond to

---

individual learners' needs. The programme set out to be learner-centred and responsive but it also needed to cover those essential elements that would enable learners eventually to pass a national test. It recognised the existence of different literacies used in different contexts and tried to give learners a sense of these by focusing in each unit on the different spheres in which people operated. The frame-work specified themes, skills, and grammar elements, beginning with the process of learning (Learning how to learn) in Unit 1, and then moving from the literacy of home (Me and my family) in Unit 2, to the immediate locality (My village) in Unit 3, to more formal literacies used at district level (My district) in Unit 4, and national processes (My country) in Unit 5.

The programme was accompanied by an extensive teacher's manual that guided teachers through the processes of learning and provided many example exercises. Teachers were also encouraged to identify and use material from the local environment as the basis for their reading and writing activities.

The design and implementation of the CELL programme illustrated a number of dilemmas associated with curriculum design, such as the tutors' needs for structure and support, and the difficulty of following learners' needs while still meeting the externally set outcomes associated with a formally recognised certificate. While the first-year evaluation showed tutors and learners preferring the model over the former content-driven curriculum, both groups struggled to cope without specified material and learner workbooks.

Source: unpublished consultancy report to the British Council, 2004

Box 13.3: Nirantur's programme for rural women, India

Nirantur, a resource group for women and education based in Delhi, worked with Mahila Samakhya – a pilot project launched through the Department of Education and committed to the empowerment of women, to develop a women's literacy curriculum. Their objective was to help women to develop a critical understanding of their life situation, to access information, and to initiate collective action towards changing their lives. There was no existing curriculum specifically for women and while the curriculum developed for children was a useful guide, it did not reflect the women's lives nor address gender issues.

Nirantur and Mahila Samakhya built a new curriculum around the basic concerns that structured women's existence: land, water, forest, society, and health. These themes provided scope for analysing the local environment and looking beyond it to how other cultures deal with these things, and to global as well as local issues. The curriculum was designed to challenge notions of 'this is how things ought to be', and to show how traditional structures are socially determined rather than 'given' or 'right'.

Language and maths were included within the five content areas, but also taught separately in order to look specifically at language-related concerns and at mathematical competencies in a sequential order. The developers justified the independent teaching of language sessions in order to be able to focus on spelling, grammar, and language and mathematical discrepancies without breaking the flow of the information sessions.

The programme started with village-mapping activities, and a series of activities associated with this. Tutors organised subsequent content into a logical progression, delivered through 'lessons' planned between them in groups, each lesson linking to the previous one in terms of content and skills. Lessons were accompanied by texts written specially for them by the tutors and recording the material they were discussing. Different tutors progressed through the content areas in different orders according to the direction taken by discussions. In this way a structured content could be delivered flexibly, responding to issues raised by different groups of learners.

Language-related competencies and guidelines for language teaching were worked out in the preparatory phase and described the language skills that learners were expected to achieve. These covered reading, writing, and comprehension, visual and diagrammatic language, analytical and communication skills, and numeracy. Tutors were given guidelines which included using a mix of Hindi and local languages, not formally teaching grammar, maintaining parity with the formal system, linking language teaching with other content areas, and encouraging self-expression and creativity.

The numeracy curriculum was developed on the premise that most women had good mental arithmetic skills and intended to build on these as well as to obtain some equivalency with the formal system. It included numbers, place values, the four basic mathematical operations, fractions, percentages, and decimals. It also included spatial concepts – mapping; area and volume; ways of representing data through graphs, diagrams, and pie charts; and measurement of distance, weight, and time.

Source: Nirantur 1997

Implications for planners

Both of the case studies cited above are examples of innovative approaches to designing curricula which are meaningful to participants and provide a way of structuring and organising material that tutors can follow. Bringing the two together is not an easy task. There are many examples of literacy curricula throughout the world that specify exactly what is to be taught in every lesson of every class, almost to the extent of scripting what a tutor should say. The success of these programmes is limited. While they provide security for tutors they rarely meet the needs of the learners involved and are often adopted on a rote learning and repetitive basis. There are also examples of programmes in the UK and elsewhere where volunteer tutors, with limited training and almost no curriculum outline, work with individuals on a one-to-one basis, responding entirely to their needs. The success of these depends very much on the individual ability of the tutor and their relationship with the learner involved.

Any curriculum designed on a larger scale will need to find a balance between a range of competing factors, many of which are not easy to resolve. These include:

- Sufficient structure to support an inexperienced tutor with sufficient flexibility to respond to individual learner need.
- Awareness of the different literacies used locally and a means for providing a range of texts for learners to use.
- Clear objectives that meet the needs of programme planners and funders but take into account the views of a broad range of stakeholders and of the learners themselves.
- The costs of designing a curriculum and its applicability beyond its immediate locale.
- The approach to literacy – skills, tasks, social practice, or critical reflection.
- The curriculum model that will best reflect the chosen approach and where this lies on a continuum from content/product to process/praxis.
- The people best placed to be involved in the design, and the skills they will bring with them, from an understanding of literacy and adult learning to an understanding of learner needs and local context.

Further reading

A. Rogers, *Teaching Adults*, Milton Keyens: Open University Press, 1986. This is a guide to the major issues faced by teachers of adults, including definitions and discussions of content and methods. It outlines five broad stages in developing curricula.

J. Oxenham and R. Hamed, 'Lessons from a Project in Capacity Enhancement for Lifelong Learning', Cairo: Social Research Centre Cairo and American University in Cairo, 2005. This is a report of a comparative evaluation.

L. Stenhouse, *An Introduction to Curriculum Research and Development*, London: Heinemann, 1975. This is a classic statement of a process approach to the theory and practice of curriculum making. Chapters explore the nature of the curriculum problem; the content of education; teaching; the school as an institution; behavioural objectives and curriculum development; a critique of the objectives model; the process model; evaluation; a research model of curriculum development; the teacher as researcher; and the school and innovation.

Nirantur, *Windows to the World: Developing a Curriculum for Rural Women*, New Delhi: Nirantur, 1997. This gives an account of their process of curriculum development, produced by the organisation themselves.

R. S. Caffarella, *Planning Programs for Adult Learners: A Practical Guide for Educators, Trainers and Staff Developers*, San Francisco: Jossey-Bass, 1994. This is just what the title says – but has the advantage over many manuals in this area in that the underlying model is dynamic and interactive and avoids some of the problems with linear planning models. The guide is clearly written with plenty of worksheets.

14

Resources for literacy

This chapter outlines the range of resources (written, visual, oral, and actual) that can be used in the development of literacy. It will discuss the value of different kinds of resources, how these follow on from curriculum design, and their relative advantages and disadvantages. It will offer some guidelines on how they might be chosen or produced.

The range of resources that can be used in the teaching and learning of literacy come from a number of different sources. They include texts that have been specially designed and produced for adult literacy learners, materials that are produced for use by children in schools, materials produced by learners themselves or written and designed locally, and everyday materials that people use in other areas of their lives. A literacy facilitator needs to be made aware of the range of material they might use, and be shown how to work with this during their training, and it is difficult to consider facilitator training, curriculum design, and resource identification separately from each other.

Different approaches to literacy also have implications for the design and selection of resources. A 'literacy as skills' approach places more emphasis on teaching pre-determined sets of skills, while a 'literacy as social practice' approach is more concerned with building a range of literacy practices for use in everyday life. Therefore a skills approach will often involve a curriculum that specifies particular materials which are specially written for the different stages of the programme. A social practice approach may contain a more flexible curriculum that incorporates some of the documents that people meet in their everyday lives.

While some of the research cited below clearly shows the advantages of some resources over others, most materials – even those written for school use – can be valuable, if critiqued and used actively alongside other forms of communication (speaking, listening, discussion, debate). Where materials are linked in with people's real literacy tasks, and questioned rather than just used as exercises for passive reading, they can support broader contextualised learning. Groups can discuss the content of literacy texts and the way that they have been presented, or redraft texts that they find difficult to understand. The way that material is used is often more important than the material itself, and tutors should encourage learners to interrogate material rather than to accept it, if they are to become familiar with the different uses of written texts.

The Oxfam book *Adult Literacy: A Handbook for Development Workers* (Fordham *et al.* 1998) contains a diagram which groups the range and use of different types of materials (see Figure 14.1).

Figure 14.1: Literacy materials: 'special' and 'ordinary'

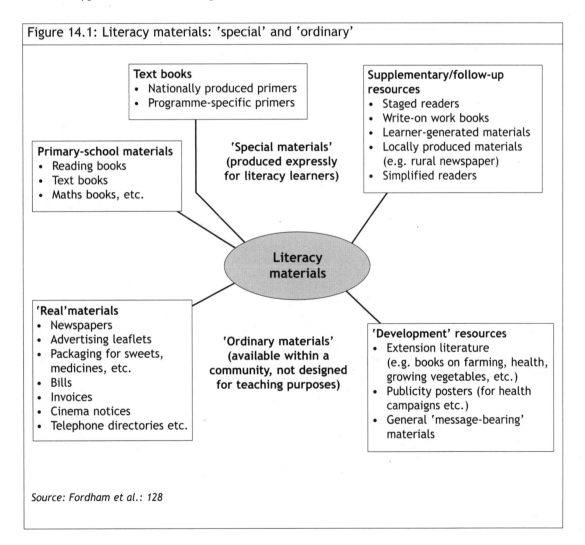

Text books
- Nationally produced primers
- Programme-specific primers

Supplementary/follow-up resources
- Staged readers
- Write-on work books
- Learner-generated materials
- Locally produced materials (e.g. rural newspaper)
- Simplified readers

Primary-school materials
- Reading books
- Text books
- Maths books, etc.

'Special materials' (produced expressly for literacy learners)

Literacy materials

'Real' materials
- Newspapers
- Advertising leaflets
- Packaging for sweets, medicines, etc.
- Bills
- Invoices
- Cinema notices
- Telephone directories etc.

'Ordinary materials' (available within a community, not designed for teaching purposes)

'Development' resources
- Extension literature (e.g. books on farming, health, growing vegetables, etc.)
- Publicity posters (for health campaigns etc.)
- General 'message-bearing' materials

Source: Fordham et al.: 128

A study by Fingeret (1991) found that students learned more effectively when the materials they were given reflected or incorporated their prior experiences. Like Freire, she recognised not only the power of generative themes (Freire 1972), but also that adults have a limited amount of time for attending classes and prefer to be working on material that relates to their broader responsibilities as citizens, employees, and parents.

Real materials or special materials?

Rogers *et al.* (1999) suggests ways of integrating both special and real materials into literacy classes, taking up proportionally different amounts of class time. His diagram (Figure 7.1 on page 83) indicates that while individuals or groups may start by predominantly using primers or 'special' materials, these can from the beginning be linked to, or presented alongside, other everyday texts. As learners become more confident, the use of everyday texts and tasks can be used more and more in learning situations until eventually these become the focus of group discussions (see Figure 14.2, for example).

Figure 14.2: Shop sign from Biu, Borno State, Nigeria

Source: personal photograph, McCaffery

This idea is supported by research carried out for the National Center for the Study of Adult Learning and Literacy (NCSALL) in the United States (Stascz *et al.* 1994). The research was based on an early survey which highlighted the differences between the use of 'authentic' and decontextualised' materials. The survey divided the range of possible materials into groups of similar real (or authentic) and specially prepared materials, and placed programmes using them on a continuum ranging from 'highly life-contextualised' to 'highly life-decontextualised'. The points of the continuum were explained as:

- *Highly life-contextualised*: programmes that use no skill books, have no set curriculum, use realia, newspapers, journals, novels, work manuals, driver's licence materials, etc. Programmes that are strongly focused on authentic materials that are relevant to the students' lives and reflect students' needs. For example: newspaper and magazine articles, short stories, children's books, newsletters sent home from school etc., but no basic set text.

- *Somewhat life-contextualised*: programmes that mention skills and may use some published textbooks and workbooks, but where student work is heavily concentrated on real-life texts and issues, including lots of life-based materials – newspapers, brochures, flyers.

- *Somewhat life-decontextualised*: programmes that are more highly focused on skills, with the majority of activities focused on phonics work, grammar work, workbooks, etc. Mostly published textbooks and workbooks, with limited use of authentic materials or activities. Instructional materials or pre-planned tutor guides.

- *Highly life-decontextualised*: programmes that have a set curriculum with a focus on skills, phonics, flashcards, etc. Most, if not all, materials are from publishers, with almost no mention of authentic materials or activities. Can include corresponding teacher workbooks and student workbooks, phonetic drills, reading word lists, sentences and stories, spelling practice.

Follow-up research, carried out in 2005, looked at changes in the literacy practices of adults as a result of attending adult literacy classes. The research measured the impact of literacy programmes by the frequency of a learner's use of new literacy skills in their daily lives after the classes had ended – rather than through achievement tests.

The results of the research showed that students who used real-life literacy texts while learning continued to do so in the longer term. Those learners who were introduced to newspapers in order to find out about the news, or manuals in order to learn how to undertake a task, were more likely to continue to use them for these purposes. Similarly, those learners who used some real-world texts, but not necessarily for the purposes for which they were designed (rather for role-play or gap-fill activities for example) did slightly less well in sustaining long-term literacy practices. The study concluded that if adult students are consulted on which texts and activities are important to them, feel a sense of ownership in their learning, and learn the skills of reading and writing through real-world texts for real-world purposes, they will be more likely to apply their reading and writing abilities in their lives.

Though not conceptualised as such, the use of real everyday materials was the general practice in England in the 1970s and 1980s. It was a practical way of addressing students' real learning needs and provided the basis for learning. Mace (2005) analyses and describes in detail the reading and writing tasks people have to undertake in their daily life; for example, seeking employment or wishing to train to become a hospital volunteer and needing to be able to:

- sign the register;
- read and complete three different forms for a surety pass, to get photographs, and to claim travel expenses;
- read and understand signs about injections.

Rogers (2005) also discusses the use of real materials in literacy classes and like the NCSALL study, he links the use of authentic materials to authentic tasks. Rogers also suggests that newspapers need to be read to find out about the news or the weather, driver's manuals to prepare for an actual driver's test, and job applications read and filled in as part of real-life job searches. In another study, also undertaken in the USA, Hunter and Harman (1985) found that 'maximum use' of real or authentic materials clearly showed higher levels of student achievement. Tutors in Ireland are highly committed to this approach and believe that this strong focus on helping students master the texts they need to read is an important factor in both attendance and achievement. Other researchers have found that student writing based on their own lives has increased writing skills (Stascz *et al.* 1994; D'Annunzio 1994 in NCSALL 1998).

While these results are important, they are based on studies undertaken in the USA, and basing initiatives on them can cause problems for planners of programmes in areas where written materials are scarce and tutors have limited education themselves. Large classes where there are few facilities to reproduce copies of 'real texts' are not easily organised around authentic materials and tasks. Special materials which simulate real-life situations like tax forms, unemployment benefits, and land registers can be developed with the involvement of teachers and learners, and produced on a mass scale, but care needs to be taken that they do not become decontextualised. Once activities and materials are mass-produced and mass-prescribed, they become increasingly distanced – or decontextualised – from the lives of individual students. In a large group, with people of different ages, this could easily happen. Once material is produced for a region, or on a national scale, this becomes even more likely. For example, a class based on the use of bank accounts (opening an account, writing a cheque, reading a statement), would be very useful for someone about to do this, but not at all relevant for those students who do not have bank accounts or are unlikely to have one in the near future. Even in a rural area where people's lives have a similar pattern, pre-prepared material does not take account of changes that may happen over time.

However, getting hold of individual examples of real documents for participants in a large class is plainly difficult in places where copying facilities are not available. If materials are to be used, they generally do need to be reproduced in advance on a large scale. Some tutors have experimented with 'twenty things to do with the text written on a match box' and worked creatively with shop signs and soap packets; but while these may be real materials, few of the exercises are actually real tasks.

Other programmes have tried to respond to individual students' literacy needs and work with student-generated, student-provided, or student-requested texts. The REFLECT programme creates texts with learners through constructing matrices (see Chapter 8). Learner-centred or empowerment programmes have asked students to bring in the things they want to read. In India a literacy class was built around film posters that students were keen to read. Groups were given folders and invited to fill them with flyers advertising new films to be shown in the area each week. They began by identifying letters and then the key names of stars and went on to read the admission prices and synopsis of the film. In South Africa women wanted to read mail-order shopping catalogues and brought these in with them, cutting up pages and sharing them between people in the group. Both programmes were successful in getting students to read and use the material they brought, but the range of different literacies that can be used in this way is again limited to material that is available or mass-produced in the area.

Working with special materials

Primers

Primers are discussed extensively in Chapter 5. They can be produced either at a national level, to be used in a range of different programmes across a country, or designed for a particular programme. Primers construct language in a particular way and present it in a mechanical, progressive form (moving from letter to word to sentence) which does not necessarily reflect the way that language is used. Even though they tend to be designed for adults, may carry development messages, and make reference to other literacy tasks (making a telephone call, recording agricultural inputs), they take an approach to learning that is reminiscent of school and as such less appropriate for adult learners.

On the other hand, they do provide a familiar way of approaching learning for people who have been to school, and an often envied 'school type' experience for people who haven't. They also provide a fixed lesson format for new or inexperienced teachers and a record of class activities that learners can take home with them. For large-scale campaigns or programmes tied to a particular development approach, they may seem to be the best option. However, large numbers of primer-based literacy campaigns across the world have failed to improve the literacy practices of people who have been involved in them, and there are some important lessons to be learned from this.

Primers tend to be produced by 'language experts' or people who are highly literate themselves, and may not be able to view the world through the eyes of a literacy learner. The development of key learning texts should include the view of new readers or people who will eventually be part of learning groups. Field testing a finished product is not the same process as basing the development of it on some research into how and what people want to learn; where possible these voices should be included from the beginning.

But pedagogical material specially prepared for classes inevitably selects knowledge, and in doing so prioritises some perspectives and pieces of information above others. New teachers or learners often view texts as containing some kind of inherent truth and are often reluctant to challenge written materials. Primers or educational workbooks are more often seen as something to follow rather than to question. This is likely to lead to a passive rather than an active approach to reading. There are numerous examples of people learning to read their workbook but not being able to apply that learning elsewhere.

Primers need to incorporate questions as well as didactic messages, and exercises that link their content to broader literacy tasks. These can include things like going outside the class to identify different examples of the new letters that have been taught (car number plates, shop signs), collecting and matching real materials (packaging, newspapers, magazines) that contain similar words, or linking new learning to personal and local information (writing names). Each lesson can be planned to end with a discussion (rather than just beginning with one such as debating the 'theme' or generative sentence of the day). Such questions can include 'how is the situation described similar to what we know here?'; 'in what situation might you use these words or sentences?'; 'how would you say or write things differently if you were writing to a friend, family member, or local official?'.

Primers tend to be used as the sole reading material for a group of learners, rather than as one example of things to be read. They may need to include in them guidance for teachers about other texts and communication activities that can be used alongside them. If links are made to other real materials and actual literacy tasks, the fixed language of primers is more likely to be seen as one form of writing in the context of people's lives. Learners need practice from the beginning in recognising the different formats, fonts, and typefaces that appear locally, and in understanding how literacy might support other forms of communication they are already using.

Whether to use an existing nationally produced primer or to develop a primer specifically for a new programme has important resource implications for programme planners. If an existing workbook is available, it may be more useful to produce supplementary materials that have another function aside from the teaching of letters and words. This could be in the form of a series of health messages to be challenged and questioned, photographic examples of related literacy tasks (such as forms to be filled in, cheques or account sheets), story or comic books, or easy reading material. If learners are to understand the use and conventions of different literacies it is more useful for them to access different kinds of materials than to be introduced to a single school-based literacy text.

An analysis of literacy primers undertaken in India (Dighe *et al.* 1996) indicated a number of reccurring patterns. The primers tended to treat their learners as people with 'empty minds', and rather than linking development problems with the reality of landlessness, low wages, and lack of access to services, they concentrated on teaching people how their lives could be improved.

As such people were blamed for their own poverty rather than invited to consider different reasons for it. Texts were didactic, talking down to readers who were supposed to accept rather than question the messages they provided.

Using materials from primary school

Many countries have a language policy of using students' mother tongue or first language in primary schools and in initial adult literacy classes. Where there is limited material available in indigenous languages, adult literacy classes have considered adapting or adopting primary school texts. Although this material tends to be written for children in a very simplified format it can, if used appropriately, form part of an adult literacy class.

Students in family literacy classes, and adults wanting to read to help their children, have some interest in the content and format of primary school materials. Providing they are presented to them as adults and as parents rather than delivered as core reading materials, they can be encouraged to critique as well as to understand what their children are learning. Supplementary materials, produced to be used alongside primary school workbooks, can suggest activities for parents to support their children's reading at home, and introduce other texts such as school notices and timetables, letters that might be written to the teacher, or school reports and tables. Similarly supplementary materials can make links between the content of a primary lesson and other aspects of adult life.

Other materials found in schools (maps, maths books, science materials) can be used as valuable source materials for literacy workers, providing they are able to help learners to critique them and to relate the content presented to aspects of their own lives. Research on primary school textbooks has shown how they, like primers, situate learners as passive recipients of knowledge, and focus on over-idealised situations of democracy, good neighbours, and good governance in a very simplistic way. The majority of primary school texts represent the values and beliefs of certain dominant sectors of society while ignoring others (Dighe 1995). Once learners are made aware of bias in texts, all material is potentially useful as a prompt for discussion.

Easy reading material for new learners

There is a debate within the literacy field about the importance of easy or adapted reading material for new learners. In some countries with a developed literacy environment (South Africa, Australia, the UK), easy adult reading material, sometimes in dual-language texts, is produced to help develop literacy practices among those completing literacy classes. In other countries post-literacy classes consist of a series of simplified texts dealing with follow-on activities such as income-generation projects, poultry rearing, basket making, or agricultural extension.

There is an argument that clearly written, simplified texts, produced with illustrations and limited words to a page, can begin to present complex ideas in an accessible format. Studies in readability indicate that line length, simplified scripts, the size of different typefaces and so on will help to either encourage or discourage someone from reading. Other arguments suggest that learners will read material they are interested in, and that they can access complex texts and language if it deals with issues they are familiar with.

Some programmes have tried to work with providers of real materials, as well as with literacy learners and tutors. The Community Literacies Project Nepal (see Chapter 7) was based on the premise that increasing literacy in communities was the responsibility of those designing and writing formal and informal documents, as well as those learning to read them. They worked with newspaper editors, council employees, producers of health information, and those working in other information-based fields to look at reproducing or rewriting public documents in order to make them easy to read. Other projects (e.g. the Kenyan post-literacy project in Box 14.3) have also tried to influence news and media channels to highlight the needs of new readers. Other projects have worked with learners to rewrite official documents such as marriage contracts or land rights that they need to sign, but in their existing formats are unable to understand. There are a number of conventions that in most languages and scripts have been shown to make texts more accessible.

Guidelines for writing easy-to-read materials

Writing easy-to-read materials entails using an adult, culturally sensitive format while making the information as easy to understand as possible. Most people remember no more than three to five ideas when they read something, and too much information in a document or on a page can confuse readers so they don't remember anything at all. Get to the point as quickly as possible and follow these guidelines:

- Focus on the most important things readers need to know and remember. Technical information or explanations of words can be boxed separately so that the flow of the text is not interrupted.

- A short list of points or subheadings at the beginning of the document can help readers to review what they need to know, and it reinforces what they are learning.

- Examples can be used to reinforce new concepts, illustrate ideas, and explain words that are difficult to understand. Try not to use technical jargon and terms in the main text, but use the words and language that readers will use in their everyday lives.

- The cover page or title page is your first chance to 'grab' your readers and let them know what the document is about. It should indicate the core content in a few key words or phrases. It should also identify the intended audience. Choose illustrations that are appropriate for the people you want to read it, and as far as possible reflect local customs and traditions.

- Organise and present the information in the document from a user's perspective and in an order that makes sense to the reader. Try to 'chunk' bits of information in ways readers will remember, or in the way they will use it. When describing a process (repairing a fuel pump for example), describe the steps in the order the reader will need to know or use them. In a list of information or points, give the most important information first. In a reference document, such as a book showing common diseases in animals, make sure readers can easily locate important information if they need to look at it again.

- Make important information easy to find. Use headers to emphasise sections. Include summaries at the end of chapters or sections to help reinforce important points. Headers and summaries also serve as a way to repeat important information for readers.

- Make action steps or desired behaviours stand out. Readers should know immediately what they need to do and how they should do it. Keep sentences short but consistent. Average sentence length should be about 15 words or fewer. Words with fewer syllables may be easier to read than longer words, but people will recognise complex words that are familiar to them.

- Use colloquial language that people will understand and terms readers use in discussion (they may say 'shots' instead of 'injections' or 'immunisations'), and a conversational style. Always try reading a written text out loud to see how it sounds to someone else.

- Use active rather than passive sentences (e.g. 'Keep rabbits in closed pens', rather than 'Rabbits should be kept in closed pens'). This helps the reader to imagine going through the experience at the same time as reading about it. Be direct, specific, and concrete, and as interesting and accurate as possible. Use personal pronouns to help readers realise how the information applies to them.

- Try using a dialogue or story format, or testimonials and statements from people that readers will relate to. People learn and remember better if they interact with the material.

- Each page should be interesting to look at and should draw the reader's attention to what is important. White space on a page and limited information can make the page easier to read. Layout is almost as important as the content and should be clear and comfortable. Wide margins and generous spacing make a text more accessible. Text should be in blocks with a limited number of lines per page.

- Pictures help attract attention and reinforce the text. They should be simple, realistic drawings or photos that help to illustrate what is going on. Pictures that decorate the page but don't help to illustrate the meaning can distract the reader. The quality of the picture is reduced each time a page is copied, and photos and complex drawings should be avoided if the material will be reproduced.

- Avoid graphs and complicated charts. They are often difficult to understand, and beginner readers have a lot of trouble trying to extract information from them. Use words to explain the key information in a graph. If you must use a chart, make it no more than three columns across and three rows down, and include some directions about how to read it.

Working with real materials

Newspapers and journals

Newspapers, as sources of text available in most areas, have often formed the basis of literacy classes. Tutors have constructed exercises for learners using headlines, photographs, captions, or short articles. Newspapers are often available in multiple copies and can form the basis of small-group or whole-class work. Local or national news are both key sources of information and a strong case could be made for the production of easy-to-read versions. The audience for easily understandable news and information about society is probably even larger than the audience for books. Many people have difficulty in understanding regular news channels. Articles in newspapers are often too long, written in a language that is too difficult, and contain too many specialised terms. Persuading local editors of the need to produce weekly versions of the news for new readers is one way of both enriching the local literacy environment and introducing new readers to longer-term literacy habits.

Newsletters or newspapers for literacy learners might include material written by new learners or simplified accounts of local or national news. These might be photocopied and distributed through a local literacy provider or produced on a regional or national scale. In Pietermaritzburg (South Africa), the *Learner Echo* was produced as an insert in a national newspaper, and also distributed on its own through literacy classes. It was funded by the national newspaper as a way of engaging new future readers and paid for through advertising. In remote areas of Nepal where there was limited access to publishing resources, villages developed wall newspapers that were written by hand and displayed in the village for people to use. They contained information, stories, drawings, and advertising of local events, and were an important resource for literacy learners. The danger with any specially produced materials, particularly those developed periodically, is that they are difficult to sustain. While they may meet a need for a time for a particularly active literacy programme, they take funds and time to keep going and are often tied to short-term projects. Getting the providers of national newspapers to take this on, and making news reading an integral part of people's lives, is one approach to ensuring the sustainability of materials and of literacy practices.

Developing learner-generated materials

The development of student writing in the UK and learner-generated materials (LGMs) in the global South is described in Chapter 8. In the UK, the student writing movement became associated with a more radical and politicised approach to literacy; in the South LGMs were linked with community development, empowerment, and the desire for change. In the South the term LGM has been used for both 'learner- generated' and 'locally generated' materials. While both have been used in empowerment programmes, and should have greater local and contextual relevance for learners, the first group are developed *by* learners and the second group *for* them. According to the research cited above, both groups are preferable and more effective than those materials developed by experts outside the area in which they will be used.

Developing materials with learners themselves can be a valuable learning process, and there are different examples of ways in which this has been done. A study in Nepal talked about a 'process' and a 'product' approach to creating material with learners (author's unpublished case study, Sankushaba, Nepal,1996). The first of these focused on the process of writing as a learning tool. Participants in groups learned to write by writing.

Students do not have to generate material by writing it down themselves. They can discuss a subject with the tutor and then decide to write all or some of it down. They can be helped to write or they can tell the tutor what to write. This is called 'scribing'. A few pages or just a few sentences may be written down. The tutor can then write it out clearly or type it up. It can be the text for an individual to develop their reading skills or, if facilities are available, it can be duplicated and read by the whole group. The process is easier when there is more than one tutor in the class or circle, or volunteers are available to 'scribe' the stories, but the method can also be used in a group. The group suggests a topic and different people suggest what should be written, as the tutor writes what they say on the blackboard. In this way a group story is built up. The students can copy the whole story off the board, or a single sentence or a few words, depending on their level. This is not dissimilar to the Language Experience approach used for many years as a learning method in the UK. Participants repeat sentences or texts they want to see written down, facilitators write these for them, and the texts form the basis for their learning.

Figure 14.3: Learner-generated materials, Nigeria

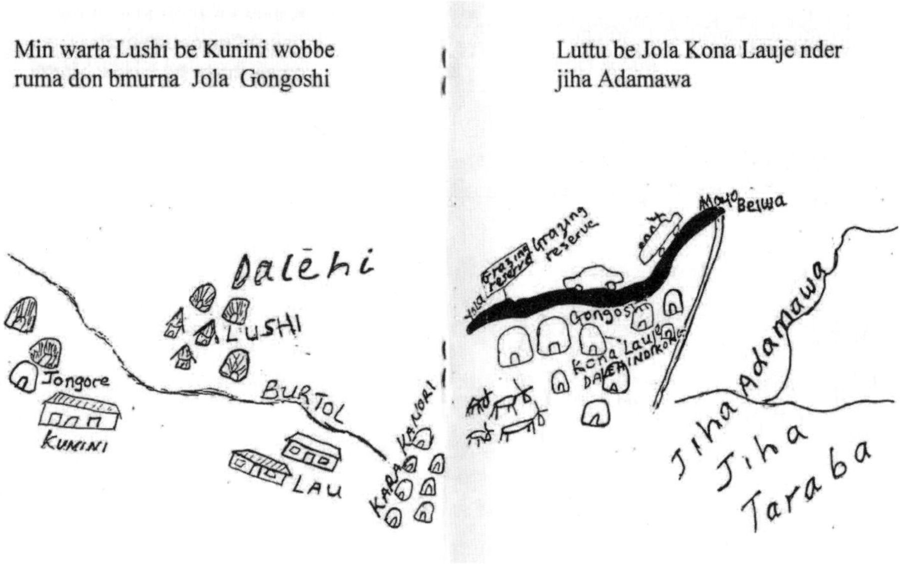
Min warta Lushi be Kunini wobbe
ruma don bmurna Jola Gongoshi
Luttu be Jola Kona Lauje nder
jiha Adamawa
Dalēhi
LUSHI
Jongore
KUNINI
BURTOL
LAU
Grazing reserve
Mayo Belwa
Gongoshi
Kona
Lauje
Adamawa
Jiha
Jiha Taraba

This story was first told in the Fulfulde language to explain why the nomadic clan move from one place in the dry season to another in the wet season in order to find grazing for their cattle. The story was then written down and illustrated and later published.

Source: British Council Community Education Project in Nigeria 1997-2001.
© Musa Yuguda et al. 1997

In a product approach the emphasis is on the producing of materials that can then be read by other new learners. However, the writing has an intrinsic value of its own. Individual and group stories record a community's folk tales, activities, and history. For example, *Bat Colony* by Oliver Chuku (1997) describes how a hundred years earlier, bats flew into his community in south-east Nigeria and colonised two large trees. Nothing was able to shift them and they still provide a continuous source of food for local people. Sometimes the stories are valuable in explaining a community's actions to others. *Why We Move* by Musa Yuguda (1998 – see Figure 14.3) explains why the Fulani pastoralists move from one location to another according to the seasons. A collection of stories written by literacy students in the Hackney Reading Centre *Every Birth it Come Different* (1980) was then used in training midwives to appreciate the diverse customs surrounding child-birth in the very diverse population. The content can also be practical – how to grow runner beans or which medicines to use to treat cattle.

Student writing can be used by literacy programmes in many different ways:

- as a reading text for an individual;
- as a text for a whole group;
- as a collection of writing or 'scribed' stories for an informal group magazine;
- as contributions to a 'scheme' magazine, either informally or formally produced;
- as published collections of student writing;
- as a poster;
- as a small book.

All these examples can be done very simply, either as single copies or photocopied for the author's group, or they can be published for a wider audience. In this case the writing has to be edited so it is clearly understood by others outside the immediate community. It is preferable if the students themselves select writing to go beyond the community and help to edit it, as this is a learning process in itself which enables students to understand and appreciate how published material is produced. The author (the literacy student) should always retain the copyright.

Generating materials with students is a method for making more texts available at local level in local languages and is a way of capturing and valuing indigenous knowledge. The Kenyan Adult Education project in Box 14.3 is one example of this.

Box 14.3: Kenyan post-literacy project

A project in Kenya supported by GTZ (an international co-operation for sustainable development operating worldwide) helped learners to produce their own texts in order to record indigenous knowledge. This formed part of a 'post-literacy curriculum' and involved networking between NGOs to share experiences and resources. The project both collated, adapted, and re-printed, materials for use by post-literacy learners, and purchased learning materials produced by commercial agencies and considered by learners themselves to be relevant and suitable.

The project involved representatives from print and electronic media as partners. This helped them, as producers of print materials, to learn more about adult education, and improve its profile in the press. Members of the press became sensitised to the issues in adult education in general, and to the objectives and processes of the post-literacy project in particular.

Under the theme 'Talk a book', learners recorded local knowledge in a variety of thematic areas. The process of talking a book recognised the richness of indigenous knowledge and traditional culture, including the oral traditions of the people. The documented insights of local people contributed to the repertoire of learning resources generated by the project for future use. The development, production, and distribution of post-literacy materials meant that learners could be heavily involved.

The project concluded that there were value-added benefits which emerged from the adoption of an integrated approach to adult literacy, but that need for literacy should emerge from the processes of meeting other priority basic needs. It also established that recognition of the learners' previous knowledge and experience helps to facilitate learning. The project demonstrates the need to balance learners' knowledge and needs on the one hand with the common project parameters such as objectives, resources, and scope on the other. The staff worked with learners' expectations and aspirations in order to try to facilitate change.

Source: Thompson 1999

A post-literacy project in Sudan was extremely successful in using this method to make more texts available locally and in three languages; Arabic, Tigrinya, and Dinka (see Box 14.4).

Box 14.4: Building literacy with SOLO press 1999-2000

This was a pilot project in community literacy in four areas of Sudan: Khartoum, Gezira, Gedaref, and Kassala States. The objectives were to:

- provide sufficient suitable reading materials for those in refugee and internally-displaced people's camps to build their literacy skills;

- encourage a reading culture by involving participants in the process of creating reading materials;

- promote and support community-driven literacy initiatives.

The rationale for the programme was that 15 years of conventional literacy instruction using primers had had little effect. There was a significant drop-out rate, significant repetition rate, and a significant lack of suitable reading materials to build literacy skills.

The process is to mobilise the local community through participatory rural appraisal and form reading and writing circles of around 20-30 members. These were led by Community Liaison Workers (CLWs). Friends join and support the circles. The circles meet about twice a week for a two-hour session to discuss and write. They then discuss the written material, edit it, develop it further, discuss it again, and re-edit. They then select pieces of work that might be suitable for publication and illustrate them for printing and distribution by SOLO Press. *Discuss, Write, Do* is a self-study handbook to be used jointly by facilitators and the circle participants, which guides them through the process from discussion to production. The handbook can also be used by others who wish to produce their own materials.

An initial 26 circles expanded into 140 circles under the supervision of group leaders, and attracted people of a wide range of educational levels. The circles began to participate in community literacy activities. Six thousand people benefited directly and 20,000, of which 75 per cent were female, benefited indirectly.

Twenty-three separate publications have been produced on a range of subjects. These include *Liberty, Mariam and the Daughter of Omran, Practices Harmful to Personal Health,* a collection of stories, and six issues of a magazine. In all 53,000 copies were distributed.

Participants became empowered, gaining self-respect and a feeling of project ownership which has enhanced sustainability. SOLO has become a fully fledged printing service.

Source: Hashim Abuzeid and Abdulah Kom-Kodi, SOLO, Khartoum (Presentation at the Meeting of Experts, Cairo 2005)

In Nepal, workshops were held with participants to help them to produce materials that were both personal and informative. The writers found publishing to be an empowering experience. People who read this material strongly preferred it to professionally developed materials, finding it easier to read, more enjoyable, and more inspirational. Both the writers and the readers felt that producing their own materials validated them as knowers. Texts which were developed around specific development themes motivated readers to get involved in local community or development projects. Writing and distributing learner-generated materials in itself seemed to be an important process in shifting learners of literacy from passive recipients to active doers.

Distance materials and information and communication technology

While access to information and communication technology is still limited to certain parts of the world, there have been huge developments in the creation of distance, interactive, and web-based literacy materials. Many of these are resources for the tutor, with additional worksheets that can be printed off or adapted for learners. Some countries (Australia, the USA, South Africa), however, have developed interactive sites especially for learners to use. Some of these contain newspapers or online journals with local or national news stories as well as games and exercises for learners to complete. Others consist of worksheets that learners fill in online; they can find out immediately whether or not they have got a question right. These kinds of materials have also been developed extensively in primary school, and use images or sounds to reward a right answer or indicate a wrong one. They can be used to support literacy classes or as a distance resource in places where there is no tutor available.

China, India, and Mexico have conducted adult basic education using radio and television broadcasting, and many literacy programmes have made extensive use of radio advertising. Locally produced interactive radio instruction and community radio can include exchanges between programme providers and learners who are encouraged to write in, and can be valuable for widely scattered or travelling communities where it is difficult to organise classes. Cuba's 'Yo, sí puedo' programme uses radio and video to support literacy teaching, and has been adopted in several Latin American countries and New Zealand.

While there is huge potential for producing materials on computer, the cost of these means they are only justified if used on a large scale. There is an immediate danger that they then become 'highly life decontextualised' and less relevant to learners. Producing these for tutors, who have been taught how to adapt them for learners, is often a more economical way forward. While this does depend on having a developed infrastructure and computers and printers available for tutors or facilitators to use, it does mean they can be offered a wide range of possible material that they can then modify to represent the local context. They can also involve participants in choosing which of these are most appropriate to them.

Implications for planners

Research carried out in different areas does seem to indicate the importance of using real-life literacy activities and texts in literacy learning. While this does not need to be all of the time and real materials can be used alongside pre-prepared literacy materials, there is a correlation between time spent learning through real materials and long-term literacy use. However, making real-world materials available on a large scale for use in classes presents particular challenges for tutors working in rural areas with low infrastructure.

Tutors need training and support in identifying and using the different kinds of resources that do exist. Learners will benefit from a range of different kinds of texts and these can include broadcast material used as a stimulus for writing or discussion. Learners should also be encouraged to produce or adapt their own resources or critique those texts that are available; this will also require substantial tutor training. Overall it is more important for learners to work actively with texts (through adapting, questioning, rewriting) than to work passively and by doing so they will begin to use, rather than just to read or to listen to, the resources they have available.

Making links with those organisations producing written or broadcast material locally, whether official, developmental, or commercial, can be a real advantage. Producers of materials might be encouraged to take the needs of new readers into account and to make copies of their materials available to literacy providers. Networking with other literacy or community-development organisations is also a way to share resources and to help learners to engage with the development messages of other agencies. If literacy activities can be embedded into broader local activities, they are more likely to be sustained.

Further reading

A. Rogers, 'Adult Learning and Literacy Learning for Livelihoods', available at: www.uea.ac.uk/care/Recent_Writing/COLLIT4.pdf (last accessed June 2007), 2005. This is a discussion of the relationship between literacy and livelihoods using examples from the UK and Bangladesh.

C. Meyers, 'Learner generated materials in adult literacy programs as a vehicle for development: theory and practice in case studies in Nepal', Ph.D Thesis, University of Massachusetts, Amherst, available at: scholarworks.umass.edu/ dissertations/AAI9639002/ (last accessed June 2007), 1996. This is a doctoral thesis analysing the use of learner-generated material in Nepal.

E. Jacobson, S. Degener, and V. Purcell-Gates, 'Creating Authentic Materials and Activities for the Adult Literacy Classroom: A Handbook for Practitioners', Boston, MA: NCSALL, available at: www.ncsall.net/fileadmin/ resources/teach/jacobson.pdf (last accessed June 2007), 2003. This is a practical handbook based on research in the USA and providing extensive advice to teachers on how to create authentic and contextually specific materials for their learners.

H. Abuzeid and A. Kom-Kodi, *Empowering People Through Education*, Sudan Open Learning (SOLO), 2005.

J. Mace, *The Give and Take of Writing: Scribes, Literacy and Everyday Life*, Leicester: NIACE, 2002.

NCSALL, 'Understanding What Reading Is All About; Teaching Materials and Lessons for Adult Basic Education Learners', developed with Ashley Hager, Barbara Garner, Cristine Smith, Mary Beth Bingman, Lenore Balliro, Lisa Mullins, Lou Anna Guidry, and Susan McShane, Cambridge, MA: NCSALL, available at: www.ncsall.net/fileadmin/resources/teach/ uwriaa.pdf (last accessed June 2007), 2005. This is a series of lessons designed to help learners to understand the components of reading, and for teachers to use with their classes.

15

Training and supporting
literacy educators

*The quality and effectiveness of any adult education programme obviously
depends crucially on the 'coal face' workers, namely the class instructors
or facilitators: it is they who actually teach or interact with the intended
beneficiaries.*
(Oxenham 2004)

This chapter considers the training and the support provided for people who
work in literacy and numeracy programmes. It looks at who they are, how they
are selected, the different levels of education they may have, and the conditions
of their work. It asks who will train the trainers? It draws attention to some of
the issues around culture, language, and gender in training. The chapter
concludes by suggesting some guiding principles for planning and delivering
training.

Literacy educators

Literacy educators, both women and men, come from many backgrounds and
walks of life; some are full- or part-time professionals in literacy; very many
more are part-time, either paid or volunteers. They may be university students,
students training to be school teachers, housewives, young women with few
culturally acceptable employment opportunities, or men unable to find other
employment. They are variously described as instructors, teachers, tutors,
facilitators, and when unpaid, as volunteers. They have many and varied
experiences and different levels of education.

In the Introduction we explained why we sometimes use the term tutor or
facilitator in this book. However, in some programmes literacy educators are
called 'instructors' and in many programmes 'teachers'. Each of these terms can
be broadly linked to one of the four basic approaches to literacy outlined

previously – a skills-based approach, a task-based approach, a social practices approach, or a critical reflection approach. The different approaches require different skills and knowledge and therefore different approaches to support and training.

People working in the field of literacy can broadly be divided into five categories:

- part-time local literacy educators, very often women and also some men employed as instructors, teachers, tutors, or facilitators, or as unpaid volunteers
- full-time male and female teachers taking literacy groups as part of their duties, for a small extra stipend or voluntarily
- full-time or part-time NGO literacy staff
- full-time or part-time 'development' or 'extension' staff
- full-time, formally qualified educators employed in adult basic or non-formal education.

Part-time local literacy educators

Instructors

The term instructor implies someone involved in the transfer of a skill – instructing someone how to do something. It is used in employment training centres where people are trained in practical skills and crafts. When used in a literacy programme, the word instructor suggests a formal and traditional class, or a competency and skills-based approach. The term implies a level of subject knowledge and a need for training in teaching and learning techniques in order to impart the skills to someone else.

Teachers

Many programmes prefer to avoid the use of 'teacher' as it is a reminder of school experiences, and school was not a positive experience for many of the participants in adult literacy classes. Indeed, the fear expressed at coming to literacy classes can be the fear of going back to school. Many people who teach in schools are also involved in adult literacy programmes and consequently think of themselves, and are thought of, as teachers. The expertise and pedagogical knowledge of a good teacher are essential to the success of a literacy programme, but the use of the word 'teacher' can bring back bad memories. Programmes therefore often use the word 'tutor', though in fact they may have the image of a teacher in mind – that is someone who has a good knowledge of the subject to be taught and teaches it to uncritical learners. The use of the word 'teacher' needs to be carefully considered.

Tutors

The word tutor can be used in whichever approach to literacy the programme adopts, but it is most commonly used in the social practice and critical reflection models. A tutor helps someone learn something they want to learn, rather than teaching someone something they don't know, but which it is perceived they should know. As stated earlier, tutors tend to work collaboratively with participants in the literacy group to identify and achieve their learning needs and aspirations. Tutors will be trained in a range of pedagogic skills and have the ability to help learners identify what they want to learn, and together develop strategies and activities to achieve these. In other words tutors help participants learn what they want at their own pace, in their own way.

Facilitators

The term facilitator can also be used in the social model of literacy. It encompasses the idea of 'facilitating learning', but is more commonly used in the more radical approaches to literacy. Programmes that are consciously linked to empowerment, community development, and social change nearly always use the word facilitator. The concept was taken from popular education and community-development work and gradually applied to literacy programmes, particularly those linked to community development such as ActionAid's REFLECT (see Chapter 8). It is also used in post-conflict situations, particularly when literacy is combined with conflict resolution as in several programmes in Sierra Leone and south Sudan.

Volunteers

Many programmes rely on unpaid volunteers, who sometimes get expenses reimbursed. Sometimes volunteers are responsible for large groups of over 30 learners. In other programmes volunteers assist paid tutors by working with small groups or individuals. While this may save money in the short term, if they are to be effective, volunteers have to be trained, well-supported, and seen to be valued. In the long term the use of volunteers may not reduce costs.

Professional staff

Full-time teachers teaching literacy either voluntarily or as part of their duties

In many countries teachers, usually primary school teachers, often teach adults in the afternoons or evenings. This can be part of their duties, additional paid work, or a voluntary activity to help the community. Such teachers are very valuable and much needed, but teaching adults requires skills that are different from those required to teach children. Teaching adults requires an understanding of adults' motivation, and an appreciation of their life experiences, the real-life literacy and numeracy tasks they will encounter, and the financial constraints and responsibilities which may limit the time they have available. Teachers have to recognise that unlike many children, adults do not have to attend and will leave if they do not feel they are gaining what they came for.

Full-time or part-time NGO literacy staff

Many NGOs, both national and international, run literacy programmes. Many also run their own training programmes. ActionAid is possibly the best-known international NGO organising literacy programmes; their programme REFLECT is run in over 90 countries. Education Action International (formerly the World University Service) organises literacy programmes in conjunction with overseas partners. The US-based CARE and World Education run programmes in Yemen and Egypt. BRAC (Bangladesh Rural Action Council) is a very large national NGO which runs programmes in Bangladesh. Nirantur runs programmes in India. Other organisations like DELES in Nigeria are smaller but nevertheless include literacy as part of their development activities. All these organisations train their literacy educators. Sometimes literacy is part of a staff member's duties; sometimes staff are specifically hired for the literacy programme. A few may be full-time, many are part-time. Most of the NGOs adopt a social practices or transformative approach to literacy, and their training and their staff-selection criteria reflect these approaches, which combine well with their community-development objectives.

Full-time or part-time 'development' or 'extension' staff

Both governments and NGOs often include literacy as embedded in, or as a component of their programmes, rather than running programmes solely devoted to adult literacy. If literacy and numeracy is embedded in this way, both NGO and extension staff – that is those working directly with the people concerned – will need to be trained either to run separate literacy and numeracy groups, or trained how to incorporate literacy and numeracy into their agricultural, health, family-welfare, or income-generation programmes. Income generation is often a component of programmes run by women's associations and numeracy is an important element in these. Similarly, women's associations aiming to empower women will cover the literacy and numeracy involved in running an organisation. In these and other instances, literacy is 'second' – literacy is a means to achieving the primary objective.

Full-time formally qualified teachers in adult basic education or non-formal education

The trend is increasing towards professionalising and institutionalising training for literacy and numeracy staff. The aim is to improve the standard of teaching and learning in order to improve learning outcomes and also to raise the status of the profession. As a result many countries, particularly in the industrialised world, now require tutors to have formal qualifications. Courses leading to formal qualifications have many different structures, but there are two basic models:

1. Accredited full- or part-time courses for future literacy and numeracy teachers organised by formal institutions such as colleges and universities.
2. Initial teacher education courses to which specialist modules in adult literacy and numeracy are added.

In-service courses for practising teachers are also being developed along similar lines. Courses such as these for both new and serving teachers are run in several countries including the USA, South Africa, and the UK.

Working situation

The working situation of most literacy educators needs to be significantly improved. Whether instructors, teachers, tutors, or facilitators, few literacy educators have full-time positions, good conditions of service, or good career prospects, even in the industrialised world. Most are part-time and paid by the hour for the groups they teach. In some countries tutors have to recruit their learners themselves and can open a group only when they have recruited a certain number. In Nicaragua during the Sandinista post-revolutionary period, university students were recruited in a national campaign to teach non-literate people. In the 1990s Egypt engaged unemployed graduates in order to provide them with work for a year. At the present time literacy educators are one of the least supported groups of educators worldwide. They receive little, if any, regular remuneration, lack job security, and enjoy few training opportunities and little ongoing professional support.

Selection of literacy educators

Different programmes have different ways of selecting their educators. How they select, and the criteria for their selection, to some extent depends on which approach they are using. Whatever the educators' background or position, they should have the skills, attitudes, and knowledge required for working in adult literacy and numeracy. All those wishing to become literacy and numeracy educators, whether they are called instructors, teachers, tutors, facilitators, or volunteers, should:

- be competent and fluent in reading and writing the language of the literacy programme and the language of the learners, and/or competent and confident in maths and numeracy;
- be excellent communicators;
- be able to relate to the participants, their lives, and their issues.

The attitudes that educators bring to learning and teaching and to the participants are possibly as important as the skills and knowledge they possess.

> [You] need know why students are in the classroom. You need psychological insight into the problems people face, the backgrounds they have and the choices they have to make. You need empathy and empathy requires insight. Three quarters of being a teacher is building rapport, and that can't be taught.
> (Lucas *et al.* 2004)

Skills and knowledge can be taught; attitudes can be deeply ingrained and hard to change, so it is essential that tutors understand and relate well to literacy participants.

There is considerable variation in the level of education required for prospective literacy educators. Planners need to give careful consideration to this. Educators are normally expected to have a certain level of formal education, to have at least completed primary school, and preferably to hold a certificate of secondary education. Some are university graduates and post-graduates. People with the highest levels of education are not always the most sympathetic to those who have very little or no education. Theoretical knowledge does not always translate into good classroom practice.

People with the required level of education or knowledge may not be available in some areas, often rural areas, where schooling is limited. In this case tutors will either have to be persuaded to travel daily from the towns and urban centres into the rural areas, or to move to the rural communities. Some people from urban areas who teach in rural communities are excellent, others have little understanding or sympathy with rural life, and resent it. If this is the case, they are unlikely to be good literacy or numeracy tutors.

In remote rural or mountainous areas in north-west Pakistan, Yemen, north-east Nigeria, and in similar areas in other countries, there are very few women who have had educational opportunities. As a result, few women have sufficiently good language, literacy, and numeracy skills to become tutors. In some places there is also a strict division of the sexes, and though there may be educated men in the community, custom prevents them from working with groups of women unless they are related to them. In such circumstances different approaches have had some success. Women with low levels of education, sometimes young and unmarried and sometimes older, are recruited and provided with high-quality initial training to enable them to work with people just beginning to learn. In some places complementary educational programmes are provided to raise women's level of general education before they are trained as literacy tutors. After the initial training they are provided with considerable ongoing support. While the education level may not be as high as is desirable, the connection with and empathy for their own communities is a very positive factor.

Similar difficulties in recruiting tutors can exist in post-conflict societies where the education structure has collapsed, schools have closed, and many teachers have fled or been killed.

Training methodologies

Training will be orientated to one of the four approaches to literacy: skills, tasks, social practice, and critical reflection. Trainers will need to be in tune with the philosophy underlying the particular literacy programme. Training that is formal and rigid is unlikely to be effective in a participatory programme designed to promote community objectives. If the programme adopts a social model of literacy, training consisting of a series of lectures will not be appropriate; this would send the message to trainees that the teacher is the source of all knowledge and the trainees have nothing to offer. The trainee is then likely to assume the same attitude when working with literacy learners.

Training for skills-based and competency-based programmes

The use of adult literacy primers as the main teaching tool is very widespread. Many training courses train tutors to use these effectively and provide guides which detail exactly what should be covered in each session. An alternative to using primers in a skills-based approach is to develop a schema of literacy and numeracy skills and competencies to be mastered in a series of stages.

The demands of the labour market and the perceived demand for literate workers has led some countries to adopt a competency-based approach which can measure the level of literacy or numeracy a woman or man has acquired. In South Africa, the Adult Basic Education Training (ABET) has a series of levels in which the standards and what is required to achieve them are clearly laid out (see Table 15.1).

Table 15.1: South Africa – ABET training standards	
TITLE 2: READ AND RESPOND TO A RANGE OF TEXT TYPES	
Specific Outcome 1	**Specific Outcome 2**
The learner will be able to understand the literal meaning of the text	The learner will be able to relate text to own experience and knowledge
Assessment Criteria	**Assessment Criteria**
We know this when the learner:	We know this when the learner:
1.1 *Identifies* main ideas, topics and messages	2.1 *Draws and responds* to text using own experience
1.2 *Finds and recalls* surface/ literal content	2.2 *Expresses conclusions and opinions* derived from reading
1.3 *Finds and recalls* visual or graphic information	
Source: ABET 2006	

In the UK a national adult literacy curriculum was drawn up which closely mirrored that for school children, and identified what should be learnt at each stage. In this competency model, the tutors are expected to be sufficiently creative to devise their own materials to arrive at specified and externally agreed outcomes. How they achieve these outcomes is flexible. They will need to be trained on the skills required at each stage, and on different and innovative ways of relating these to learners' lives and literacy and numeracy requirements.

Training for task-based literacy programmes

The tasks for which literacy and numeracy are required are many and varied. A training course should enable the literacy and numeracy tutors to achieve a balance between helping participants acquire generic reading, writing, and calculating skills, and the particular skills required for the particular tasks in the particular context. The skills required in industry, commerce, or agriculture will be different from those required for child care, hygiene, and health.

Ideally, the people training tutors for task-based schemes will know something of the context, in order to enable trainees to relate the literacy and numeracy to the tasks. It may not always be possible to find one person who has knowledge of literacy and numeracy and of the area in which the skills will be used. Sometimes two trainers will be required.

Alternatively, if the literacy and numeracy is embedded as part of a wider skills programme, the skills instructor can be trained in adult literacy and numeracy, or the literacy instructor can be trained in how to link the literacy and numeracy to the relevant skill training. The Irish literacy association, NALA (The National Adult Literacy Agency) provided training for literacy staff in youth training centres, enabling them to link the literacy and numeracy to a range of skills courses such as woodwork, horticulture, catering, and fashion.

A task-based literacy programme may be based on adult primers. The primer might include information that the provider, donor NGO, or government feels that participants need in order to improve their lives. The training would reflect this approach.

Training for social practice programmes

The social practice approach views literacy as a variety of social practices dependent on the specific cultural and social situation. The social practice model is learner-centred. The tutors will need to know how to determine the literacy needs and aspirations of the learners, be trained in methods of participatory and active learning, and understand how to use these as well as why they are important.

In some programmes, students not only engage in dialogue over their learning but direct it, deciding what they want to learn. Tutors should be shown how to take a student's learning goal such as reading a hospital appointment card or writing a receipt, and break it down into learning objectives, planning activities to achieve these. This is a much harder task than teaching students the sounds of the alphabet or vocabulary as set out in primers. It demands flexibility, imagination, creativity, and a high level of commitment. This involves the trainer demonstrating a wide range of strategies and ideas to meet both individual learning needs and the needs of the whole group.

Training in the techniques of PRA should be included in training for the social practice model of literacy. Tutors should be provided with the tools to identify the literacy and numeracy used in the community and to gather social, economic, and cultural information about the area.

Training for critical reflection, transformation, and change programmes

In this model, facilitators will need many of the same skills as for the social model. Training will be required to enable them take on the broader aspects of social change as a conscious goal in order to help people 'decide what they want to accomplish, remind them of their responsibility in achieving it and encourage and help them to complete an agreed activity' (Prenderville 2004:13–14).

Trainees will also need to recognise

> *the value of each person's contribution, encouraging the active participation*
> *of each group member in identifying and utilising skills and experiences,*
> *creativity and analysis ... [which] enables groups and individuals to plan*
> *for development and change.*
> (*ibid.*)

The facilitator role goes beyond that of helping people to acquire the skills of literacy and numeracy. Facilitators are required to develop, organise, promote, negotiate, and advocate. An understanding of group dynamics and how groups operate is essential.

Difficulties and conflict are almost inevitable in a group. Facilitating is not an easy option. It requires the facilitators to think about their own skills, values, beliefs, and experiences. This involves self-reflection and self-analysis. It also requires the facilitator to 'know when to stand back' to allow participants to express their views and to ensure everyone is heard. A good facilitator is trained to manage disagreement and even conflict and enable the group to progress, even though views may differ. As happened in Brazil, facilitators may be required to promote the ideals of democracy, human rights, and citizenship and 'develop a critical and contextual understanding of reality for the conscious transformation of reality' (Singh and McKay 2004).

Training facilitators for a transformation and change approach to literacy must model the expected practice within the literacy group. The training must be participative and active. Many of the ideas are adapted from community-development practices and exercises derived from programmes such as 'Training for Transformation' (Dighe 2004). Ouane *et al.* (1990) point out that the majority of personnel working in literacy bring with them the views, methods, skills, and values of the formal system, and even if they have no experience as teachers they fall back on their own experience as students. DELES, a Catholic community-development organisation in Nigeria, developed excellent training for facilitators which was utilised in the DFID-funded Community Education Programme. This focused on changing attitudes, group cohesion and co-operation, and enabled facilitators to tackle difficult issues such as gender equality. The exercises were written up in a small handbook. The Irish NGO Combat Poverty has produced an excellent handbook to assist facilitators in developing their skills.

The training for critical reflection and transformative literacy may include the Freirean psycho-social model of literacy. Facilitators must be shown how to take topics and generate discussion and analysis, before moving on to the technical aspects of reading and writing that the topic incorporates. Topics may be provided as in the primers in the Nicaraguan and South-West Africa People's Organisation literacy programmes of the 1980s, or derived from small-scale PRA research and community analysis as in REFLECT, community-development, and post-conflict programmes.

A REFLECT programme following the mother manual requires the drawing up of a programme relevant to the particular area. Training for REFLECT programmes varies. In most cases local tutors assess the area and the needs of the learners and decide on a series of maps, diagrams, and matrices illustrating the situation. The vocabulary and text are drawn from these. Word cards and pictures are sometimes prepared in advance. The programme is flexible and can take into account the situation in a particular locality. Thus each training programme is slightly different.

Initial training

The majority of literacy programmes place great importance on a short period of initial training. The majority of training for grassroots tutors and facilitators is two weeks or less (sometimes much less: three days in the Ugandan government literacy programme). The initial training course is the foundation on which other training and support rests. Some of the areas to consider in planning initial training include:

- accredited or non-accredited training, a certificate on completion of the course or on reaching a required standard
- the length of training and whether residential or non-residential
- the programme's ideological and methodological frameworks
- the number of trainees, cost, location, frequency
- the availability of trainers with in-depth knowledge of the theory and practice of literacy and numeracy
- trainees' educational level, time availability, and financial constraints
- training materials and/or handouts.

A short course cannot cover all aspects. Decisions need to be made as to what should be covered initially and what can be covered on in-service or refresher courses. The training will be planned to achieve the desired outcomes, which will to some extent depend on the model of literacy selected for the programme. Some generic topics to be covered in training include:

- the programme's underlying ideology, methodology, and methods
- theories and principles of adult learning
- the skills, attitudes, knowledge, experience, and motivation literacy participants bring to the learning situation

- practical teaching strategies and techniques for teaching literacy and numeracy
- planning courses and planning individual sessions
- assessing progress
- using appropriate learning materials
- gender, minority, and language issues
- evaluating and improving own teaching.

It is important that the training is orientated to the model of literacy the programme has adopted, that it reflects its values, and demonstrates its methods. UNESCO (2006) stresses the 'absolute necessity of ensuring that the content, methodologies and envisaged outcomes of training are consistent with the intentions and goals of the locally defined needs and programmes'.

In addition to the generic outcomes, possible outcomes for the different approaches might be that tutors:

1. In skills-based approaches

- know the competencies learners need to achieve at each level;
- have the ability to develop strategies and activities to achieve these;
- are able to use relevant adult primers effectively.

2. In task-based approaches

- understand the context in which the skills will be used;
- know the specific literacy and numeracy tasks the learner will need to carry out;
- are able to use relevant adult primers effectively.

3. In social practices approaches

- know how to analyse the social, economic, cultural, and political context using PRA tools or ethnographic techniques;
- can confidently work with participants to identify learning goals and develop strategies and learning activities to achieve these;
- can work with mixed ability groups at a range of levels;
- are able to manage groups and generate discussion and dialogue;
- understand and are able to use the Freirian psycho-social approach;
- have an understanding of and are able to use the REFLECT approach;
- have excellent facilitation skills.

4. In critical reflection and transformative approaches

The training outcomes will be very similar to the social practices approach but in addition facilitators will need to:

- have a sound understanding of the theory and practice of community development;
- understand and use the REFLECT literacy programme and related ActionAid community-development programmes;
- have the ability to generate dialogue, discussion, and critical thinking;
- have a good understanding of group dynamics and be able to resolve group differences and tensions;
- have the ability to motivate and manage a group to reach an agreed goal;
- know how to support and facilitate change identified by the group.

The length of initial training and the amount of in-service training will vary according to the priority accorded both to the literacy programme and to the training of literacy staff and to constraints on human and financial resources.

Models of training

The British Council Community Education Project in Nigeria (1996–2000) adopted a four-stage training model of:

- initial residential training for tutors
- observed field experience
- follow-up training
- second-level specific training (monitoring and evaluation; materials production)

The Nigerian model was interesting as it required the trainer to observe the trainee tutors working. Their observations determined the content of a week of follow-up training three months later. After approximately six months, tutors judged to be particularly effective were provided with further training on developing literacy materials and on monitoring and evaluation (Ezeomah *et al.* 2006: 231–58).

Training in the CELL project in Egypt was more complex and comprised:

- a training needs analysis
- a training course to develop a central group of core trainers
- three initial residential training courses each (for tutors from two governorates) carried out by the core trainers, General Authority for Literacy and Adult Education (GALAE) branch officers, and university personnel
- monthly support meetings with branch personnel.

An interesting feature of this programme was the high number of people trained simultaneously. This involved training over 200 tutors attending a central location for two weeks and was possible by subdividing them into three large groups of around 70, and subdividing again for group work. This is a very different model from training a maximum of 30 tutors at any one time, as in the UK and elsewhere. Another interesting feature was that in a very religious Islamic environment only a very few women tutors were unable to attend residential training.

Training methods and styles

Training styles will vary according to the ideology and underlying methodology. Training for the task-based and competency-based approaches is likely to be more formal, sometimes following a 'lecture' mode in which the trainer is assumed to be the expert. Training facilitators in the social-practices and critical-reflection models will tend to be informal, interactive, and participative, and will recognise and draw on the skills and knowledge trainees bring to the training. This is diagrammatically represented in Figure 15.1. The training-room layouts used will provide a model for trainees in how to arrange *their* rooms – formally or informally – and will in the same way reflect their view of whether the literacy students bring something valuable with them or are 'empty vessels' to be filled with knowledge.

Formal and informal training styles and formal and informal programmes will not always correspond exactly, and there is likely to be considerable overlap. For example, the training in Egypt on the CELL programme contained both lectures by an academic and group-work facilitated by programme managers.

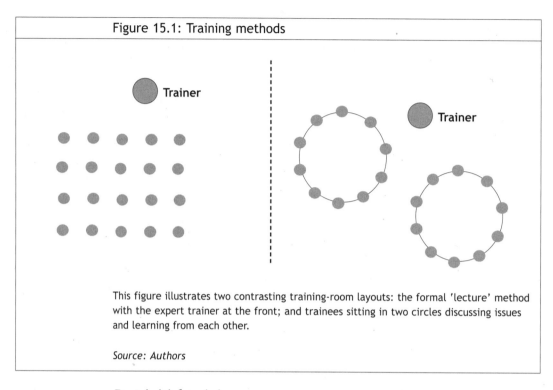

Figure 15.1: Training methods

This figure illustrates two contrasting training-room layouts: the formal 'lecture' method with the expert trainer at the front; and trainees sitting in two circles discussing issues and learning from each other.

Source: Authors

Post-initial training support

In both Nigeria and Egypt, considerable support was provided to tutors after their initial training. During the project period in Nigeria the national consultants and project managers regularly monitored progress. In Egypt there were regular meetings with General Authority for Literacy and Adult Education (GALAE) branch officials and project organisers and short 'refresher' courses.

However good the initial training, it is not sufficient. In-service and refresher training as well as continual support is always required. This can be organised in many ways: monthly meetings of tutors and organisers to discuss issues, or workshops on specific topics, and the provision of resources and materials.

Newsletters and magazines can also play an important part in enabling tutors to feel part of a larger organisation as well as providing them with news about activities and with learning and teaching strategies. Two examples of such magazines are *Community Literacies*, the newsletter of the Community Literacy Project Nepal, and *CEP*, the magazine of the Community Education Project, Nigeria. Both of these were produced for internationally funded projects. Such magazines are not always considered necessary when financial resources are restricted, but it is an important option worth considering.

Support can also be provided for literacy educators through distance methods. In South Africa the Adult Basic Education and Training (ABET) programme provides detailed workbooks with very specific instructions as to how to develop and manage a literacy group. The advantage of such a programme is that it can reach many more people than face-to-face learning or training. The International Educational College in Cambridge, UK worked with the Sudan Open Learning Organisation to develop an excellent manual on how to develop literacy skills, aimed at both learners and facilitators working together.

Radio, television, DVD, and video are also used, although perhaps less than might be expected, given the general widespread use of these media.

Trainers and trainers of trainers

If the success of a literacy programme depends on the quality of the tutors, the quality of the tutors depends on the quality of the training they receive. Key questions to consider are:

- Who should train trainers and trainers of trainers?
- How are they selected?
- What qualifications should they have?
- What practical experience of literacy and numeracy should they have?
- What theoretical knowledge should they have?

Much of the initial short training described above is carried out at local level by experienced practitioners or specially trained cadres of training experts, programme managers, lecturers at local universities or colleges, and national or international consultants. Very little research has been carried out into the training, qualifications, or experience of those who train literacy and numeracy tutors or those who train the trainers. UNESCO (2006) suggest this is an area of great weakness. Many writers have commented on the poor quality of training provided (Shah 2004, Dighe 2004, Carr-Hill *et al.* 2001, and Riddell 2001).

Training frameworks

In some countries, particularly industrialised countries, more formal training is being developed through extensive full- or part-time courses for new entrants to the profession, and in-service courses for experienced tutors who may have no qualification in adult literacy and numeracy. In some countries a complex 'hierarchical' structure of training is developing (see Figure 15.2).

Ideally the three levels of training identified in Figure 15.2 and the whole training structure would be framed by a national training policy. Most countries do not have such policies but a few, like Tanzania, do. In Tanzania, Brazil, Botswana, and Egypt tutors have to undergo a certain number of hours of training before taking groups. In national programmes different target groups may require different approaches. These differences may relate to gender, culture, geography, or work.

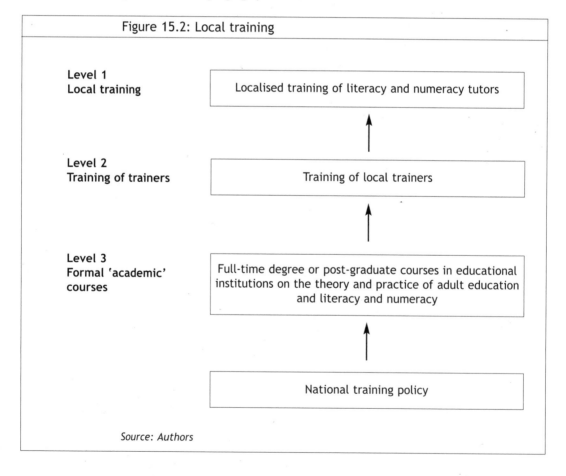

Figure 15.2: Local training

Level 1
Local training — Localised training of literacy and numeracy tutors

Level 2
Training of trainers — Training of local trainers

Level 3
Formal 'academic' courses — Full-time degree or post-graduate courses in educational institutions on the theory and practice of adult education and literacy and numeracy

National training policy

Source: Authors

However, the development of extensive Level 3 'professional' training courses (as well as an increase in research in universities) suggests that a firmer intellectual and theoretical base is developing. These Level 3 courses are for people interested in entering, or already working in, the field of literacy and numeracy. They are normally organised by universities and colleges and can be undergraduate courses covering all aspects of working with adults, initial teacher training courses covering literacy and numeracy for adults, certificate or diploma courses, or post-graduate degree courses. The courses are accredited and those passing receive the appropriate degree, diploma, or certificate. Different courses are targeted at different audiences.

One example is the Advanced Diploma for Educators of Adults, a National Qualifications Framework Level 6 qualification provided by the University of the Western Cape, South Africa for a broad range of professionals involved in adult learning (including ABET facilitators, development practitioners, and health practitioners). The entry requirement is a degree or equivalent qualification and a minimum of two years' professional experience. The course is structured around eight modules which include:

- Adult Education and Social Transformation
- Adult Learning Theories and Practices
- Organisation Management and Development
- ABET
- Evaluative Research

The University of the Western Cape also runs a Diploma in Education, Training and Development: Workplace Learning, a Higher Diploma, and a Higher Certificate in Education, Training and Development: Adult Learning.

In some countries generic professional courses in education are a base to which specialist courses are added. The generic courses may be for any level of teaching or particularly for the post-school sector. The latter would include the theories of adult learning.

Recent research carried out by the National Research and Development Centre on Adult Literacy and Numeracy (NRDC) in the UK found that 'Some teachers of literacy and numeracy lacked knowledge of the subjects they were teaching' (Moser 1999 cited in Lucas *et al.* 2004). The research suggests specialist courses in formal institutions should include the following areas:

- *subject knowledge* – sound knowledge and competency in language, linguistics, and /or mathematics and numeracy;
- *theoretical knowledge* – theoretical and conceptual understanding of literacy and numeracy and adult learning;
- *practical pedagogy* – knowledge of practical teaching strategies and techniques in teaching these subject areas;
- *teaching competence* – be good teachers themselves able to model sound teaching techniques.

A series of studies in the UK highlighted the importance of integrating knowledge of the subject and learning and teaching skills into training and professional development. They noted that teacher educators need both a firm grasp of their subject and a firm knowledge of how to teach it:

> The numeracy study concluded that teacher educators not only need a firm grasp of the subjects they teach and of the best way to teach them, they also need to be on top of their subject specific pedagogic knowledge, similarly teaching reading ...requires an understanding of both pedagogy and subject.
> (Vorhaus 2006)

The research report (Lucas *et al.* 2004) notes that several effective approaches to the teaching of reading, such as phonics and developing fluency, were hardly ever seen. A set of standards has recently been developed by the Further Education National Training Organisation (FENTO) to systematise both the generic and the specialist standards required of literacy facilitators. The specialist standards include for example a knowledge of phonetics, phonology, and sound–symbol relationships; construction of complex sentences; the functions and conventions of punctuation; a knowledge of specific learning disabilities and learning difficulties that restrict language acquisition and development. The standards also include aspects of speaking and listening such as using a range of delivery techniques to enhance communication. The report notes that it is essential that those teaching these courses have the requisite theoretical and practical knowledge but it also notes that people with these combined skills were not always easy to find.

Such formal courses and training are validated by government or designated bodies. Trainees gain certificates on successful completion of the course. Assessment can involve course work and an exam or alternatively submitting pieces of work and demonstrating teaching and facilitating skills. The methods of assessment, whether formal exams, coursework, or teaching, can all be judged internally by the course trainer or externally by a validating body.

Certification aims to provide a nationally agreed standard. Once trained to an agreed standard, a tutor can move from one literacy programme to another.

It is likely that training will continue to be formalised and this will have positive aspects. However, the flexibility, responsiveness, and participative processes of much localised training should continue and be highly valued.

Cultural, language, and gender issues

Whether training is formal or informal and whatever approach a literacy programme adopts, all training should include culture, language, and gender issues. People from different cultures have different ways of thinking and learning. This includes not only what the learner brings to the learning experience, but also indigenous knowledge, language, and culture and the identity of the learner in terms of 'class, gender, religion and race' (Ouane and Glanz 2005).

Cultural issues

People think and learn in different ways (Ouane *et al.* 1990). In areas where schooling is limited people will have learnt from their elders by copying or practising the skills they require. They will have acquired the history of their community through oral traditions. Trainers will need to take particular care in stressing the importance of valuing the skills and experiences of groups excluded from the mainstream, such as the Dalits in India and Nepal, Gypsies in the UK, nomadic pastoralists in sub-Saharan Africa, legal or illegal migrants, internally displaced people, and religious minorities. These different cultural contexts need to be addressed in the training and above all, tutors and facilitators need to respect and value the traditions learners bring to the learning situation even if they are very different from their own. Ideally people from these groups will be trained to work with their own people.

Language issues

Language issues are often ignored or glossed over. Training may be for mother-tongue teaching, dual-language teaching, and regional and national language teaching. Whatever the programme, the trainer must be able to communicate effectively with the trainee tutors and facilitators. Training is frequently provided in regional, national, or international languages rather than in the local language. One of the criteria for selection for training is often knowledge of the language of the trainer. The position needs to be reversed and the trainer selected for knowledge of the trainees' language. Trainers should always asses the language ability of the participants and ensure interpretation is available whenever necessary. Where training takes place in a multi-lingual context, there is usually someone who can translate. Training in the Community Education Programme in Nigeria (1996–2000) was conducted in English, Hausa, Ibo, Ibibio, and Fulfulde. In south Sudan English rather than Arabic was the preferred medium for training, but Arabic, Amharic, Dinka, and several local languages were also spoken. Three different scripts and seven languages were used among a group of 20 people.

Gender issues

Gender issues in training include the choice of language, the proportion of female to male tutors, cultural restrictions on women's mobility and therefore access to training, women's low self-esteem, and the need to avoid portrayal of gender stereotypes in training materials.

Training in national or international languages can disadvantage women. In many countries their knowledge of the international language is poor and their exposure to languages spoken outside their immediate community is limited. While many may appear to communicate reasonably well, their understanding of more complex or unfamiliar language may be limited. Writing skills in a language other than the mother tongue may also be limited. These difficulties need to be identified and addressed.

Cultural traditions and restrictions on mobility impact on the ability of women tutors to attend training. For cultural and religious reasons many women are only able to attend training with their husband's permission, and if the trainer is a woman and local social norms are respected. It is very difficult for women in some countries to attend residential training. Occasionally their husband accompanies them to enable them to attend.

In Egypt 90 per cent of trainers and organisers are men, yet in some governorates 70 per cent of the tutors and learners are women. In Uganda 70 per cent of the learners are women and most of the tutors and facilitators are men. Some would argue that this is of no consequence, but women and men have different experiences and different perceptions and both need to be taken into account. Moreover in societies where there is little interaction between women and men outside the family, problems and difficulties are unlikely to be taken to members of the opposite sex.

There are also gender issues around learning. Many women have very low self-esteem. To learn effectively they need to be reassured that they are capable of learning. Tutors, women as well as men, need to be trained to give constant positive reassurance and constructive feedback. As with men, women's life experience and skills need to be valued. Just as the tutor needs to recognise the skills, experience, and knowledge of the literacy participants, trainers, most frequently men, need to recognise the skills and experience of female facilitators. If they don't recognise the strengths of the women they are training, the women trainees in turn will have difficulty in recognising the skills and knowledge of the literacy participants.

Gender bias is not limited to men. Women tutors and facilitators who are not aware of sex discrimination and gender bias can have negative attitudes to non-literate women. Similarly men who are gender-aware can be very positive and supportive to women tutors and women learners.

In many programmes training materials will have been centrally determined. In others trainers will develop their own. In both cases care needs to be taken to ensure there is no gender, ethnic, or religious bias. It is important that examples of both women's and men's activities inside and outside the home are given and that illustrations show women and men undertaking a range of activities. Similarly, any excluded or disadvantaged groups should be portrayed positively.

Implications for planners

A national training policy provides a framework and quality standard in which different organisations – government departments, NGOs, community-based organisations, prisons and correctional institutions, family literacy providers, and profit and not-for-profit organisations and other providers can operate to agreed standards. It provides some assurance of quality across a wide range of possible providers. Ideally such a standard recognises and incorporates the best of government-led training and the best of NGO training.

The training of literacy educators is an under-researched area, but evidence to date suggests some guiding principles planners might consider when deciding on the extent and nature of training and support:

- A national training framework provides a structure for training.
- Training for organisers, tutors, and facilitators should be given the highest priority and the costs, logistics, and time for training and ongoing support should be built into the programme from the beginning.
- High-quality initial training and good ongoing training support is essential.
- The methodology and the methods should reflect the literacy approach adopted by the programme.
- A range of support activities enhances the effectiveness of the teaching and learning.
- Those training the trainers, and trainers themselves, should have subject-specific knowledge, a theoretical understanding of literacy and numeracy and language development, knowledge and skill in pedagogical methods, and be expert teachers themselves.

Planners and senior programme managers will have difficult decisions to make regarding training. Funding is often scarce and it is not always possible to put as much training in place as is necessary, nor are the most appropriate people always available. Nevertheless, if training is planned from the beginning and effective training and support taken seriously and considered essential, the outcomes will be positive.

Further reading

There are a number of training manuals which provide ideas and exercises for participative training for literacy educators, training in PRA and in group facilitation skills:

A. Hope and S. Timmell, *Training for Transformation: A Handbook for Community Workers*, Books 1– 4, London: ITDG Publishing, 2003. This is one of the basic resources for any participatory training. First developed in Zimbabwe, it has been widely use in many countries for community development. The activities are very useful in training literacy tutors – highly recommended.

A. Ouane, Mercy Abreu de Armengol, and D.V. Sharma, *Handbook on Training for Post Literacy and Basic Education*, Hamburg: UNESCO, 1990. This handbook is very easy to read and very clear – it takes the reader through a whole training programme.

D. Archer, and S. Cottingham, *REFLECT Mother Manual*, London: ActionAid, 1996. This is an essential manual providing trainers with an understanding of PRA and REFLECT.

J. McCaffery, F. Obanubi, and K. Sanni, *Guide for Training Literacy Instructors*, Community Education Programme, Nigeria, British Council, 2002. This is a short, practical, and easy-to-use guide which suggests activities for different elements of the training programme.

J. McCaffery, K. Newell-Jones, and S. G. Doe, *Integrating Literacy and Peacebuilding: A Guide for Trainers and Developers*, Reading: Education for Development, 2005. This is a detailed manual containing information on both areas, and suggestions and activities to use in an integrated training programme.

LABE (Literacy and Basic Education), 'The LITKIT: Resource File for Instructors/Facilitators of Adult Literacy and Numeracy', Kampala and London: LABE and Education Action International, 2003. This is a useful and very accessible low-cost guide for trainers and facilitators.

P. Prenderville, *Developing Facilitation Skills: A Handbook for Group Facilitators*, Dublin: Combat Poverty Agency, 2004. This offers excellent advice on facilitating groups – it is highly applicable to literacy groups.

Sudan Open Learning Organisation, *DWD, Discuss, Write, Do: A Self Study Handbook for Practitioners Working to Build Literacy Skills*, Sudan Open Learning Organisation with IEC and UNESCO, 2005. This is a very practical guide aimed at students and tutors working together.

UNESCO, 'Literacy for Life', EFA Global Monitoring Report, Paris: UNESCO, 221–30, 2005. This is a good summary of the current situation in training for adult literacy.

16

Assessing literacy learning

This chapter reviews the role of assessment in literacy programmes.
It considers two broad purposes for assessment: assessment for learning and
assessment of achievement, and how these different purposes require different
approaches. It then considers what is to be assessed: skills, tasks, practices,
or critical reflection imply different plans and methods of assessment.
The chapter then reviews a number of assessment methods grouped under the
two main purposes. Finally, it considers how to build capacity for assessment
and summarises the main implications for planners of literacy programmes.

What do we mean by assessment?

Assessing learning means gathering information about what learners have
learned and analysing their achievements. There are many different
approaches to assessment and even more assessment methods. Some are better
suited to a particular purpose than others. This chapter will help programme
planners think about why assessment should be part of the programme, what
should be assessed, which methods might be most appropriate, and some of
the main issues to consider when planning assessment.

Assessment of learning is not new. The first recorded school examinations
were in China around the twelfth century BC. The first recorded reading
assessments, testing oral reading abilities, were in England and France in the
fourteenth century AD. In the global North, twentieth-century education
developed a strong emphasis on standardised tests in schools and also for
adults. These were derived from intelligence tests, first developed by the US
army during the First World War (and including reading comprehension).
In the 1930s the first American functional literacy tests were conducted.
These measured the ability of adults to extract information from texts like

catalogues and telephone directories. They started a trend that continues today with tests like the IALS (International Adult Literacy Assessment) and LAMP (Literacy Assessment and Monitoring Project). More recently other ways of assessing learning have been developed and now standardised tests are only one method in the array of assessment tools from which to choose.

Many adult literacy programmes, especially the more informal ones, include no planned assessment of literacy learning at all. In omitting assessment they are failing to help both learners and tutors see the progress that is being made and areas that need further work. At the other end of the spectrum, some countries require all literacy programmes to use a particular method of formal assessment, often a test. By making 'one size fit all' these may also be missing opportunities for more thoughtful assessment that responds to particular learners' goals and expectations. Between these extremes lies a wide range of options.

In planning any assessment of literacy learning, the first step is to be clear about the purpose for assessing learning and what will be assessed. The most appropriate methods can then be selected. The following sections describe two broad purposes for assessment, and what insights and information they can provide for literacy programme managers, teachers, and learners. The two broad purposes are assessment for learning and assessment of achievement (Lavender *et al.* 2004: 15).

Assessment for learning

In this approach, assessment is designed to improve the process of teaching and learning. It is also known as 'formative' assessment, because it helps 'form' the learning programme. It may start at the beginning of the learning process to identify learning needs, continue during learning to identify areas of progress and problems, and also take place at the end of learning to demonstrate for learners themselves what they have learned. Assessment for learning can provide:

Information for tutors and learners:

- diagnostic assessment can identify specific skills and knowledge with which the learner needs help;
- self-assessment by learners can help them recognise their progress and what they still need to work on. As well as encouraging them it can build self-management and reflection that is part of becoming autonomous and self-directed learners;

- assessment of progress can help tutors and learners plan what needs to be learned next.

Quality assurance:

- reviewing reports on learning progress can help programme managers ensure that tutors plan learning in response to learner needs and adjust those plans as progress is made.

Accountability to learners:

- ensuring that learners participate in planning and reviewing their own learning

(This outline is based on Merrifield *et al.* 2001.)

Assessment of achievement

In this approach, assessment is designed to confirm that learning has taken place and certain standards have been achieved. It is sometimes called 'summative' assessment. There may be an initial assessment to identify a baseline or starting point, and further assessment after a period of time to identify progress made. Assessment of achievement can provide:

- A qualification for the learner, whether this is a school-equivalent qualification or one especially designed for adults. Qualifications may have intrinsic value for learners as a recognition of their achievement, or extrinsic value if they are recognised by employers, or for entry to further training or higher education.

- Quality assurance – ensuring that programmes are enabling learners to achieve desired results.

- Accountability for the outcomes of the learning process, whether to learners, the community, government, or other funders.

- National statistics of literacy needs and achievements. These may be important in establishing the scale of need and the value of literacy programmes for governments with many other demands on resources.

Methods for the two purposes

While assessment for learning and assessment of achievement may use some of the same methods, they emphasise different aspects of learning and are likely to use different methods, or the same methods in different ways.

Methods for *assessment for learning* are most likely to focus on the processes behind reading and writing. They might be termed 'diagnostic' in the sense that tutors use them to see how the learner is approaching reading and writing activities, and where they are having difficulties. Diagnostic methods may include, for example:

- placement and diagnostic tests such as those in Box 16.1

- analysis of reading processes, including the mistakes people make (see Box 16.4)

- learners' interpretation of meaning in texts

- environmental print tasks, assessing whether learners recognise words and symbols in their daily context (see Box 16.4)

- cloze exercises (or gap analysis), assessing how well learners can make sense of reading tasks (see Box 16.5).

Box 16.1: Screening and placement instruments from the Philippines

The Philippines Nonformal Education (NFE) System makes use of two placement tests to assist in the process of diagnosing learners' appropriate level of learning. These tests are the Assessment of Basic Literacy (ABL), and the Functional Literacy Test (FLT). Both tests are in Filipino and are designed purposely for determining the starting point/level of potential learners who wish to enrol in the NFE A&E LSDS (Accreditation and Equivalency Learning Support Delivery System). Those individuals who do not pass these tests may be recommended to complete the Basic Literacy Program before enrolling in the NFE A&E LSDS.

Instructional managers should be aware, however, that the very idea of testing could be very threatening to some learners, particularly to those who have not been involved in any learning program for some period of time. Great care must be taken when using the ABL and FLT as screening and placement instruments to ensure a supportive and as non-threatening environment as possible so that adults are able to build their confidence as enrolled learners of the NFE A&E LSDS.

Source: NFE A&E 2002

Assessment for learning may also use performance assessment and portfolios to identify learning strengths and weaknesses in order to plan further learning (these are discussed further below). Learners' own self-assessment may be an important element in assessment for learning, as it encourages learners to become more actively involved in planning and revising their learning experiences. This is used in the Philippines Nonformal Education system as well.

Methods for *assessment of achievement* are most likely to focus on the outcomes of reading or writing. They assess whether the learner can read and comprehend a text at a certain level of difficulty, spell particular words, use language conventions and grammar rules appropriately, or organise a writing activity so that it can be understood. Major methods used are described at length later in this chapter and include:

- Standardised reading tests (many of these are now based on the IALS), which use comprehension questions to identify whether a learner has understood a given piece of text.

- Performance assessment, which uses activities based on life tasks, often requiring multiple skills and knowledge areas, to demonstrate what people can do in solving problems and accomplishing tasks.

- Portfolio assessment, in which learners assemble over time a collection of their work that represents their achievements in a variety of areas and activities.

More detail on each of these methods is included below in the section on assessment methods. But first there is another question that programme managers need to consider: what exactly should be assessed?

What is to be assessed?

Depending on the underlying concept of literacy in the programme, planners might want to assess:

- skills
- tasks
- practices
- critical reflection.

Planners might choose to assess some combination of these (for example skills and tasks, or practices and critical reflection), or even all four. Not all methods are appropriate for everything, and programmes will want to select a manageable set of methods that best suit their focus.

Assessing literacy skills

Tests are the most common method of assessing literacy skills, but not the only method (performance assessment, most commonly used for assessing tasks and practices, also reveals skills).

Standardised tests are developed, tested, and normed against a specific population. Their advantage is that they are quick to carry out and they minimise demands on test administrators (and therefore training needs) because they are standardised. They produce a score that can be used to compare students to one another, track an individual student's progress over time, or measure their skills against a norm or set of expectations.

For example, in the Philippines there has been a ten-year history of developing literacy assessment tests as a screening tool (identifying initial skills and knowledge). The ABL test was originally developed for the Alternative Learning System that offers learning opportunities to out-of-school youth and adults, leading to a school-equivalent qualification at elementary or secondary levels (see Box 16.1 for more on the Philippines assessment approaches).

Curriculum tests are different in that their aim is to check whether learners have mastered the curriculum that has been taught. In the Philippines the exit tests of the alternative education system provide school-equivalent qualifications at elementary or secondary levels. The tests (using multiple choice questions and an essay) are based on the curriculum covered in the non-formal education system and are normed on grade six (elementary) and fourth year high-school students (secondary) two weeks prior to their graduation (SEAMEO-INNOTECH 2006: 115).

Whatever the test, planners should be aware that performance in a test is not always a good measure of someone's ability to use the same skills in life tasks. The transfer of skills from one context to another is not automatic and cannot be assumed: some people do better in a classroom context than they do in life, others may perform better in life tasks than in literacy tests.

Test results need to be carefully interpreted. A learner's familiarity with doing tests, knowledge of the particular vocabulary used, and confidence will all influence how well he or she performs. The level of difficulty of a text is not independent of its context. Difficulty relates not just to the text's internal characteristics (like vocabulary and sentence structure) but also to the reader's experience of the content and to the context in which it is read. For example there is much research evidence from the USA that workers can read job-related texts at a much higher level of difficulty than their reading ability revealed by general reading tests.

Diagnostic assessment methods aim to uncover the processes the learner is using in reading and writing and so may provide a more in-depth view of the learner's skills than a one-off test. Some of the diagnostics may identify particular aspects of the skills of reading, writing, and mathematics. Diagnostic methods are not used in assessment of achievement, but are very useful in assessment for learning because they reveal specific areas in which learners are doing well or need help. They provide the basis for an individual learning plan agreed between tutor and learner. Boxes 16.4 and 16.5 summarise some diagnostic assessment methods for reading and writing.

Assessing literacy tasks

Functional tests like the IALS create mini 'tasks' that aim to mirror everyday tasks like reading a label, using a bus timetable, or calculating a bill. Other task-based methods use scenarios and simulations to create similar problem-solving situations. In the Philippines the FLT, recently revised, is a purpose-designed tool for assessing functional literacy. It aims 'to document adult nonformal learning that occurs in the context of community life and everyday activities by measuring an adult's potential or capacity for various levels of thinking' (SEAMEO-INNOTECH 2006). It is used for determining the starting point of adult learners who have already achieved Basic Literacy.

As with the skills-assessment methods, it is important to bear in mind that applying skills in a real-life context is not the same as applying them in a learning group or literacy programme. As a result, the assessment may not accurately reflect learners' ability to accomplish the same tasks in their daily lives.

How well someone can complete a task depends on many factors, not just the content and structure of the task itself. Working with a group of people who have different skills and knowledge may affect an individual's performance of the task. Familiarity with the context and content of the task material may mean that a learner performs at a higher level in life than in the classroom or vice versa. Their confidence, depending on setting, also affects how well they complete the task. The confidence of working in the secure environment of the literacy learning group may mean that the learner's skills appear higher than they would be in a similar life task outside the programme.

Assessing literacy practices

Practice-based assessment aims to document how learners use literacy in their lives as well as in their learning group. Many social practice-based assessments use a framework that includes not only knowledge and skills but also other aspects of literacy learning and performance. For example, in the Republic of Ireland, NALA's Mapping the Learning Journey (MLJ) assessment framework has four 'cornerstones' of literacy learning as Box 16.2 shows.

Box 16.2: Mapping the Learning Journey, Republic of Ireland

The four cornerstones of literacy learning:

- knowledge and skills
- fluency and independence
- understanding
- range of application.

Each cornerstone contains elements. For example within fluency and independence there are three elements:

- carries out activity and task easily
- carries out activity and task consistently
- carries out activity and task independently.

Within range of application there are two elements:

- applies knowledge and skills to less familiar activity and tasks
- applies knowledge and skills in a range of settings.

Source: NALA 2005

Using the MLJ, tutors and learners identify which particular cornerstones and elements they are working on and select, for assessment purposes, specific examples of learner work to demonstrate their learning. These may include written and oral work, done in the learning group or outside, individually or as part of a group. The tutor will assess the work against the performance criteria of levels in the MLJ and review these with the learner.

More informal approaches to assessing literacy practices may include documenting through interviews how learners are using their knowledge and skills in their lives. In Mali, World Education's Sanmogoya literacy project works with parent associations. Learners take an initial literacy test, administered by an NGO fieldworker (not the literacy tutor), followed by an end-of-course test and learner evaluation. In several programme evaluations, interviews with learners reviewed the impact of participation in the programme on their activities in the parent association (taking notes, recording finances, monitoring school attendance), their involvement in their children's education, attention to health matters, effects on confidence and mobility, and family financial skills. For example, some participants had their own businesses and said they were better able to maintain their own financial records (World Education 2006: 368).

Assessing literacy as critical reflection

Most programmes taking a critical-reflection approach to literacy have aims beyond literacy. They focus their assessment less on literacy skills or applications and more on action and outcomes. Assessment methods may include:

- individual and group projects that include analysis, critique, and deliberation
- reflection logs, learning journals, and discussions that involve self-assessment and self-evaluation by the learner
- action projects that incorporate the elements of the experiential learning cycle – observing and reflecting, generalising, experimenting.

While the methods are usually based on self-assessment, they are not necessarily individual. The use of group assessment (using participatory and visual tools) may ensure that action and change within the community is documented as well as individual development.

In a family literacy project in Kwa Zulu Natal, for example, the aim is to help adults to improve their own levels of literacy while at the same time giving information and support on how they can help young children develop early literacy skills (Desmond 2006). The project uses REFLECT tools to ensure a participatory approach, and integrates literacy teaching (initially mother tongue and now also English) into sessions along with information on early literacy development and parenting. Within the unit topics the group decides what action to take to use their new knowledge, and some of these actions provide group members with opportunities to practise their literacy skills – writing to the editor of the project newsletter; maintaining community noticeboards; or writing stories about their own children and their adult lives. One result of the programme has been to bring books and reading to remote communities.

While REFLECT itself does not include literacy assessment there are appropriate methods that could be used in critical-reflection literacy programmes. The 'authentic' or performance-assessment methods described below seem particularly appropriate to demonstrate the active and reflective learning that is the goal of this approach.

Developing an assessment plan

The assessment plan will reflect both the purpose for doing assessment (for learning or of achievement), and the particular literacy focus of the programme (skills, tasks, practices, or critical reflection). There are some other factors to consider in planning the assessment, but these two are the starting point (see Box 16.3).

Box 16.3: Planning assessment		
Concept of literacy	Assessment for learning	Assessment of achievement
Skills – assessing: • knowledge • skills • fluency	Diagnostics such as: • miscue analysis* • analysing recalls* • language experience* • cloze exercises* • environmental print* activities	• standardised skills tests • curriculum-based tests • portfolios with external criteria
Tasks – assessing: • knowledge and skills applied to complete tasks	• performance or authentic assessment • portfolios with internal criteria	• standardised tests such as IALS • performance or authentic assessment • portfolios with external criteria
Practices – assessing: • knowledge and skills • fluency • range of application • understanding	• performance or authentic assessment • portfolios with internal criteria • self-assessment	• performance or authentic assessment • portfolios with external criteria
Critical reflection – assessing: • analysis • reflection • application of literacy to community action and problem-solving	• portfolios with internal criteria • reflective journals • PLA (participatory learning and action) • PAR (participatory action research)	• individual and group projects and evaluation

* See Boxes 16.4 and 16.5 for definitions of these terms.

Source: Authors

Other factors to think about in making an assessment plan include scale, what models of assessment are familiar in the culture, and requirements of accountability systems.

What can be done with assessment depends partly on the programme's scale and capacity. A small-scale programme focusing on a particular geographical area would not generally have the resources to construct standardised tests, for example, and more informal methods might be more appropriate and achievable. Larger-scale programmes across a region or country may be able to put resources into developing assessment methods and training tutors.

The 'folk models' of assessment in the local culture also affect what people expect assessment to be like. Learners may expect tests because they have been given them in school. On the other hand they may be fearful of tests because of past failures. Introducing an alien model may take more time and work, and require more training and support, than offering a method that feels more familiar to learners and tutors. A decision to use a different form may be valid, but must take into account needs for training and capacity building.

The demands of funders or government may require statistics to be produced, or disinterested evaluation and judgement by someone other than the teacher. These factors will mean that more informal assessment within the learning group may not provide what is needed.

Once a broad approach has been decided there will be more detailed planning, including such questions as:

- Frequency – how often the assessment needs to be done. This depends partly on the purposes: assessment for learning should be done on a regular basis and with every learner, but assessment of achievement does not need to be carried out frequently, or even with all learners (a sample may be sufficient).
- Consistency – how to make sure that different teachers or assessors use the same criteria in making judgements. This requires assessment to be part of the tutor-training programme and support to be regularly provided. Cross-moderation, in which tutors review and comment on each other's assessment of samples of student work, provides a way of checking on judgements and criteria used. It can be a valuable form of professional development as well.

Methods of assessing literacy learning

This section describes in a little more detail the main assessment methods that are in common use in literacy programmes. They are grouped by the two broad purposes for assessment outlined earlier: assessment for learning and assessment of achievement.

Methods for assessment for learning

Assessment for learning focuses on the process of reading and writing and analyses how the learner is approaching these. By analysing the process the tutor can identify where learners are having difficulties and can then explicitly teach these skills and knowledge.

The process of reading

The reader always has a purpose for each reading event: it may be for enjoyment or to pass the time, to find out local news in the newspaper, or to identify the information needed to fill in a form. Readers bring their prior knowledge to a new text. This includes their knowledge of the genre or type of text (a story or a report, a list of rules, or a description), the rules of language (the arrangement of text, division into words and sentences), vocabulary, and grammatical structure. Various methods allow tutors to examine what learners bring to the reading process and how they carry out the task (Fagan 1992 provides a useful review of many of these methods, and some are presented in Box 16.4).

The process of writing

The writer always has a goal: it may be to tell a story, pass on information, convince others, or share an idea. Writers bring to the process their understanding of writing styles and genres, world knowledge, and knowledge of language. They select words and create sentences to try to convey meaning. They use spelling and grammar rules to help their readers understand what they mean. Various methods help tutors analyse the process of writing (see Box 16.5).

Box 16.4: Reading process assessment – some examples

Method	What it does	Who it is used with
Environmental print tasks	Recognition of words and symbols commonly found in daily life and surroundings (to assess learners' understanding of how these are used and their meanings)	Beginner readers
Reading predictable books	Assess learners' knowledge of basic book conventions and their use of meaning and word cues from the title, illustrations, and so on. It encourages new readers to make guesses and check whether they were right, a valuable reading strategy.	Beginner readers
Analysis of reading processes – sometimes called miscue analysis	Reveal the decisions that readers make as they read and how they try to resolve problems. The tutor records the mistakes learners make as they read aloud and looks for patterns that can identify consistent mistakes. These can be the focus of future teaching.	Progressing readers
Interpretation of meaning – sometimes called analysing recalls	Shows how a reader links information in a text with their prior knowledge in order to make sense of it. Analysing recalls can determine whether the reader relies mostly on information directly stated in the text or interprets it using inference, synthesis, and prior knowledge, and how much he or she misinterprets or uses contradictory information. Good readers use both direct information from the text and interpretation.	Progressing readers

Source: Authors

Box 16.5: Writing process assessment – some examples		
Method	What it does	Who it is used with
Language experience activity	The learner tells a story or talks and the tutor writes it down. The text is used for reading practice. It enables tutors to analyse how readily someone can generate narrative ideas, their spoken vocabulary, and their knowledge of written text conventions.	Beginner readers and writers
Cloze exercises (or gap analysis)	A short text is used in which some words are replaced with blanks that learners are asked to write in. This allows tutors to explore how learners think through sentences and whether they can make informed guesses that make sense.	Progressing readers and writers
Tracking the writing process	The tutor observes learners as they write, noting where they pause, look back over what they have written, and make changes as they go along. The tutor then discusses with the writer what he or she was thinking about at the specific points where he or she paused, or looked back.	Progressing writers

Source: Authors

Methods for assessment of achievement

Standardised tests provide evidence in a specific 'test' context of performance on tasks requiring particular skills or knowledge. These tests are referred to as 'standardised' because administration and scoring are the same for all candidates. Questions are presented in the same wording to all test candidates, and answers are scored using the same procedures (including cross-checking).

Designing tests requires technical expertise. Test items must be constructed to measure a single underlying attribute (or different cognitive processes that function in unison). Features of validity (how well it measures the domain of knowledge) and reliability (consistency and accuracy of the scores) are crucial. Tests are designed to discriminate between candidates: that is their function. They may be norm-referenced (an individual's scores are compared with a representative sample of the population) or criterion-referenced (an individual's scores are compared against the domain of knowledge along a continuum). The continuum of skills may be divided into levels, although often the levels are chosen for convenience rather than because they have meaning.

Standardised tests are imperfect predictors of actual literacy performance in life (Gifford and O'Connor 1992: 4). They are more successful in predicting how learners perform in the context of educational settings. Tests usually do not take cultural knowledge into account although this can be crucial in whether or not a reader can understand particular texts. By measuring reading and writing outputs, tests do not reveal how learners might be able to apply their skills to new activities in different contexts.

Curriculum tests work best when there is a curriculum with a well-defined, internally coherent knowledge base. The test content can then be related directly to the curriculum. School teachers often use tests as a quick way of checking whether their students have memorised or mastered the knowledge or skills they have been taught.

Curriculum tests have often been criticised by literacy researchers and practitioners. Critics say they inevitably narrow the curriculum because everything in the curriculum is not assessed and they create a strong incentive for teachers to teach to the test. By creating tests for large numbers of learners for comparative purposes there is a risk that specific test content may not apply to particular groups of adults (for example tests may use an activity like reading a phone book when there is no phone book for the community and some learners will never have seen one).

Tests of any kind have also been criticised for taking apart particular components of skills and knowledge and so treating thinking and learning like a machine (Resnick and Resnick 1992: 42). The analogy is that one can build a machine by taking all the parts and putting them together according to a design. To create test items skills have to be 'decomposed' or taken apart.

They must also be taken away from the context in which they are normally applied. Critics argue that literacy is not a machine. In measuring skills and knowledge in a decomposed and decontextualised way, the most important aspects of their application are ignored. Nevertheless, tests are widely used in the North and international agencies may generate pressure for them to be used in the South to demonstrate the scale of literacy needs and the effectiveness of programmes.

Performance or authentic assessment

This approach can be used either for assessment for learning or for assessment of achievement. It attempts to create a context that is as much as possible like 'real life'. The aim is to assess what people can do in the context where a problem has to be solved, a product made, or a service provided. As a result the tasks in performance assessment are generally holistic, larger activities requiring multiple knowledge and skills (Ananda 2000).

Performance assessment stimulates learners to think, solve problems, and evaluate their work. Methods include using problem-solving scenarios, group or individual projects, performances, activities, and computer simulations. Some assessments may take place over time through an individual or group project, and others may set a task to be completed 'on the spot'.

Learners are expected to participate fully in performance assessment: deciding on their plans, reviewing their work, and taking part in the analysis and evaluation. Performance assessment is demanding of both learners and tutors: tutors have to give up some control, allowing learners to take responsibility for their learning and to work independently. Tutors become more like facilitators or coaches as learners begin to make more choices and decisions about their learning.

Differences in learners' cultural backgrounds, language, learning styles, and expectations all influence their performance in assessments. Some learners may be more comfortable than others with verbal forms of expression. Some may be more at ease with writing than others. Performance assessment offers the potential to allow learners with different backgrounds and styles to show their skills and knowledge via a range of different forms of expression. Students may write, create hands-on projects, visual and graphic representations, and verbal reports.

Assessment of performance may be:

1. Tutor-assessed: requires extensive training so tutors have knowledge of assessment and how to integrate it into their practice.

2. Assessed by an outside assessor: requires careful attention to validity (that it measures what it says) and reliability (that judgement is consistent over time and among assessors).

Tutors using performance-based assessment (whether tutor-assessed or not) need a lot of support. Support should include training or mentoring, resources, time to design assessment activities, and time to manage them. Tutors may also need space to store work in progress, when performance tasks take place over time.

Critics say performance assessments are expensive to administer, require a high degree of skills and knowledge in the teachers involved, and are therefore unsuited to the often poorly-resourced programmes of the South. Because they assess multiple skills and knowledge, they may not reveal enough specific skills and knowledge. Because the activities are still not really part of learners' life contexts, performance assessment may not necessarily be better able to represent real-life application of skills and knowledge than other forms of assessment. Nevertheless, proponents of performance assessment would argue that performance assessment is worth the additional resources needed because of their authenticity. It encourages learner involvement and stimulates problem-solving and active learning. Performance assessment comes closer to real application of skills and knowledge than other methods, which is why it sometimes carries the name 'authentic'.

Portfolio assessment

A portfolio is a collection of evidence that demonstrates what a learner knows or is able to do. Portfolio assessment is more than a folder with bits of paper in it: it both represents and evaluates the learning that lies behind the paper. Portfolios are a flexible assessment tool that might contain evidence of skills or of practices. Learners choose what they put in it – their best work, most representative work, or work they want to share with others. Some points to note include:

*   Portfolio assessment focuses on the actual learning that is taking place.
*   A portfolio is one way for learners to tell their own story – show others what they can do, what they are interested in, what is important to them.

- Portfolios are very individual. They allow learners' goals, needs, and interests to shape what goes into the curriculum and what goes into the portfolio.

- Groups can develop portfolios too: a learning group can gather together a joint picture of what the group accomplished, either acknowledging or not identifying the individual contributions to the group learning.

- Portfolios are particularly used in participatory curriculum approaches, where learners are active in creating the curriculum and making decisions about what is learned and how.

Portfolio assessment is not necessarily learner-centred, but it is a useful tool in learner-centred teaching. However, making portfolios part of a participatory approach to teaching and learning is time-consuming. One American volunteer literacy tutor involved in a portfolio assessment project wrote:

> It takes more planning to be learner centered, it takes more lesson preparation, it takes more search, both in search for materials and searching inside your student to see what it is they want to do, what kind of needs to meet together. It also takes more time for self evaluation…But I would say that the time requirements were worth it.
> (Literacy South 1997: 99)

For portfolios to be more than a collection of pieces of work, to be an *assessment* tool, they need criteria, a set of rules by which judgements are made. The criteria can be set in advance or they can emerge from looking at the work and deciding what it means. The criteria may determine the work that is chosen to go into the portfolio. More importantly, the criteria lead to judgements about the quality of the evidence; what it says about the learning achievements. Criteria can be internal and/or external:

- Internal criteria: involving learners in developing the assessment criteria encourages them to reflect on and analyse their own work. The criteria could be in the form of questions such as: 'what did you learn from this?' or 'how does this demonstrate what you have learned?' Learners could compare examples of their work from different time points to see progress over time (what has improved and what has not), and to identify what they want to practise and learn in the future.

- External criteria: the assessment criteria might be linked to external standards. For example, portfolios could be linked to the Skills for Life standards developed in England (see Chapter 5) and learners could select samples of their work demonstrating they have mastered skills like using grammar or punctuation.

Whether the criteria are internal or external, when they put their portfolio together learners often become conscious of the gaps in their work. This helps them identify next learning steps. Learners might find they don't have writing samples, or examples of using reading to solve day-to-day problems. They may identify areas where they need to improve the evidence they do have. As a result they may say 'we need to work on this'.

Portfolios are used in the Philippines alternative education system but mainly as a tool for assessment for learning rather than of achievement (for which there are tests). Learners may prepare a portfolio of ongoing work for discussion with their facilitator and to enhance their motivation. In a pilot project the NFE A&E is testing a portfolio assessment approach in which learners prepare a portfolio on a project they have carried out in a module. This is assessed for evidence of practical application of skills and understanding (NFE A&E 2002: 35).

Building capacity for assessment

Literacy managers need to build capacity for assessment at different levels within their programmes. The nature of that capacity will vary depending on the approaches taken and the experience already present.

At the overall programme level, capacity is needed to decide on assessment approaches that are appropriate for the goals of the programme and its learners. Assessment methods may need to be developed or chosen, and explanations or manuals for tutors and learners developed. Trainers of tutors will need to include assessment in their training plans. Depending on the methods chosen there may be ongoing support needed, for example peer-moderation of portfolio assessment.

Tutors will need to develop the understanding and skills needed to carry out the assessment approaches with their local learning groups. If assessment is to be an integral part of the teaching and learning process, tutors will need to understand the purposes of the assessment they are using. If these are new to them they themselves will need to become active and reflective learners as they incorporate assessment into their practice.

Finally, learners themselves need to develop the capacity to self-assess, to recognise their learning and what they need to work on, and to celebrate their achievements.

Implications for planners

Many small-scale and local literacy programmes fail to assess learning because they think it is beyond their scope, requiring professionals and tests, and perhaps that it is inappropriate for their learners. This chapter has aimed to show that there are many approaches to assessment, among which there is something for everyone. All literacy programmes should be gathering information about what learners have learned and analysing their achievement.

'Assessment for learning' is designed to improve the process of teaching and learning by working with learners to identify learning needs, track progress, and demonstrate for learners what they have learned. It can be informal, based on conversations between tutors and learners, and ongoing.

'Assessment of achievement' is more likely to be part of a wider system of assessment against standards or award of qualifications. These may parallel school qualifications or be specially developed for adults. As such there does need to be careful attention to assessment criteria, to moderation of judgements, and consistency of standards.

Assessment methods should be appropriate for the scale and purpose of the programme. The 'folk models' of assessment that learners and tutors are familiar with also need to be taken into account – introducing new approaches will take more time and work. Finally, assessment needs to fit with the approach to evaluation and accountability being taken in the programme. Resources and capacity for assessment may need to be developed, and this will take time and careful planning. Investment in developing appropriate assessment methods will pay dividends in terms of demonstrating to funders and governments the effectiveness of the programme, as well as in recognising and celebrating the achievements of learners and tutors.

Further reading

There is a series of booklets written for English school teachers by the Assessment Reform Group called the Black Box series. These focus on assessment for learning (formative assessment) and make a clear argument for its importance in raising levels of achievement. Although they are written for school teachers there are many applications to the adult literacy classroom.

Assessment Reform Group, *Testing, Motivation and Learning*, Cambridge: University of Cambridge Faculty of Education, 2002.

Assessment Reform Group, *Assessment for Learning: Beyond the Black Box*, Cambridge: University of Cambridge School of Education, 1999.

P. Black, C. Harrison, C. Lee, B. Marshall, and W. Dylan, *Working inside the black box: assessment for learning in the classroom*, London: nferNelson, 2002.

P. Black and W. Dylan, *Inside the black box: raising standards through classroom assessment*, London: nferNelson, 1998.

Part V
Making Sense of Adult Literacy

17
Conclusions

This book set out to identify key considerations in planning and implementing literacy programmes. Chapters have explored understandings of and approaches to adult literacy in different parts of the world. They have placed programme decisions within the political, social, and environmental context in which they have to be made. Assisting men and women to learn literacy and numeracy skills and to use these to enrich their lives is a clear objective, but our capacity to do this is framed by a range of factors. Sections 3 and 4 have focused particularly on the practical matters of developing and implementing literacy programmes, and each chapter concluded with practical guidelines, drawn from experience in designing and running literacy activities and training trainers. While we are primarily concerned with non-industrialised or resource-poor societies, we are aware that there are also lessons to be learned from and by resource-rich countries, so we have included approaches from many different parts of the world.

Key principles

A number of overarching concepts have framed many of the debates we have raised in the different sections of this book. These could be seen as key principles that we, as authors, feel should underlie any literacy intervention:

- recognise the importance of context;
- address questions of power and access;
- understand and apply the different concepts of literacy;
- avoid any single orthodoxy.

We discuss these key principles below and follow this with our view of some key issues and opportunities for literacy programme planners today.

Recognise the importance of context

The context of any intervention is important in determining its ethos and its shape. Literacies exist in response to particular contexts and literacy learning needs equally to take that context into account. Context at all levels is important in shaping what can be done and how. Context includes local culture, tradition, and employment opportunities; local, regional, and national government infrastructure and policies; and international policies and the state of the global economy.

The local context is important even for large-scale programmes. Planning a literacy intervention entails first having a realistic understanding of:

- the local culture and communities
- the needs and interests of potential participants and their purposes for literacy
- the gender, class, age, and ethnicity of potential participants and how this might affect their needs, interests, purposes, and ways of learning
- the purposes or intentions of the programme and how these relate to local, regional, national, and international policies.

The policy context is also important. National government policies will affect regional and local policy. International policies, in terms of education and factors in the global economy, will impact on national government policies. If the global economy is strong, a greater proportion of the richer countries' gross national product will be contributed to aid programmes. Aid policies and priorities are determined not only by politicians but also by academics, educators, and economists. The current policy of international donors is to respond to priorities expressed by donor governments. It is important therefore that those involved in adult literacy advocate its inclusion in all national development and educational programmes.

The key principle is to plan literacy programmes with awareness of the context at all levels from local to international, and to work with others to promote and advocate for literacy.

Address questions of power and access

Disparities in power and access are at the core of literacy acquisition and literacy education. Differences including gender, ethnicity, language, and cultural grouping affect people's access to school, and UNESCO has found that years of schooling is the strongest correlation to literacy skill levels. These disparities continue to influence access to learning opportunities at all ages and subsequently access to information and to income.

People least likely to have gained literacy skills are women, older people, those living in rural areas, and sometimes those from larger households. Even more likely to be excluded from education and from literacy are people with physical or mental difficulties; internally displaced people and refugees; illegal immigrants; groups living 'outside' mainstream society such as street children and homeless people; those in institutions such as prisons and mental hospitals; people who have been ill for a long time; members of minority religions; speakers of minority languages; and indigenous groups.

While it is these people that should and often do form the constituency of literacy programmes, they may still be marginalised within them. Literacy programmes have to guard against re-creating inequalities of power and access within them. There are often hidden ways in which the assumptions and expectations that support inequalities can be perpetuated. These might involve the choice of language, grouping of participants, notions of schooling or of learning, or the time or location of any intervention.

The aim of EFA and the MDGs is for universal literacy – literacy for all, not just the few. Gender disparity continues to exist throughout the world though its shape and priorities are changing. Gender mainstreaming means specifically addressing the literacy and numeracy needs and aspirations of both women and men, some of which will be the same and some of which will be different. Attention has been drawn to the importance of conceptualising gender as an integral part of the planning, implementation, and monitoring of literacy programmes – whichever approach to literacy is used. Developing a gender-integrated programme relies as much on men being gender-aware as on women being so. Gender equality entails both women and men playing equal roles and assisting others to achieve their full potential.

It is equally important to develop strategies to address the needs of all excluded or marginalised groups, though the practicalities may be different. For example, inclusion of older people in programmes may require making reading glasses available, while working with blind or deaf participants requires specialised training and often the learning of an additional language (sign or Braille). Adults with physical or mental health difficulties may need particular help to cope with mainstream programmes but may wish to be integrated as far as possible. Learners from minority-language or religious groups may need to be taught by people from their own community. There have been a number of innovative programmes working with street children or homeless people who have no stable place to live, but these have been specially designed to meet the needs of these groups who will rarely participate in a large mainstream programme.

The key principle is being aware of power disparities within society and the potential of programmes to challenge rather than to replicate these, by focusing on the needs and aspirations of excluded groups, and working with them to identify practical solutions.

Understand and apply the different concepts of literacy

The concepts of literacy that underpin a programme shape every aspect of its design and implementation. We use four primary concepts and show how they create different options, opportunities, and challenges for literacy programmes. While we as authors have a preference for a social practices or critical-reflection approach to literacy, we are aware that these can become a new orthodoxy, every bit as limiting as the old. We argue that programme leaders need to become clear about their conceptual base and make conscious choices in planning and implementing programmes. We suggest there are strengths and challenges with all the conceptual models:

'Literacy as skills' is based on the undeniable idea that reading and writing are activities that require particular sets of skills. The popularity and longevity of primers reflects the usefulness of defining what needs to be taught and learned, especially in contexts where there are few resources for training tutors and creating materials. The weakness of skills-based approaches has been in the notion that 'one size fits all', and the assumption that the skills stand alone and are transferable to any group or context. The competency approach, which has dominated in the North in recent years, breaks skills down into the smallest elements and so detracts from any holistic understanding of the broader literacy context, and is in danger of teaching individual skills in isolation from each other. A concentration on skills also avoids any questions of power and inequalities. Though some primers (such as those used in revolutionary campaigns) do explicitly address power issues, they are in a small minority. We accept the importance of mastering the skills and knowledge of reading and writing in literacy education but recognise that these are not a single set of skills applicable in all circumstances. The failure of many skills-based programmes to make any long-term difference to people's lives demonstrates that for adults, learning skills alone is not enough. The focus of literacy education must be on the application of skills by learners in their lives.

'Literacy as tasks' (often known as functional literacy) has made important efforts to link literacy with its contexts and applications in everyday life. Its appeal is in its apparent practicality, especially in terms of looking more broadly at people's livelihoods and the literacies they need to support them. However, the weakness of functional approaches has been in their large-scale, top-down design which doesn't contextualise learning for the particular participants and tends to be based around the needs of dominant groups. While a task-based approach may help people to cope with their lives, it does little to challenge or transform social structures or power relationships. Functional literacy approaches take an important step toward focusing on application, not just possession, of skills, but programmes have generally taken a narrow view of literacy tasks. They have ignored important differences rooted in social and cultural contexts. By starting from the top down in defining what is important to learn, they fail to nurture autonomous and reflective learners. Learning to carry out literacy tasks is not enough to make a real difference in lives and communities. Literacy education needs to be more responsive to the full range of literacy practices.

'Literacy as social practice' provides an understanding of literacy as rooted in particular social contexts and draws attention to the many ways in which literacies vary depending on who is reading or writing, for what purposes, and in what settings. This makes it highly reflexive and responsive but while it has been extensively theorised and grew out of attempts to make literacy pragmatic and practical, it is still relatively new as an approach for literacy programmes. Attempts to apply it to programmes in the global South have struggled with the need to overcome traditional assumptions about literacy, and to recruit and provide tutors with the training and support they require to be responsive and creative. Tutors need to be highly skilled at working with participants to identify their goals, and develop strategies and learning activities to achieve these, often with very limited resources. In many parts of the world, tutors' own experiences have been of formal, skills-based, and highly structured education. It should not be expected that tutors will find it easy to adopt an approach that is very different from their own experience; to become responsive, creative, and to value difference.

Despite the challenges, the social-practices approach has begun to offer an alternative perspective based on an analysis of the different practices in any literacy environment. The challenge is to ensure sufficient guidance to tutors, through training and support materials, to enable them to respond to the needs and aspirations of their learning groups. This may require careful contextual analysis initially and the design of an adaptable, flexible framework that helps structure the learning but leaves space for groups to indicate their own goals.

'Literacy as critical reflection' has a long history and Freire, one of its key proponents, is recognised by most literacy practitioners. However, the proper application of a critical-reflection approach has rarely been mainstreamed. Its strength lies in enabling participants to analyse and reflect critically on their society and their place within it, and in doing so to address directly the roots of power inequalities. 'Literacy as critical reflection' has the potential to transform individuals and communities. Like the social-practices approach, critical literacy depends on highly trained and experienced tutors. Literacy education does not have to be overtly political to take the radical approach of developing Galtung's 'literate, autonomous, critical, constructive people, capable of translating ideas into action, individually or collectively' (Galtung 1976, quoted by Limage 2004). However, tutors do need to be competent, confident, and able to think for themselves. While radical approaches to literacy can sometimes become another form of orthodoxy, particularly when used in campaigns, taking a critical-reflection approach entails being responsive to individual and community needs. It means encouraging learners to look beyond 'reading the word' to 'reading the world', as Freire put it. It entails working with learners to interrogate the texts they read in order to understand what lies behind them, in terms of content, context, and the way they are written. Paying due attention to skills, tasks, and practices, a critical-reflection approach to literacy can support learners to become actors in developing their own communities and societies.

Avoid any single orthodoxy

The danger in prioritising any single approach or in producing guidelines for best practice is that they can then be reproduced inappropriately. Our final overarching principle is that there should be no orthodoxy. The four approaches we have described sit inside one another and the emphasis in any programme can shift from one to another at different times. We take from the different conceptual approaches what they can offer to create programmes that work. For us the best programmes will:

- offer enough flexibility to respond to the particular (and changing) needs and interests of participants and communities, and how they want to use literacy, and to take them beyond the things they know;

- provide enough structure that both learners and tutors are clear about what is expected of them, what will be taught and learned, and how it will relate to people's lives;

- ensure good learning materials are available, either by enabling the development of local material or providing appropriate and creative programme resources;

- support learners to become independent in their literacy and learning and to be reflective learners who are aware of their goals and how to act on them;

- encourage critical analysis to encourage learners to question what they read and write. (The way that material is used is often more important than the material itself.)

Issues and opportunities in implementing programmes

Good planning, high-quality staff training, efficient administration, and consistent monitoring and evaluation are required whichever model is adopted. We explore all of these in the chapters of the book. Here we want to emphasise some key issues, and we then go on to highlight some opportunities offered by ongoing international developments.

There can be no short-cuts in planning before a programme starts. From needs assessment to thinking about sustainability, planning takes work and time; without it resources can be wasted on short-term efforts that yield little result. We advocate for planning to take account of the purposes and interests of potential participants, the broader context of environment, infrastructure, and policies, and the scale of resources for the programme.

We suggest the importance of using real-life literacy activities and texts in the learning programme. But we recognise the challenges this presents to tutors, not only in terms of their own training and skills but also in terms of practical matters like photocopying. Overall we feel it is more important for learners to work actively with a range of different kinds of text, adapting, questioning, and re-writing, than to be too purist about what those texts are.

The quality and effectiveness of any adult education programme depends crucially on those who implement the programmes – managers and tutors. It is they who actually put the local programmes and the learning in place and interact with the women and men who participate. The selection, training, and support of literacy managers and literacy educators are under-researched areas. Yet evidence to date suggests some principles to guide the extent and nature of training and support. These include:

- understanding the theory underpinning the literacy approach(es) adopted and the ability to use methods appropriate to that model;
- a level of education appropriate to the situation and the level of support they will receive;
- a knowledge of the reading and writing process and how to teach them;
- gender and cultural awareness and respect for the knowledge and experience both women and men bring to the learning situation.

Investment in tutor training and support pays dividends. Training and support for tutors should be included in terms of time, financial resources, and human resources allocated from the beginning, as an integral part of the programme.

Finally, monitoring and evaluation need to be built into programmes from the start, to ensure ways of learning from experience, improving programme practice, and being accountable to others. Monitoring and evaluation are too often seen as something to be done for outsiders – for funders or governments – rather than as a way for everyone involved in a programme to gain insights and ideas for action. Assessing what learning is taking place and enquiring about the impacts on people's lives are important tools in programme improvement. There seems to be increasing interest among funders and governments in participatory evaluation as a way to engage learners, volunteers, and staff at all levels in making use of the lessons learned from their experiences. Involving learners in recognising their own learning is part of helping them to become independent and reflective learners. Monitoring and evaluation can also help programmes check against their own perpetuation of social inequalities of class, gender, ethnicity, and other factors.

One of the tensions in adult literacy is the difficulty of knowing or proving what works in a particular area and, as is often required, of demonstrating measurable outcomes against financial investment. The pressure to evaluate programmes and, to date, the difficulty in doing so, has led to an emphasis on quantifying improvement in technical skills rather than assessing any holistic change in people's lives. Globally the use of certificates to demonstrate levels of literacy and numeracy is increasing, as is the accreditation of training and the introduction of certification for tutors. There is a general move towards the professionalisation and institutionalisation of adult literacy and numeracy and while this should mean additional funding and higher standards, it can also constitute orthodoxy and lead to programmes that are less locally responsive and less challenging of the status quo.

International developments

In contrast to this growing formality, there is a move away from the teaching of technical skills divorced from the ways in which literacies are used. There is a growing awareness of the need to ground programmes in the reality of their social and cultural contexts. International policy makers make reference to the need to focus on the literacy and numeracy required by individuals in their community rather than the skills of literacy alone. Thus the tools of ethnography and PRA are being used to identify the social, political, cultural, and economic situation of the different communities in which programmes will be based. This broader agenda is reflected in the UNESCO report 'Literacy for Life' (2005a).

Innovative ways of teaching and learning continue to be developed, including community-based, community-directed, and community-owned programmes utilising the theories of New Literacy Studies, and the methods of REFLECT as well as, for example, *Yo, sí puedo* from Cuba. In countries of the North and the South planners are looking for ways to embed literacy learning within other activities or programmes, such as nutrition, poultry keeping, gardening, or health. If literacy activities can be embedded into broader local activities they are more likely to be sustained.

The use of ICT, though still rare in some parts of the world, has enabled facilitators to be trained at a distance and learners to work on a range of activities under the guidance of a single tutor. The range of options surrounding the implementation of literacy interventions increases with the spread of technology. Mobile phones are now being used by previously non-literate communities in the remotest of areas where texting has transformed the marketing habits of small-scale farmers and the social lives of deaf people. New modes of communication are adopted and adapted by people who see ways in which these will benefit their lives, and new literacies will continue to shape the literacy terrain. Online translation and localised computers may in the future be used to support minority languages or small-scale programmes, while globalisation continues to prioritise Arabic or English.

As practitioners and authors we urge programme planners to find creative ways of operating within these tensions and to take account of the fact that nothing works everywhere all of the time. Literacy practices and literacy uses are as varied as the contexts in which they are based and the people who need or want to access them at particular points in their lives. There are no simple answers but there is much that has been learned from experience.
We encourage you to draw from the experiences of others and to continue to reflect on and learn from your own.

References

Abadzi, H. (1984) 'What We Know About Acquisition of Adult Literacy – is there Hope?', World Bank Discussion Paper 245, Washington, DC: World Bank.

ABET (2006) 'Adult Basic Education and Training for Adults', available at: www.capegateway.gov.za/eng/directories/services/11475/14911, Cape Town: Cape Gateway (last accessed June 2007).

Abuzeid, H. and A. Kom-Kodi (2005) *Empowering People Through Education*, Sudan Open Learning Organisation (SOLO).

Abuzeid Elsafi, H. and J. McCaffery (2000a) *Building Literacy with SOLO Press: Second Training Course for Literacy Workers*, Annex 2: 'Small books and writings produced in the circles', Cambridge: Cambridge International Extension College and Khartoum: Sudan Open Learning Organisation.

Abuzeid Elsafi, H. and J. McCaffery (2000b) *Training for Community Literacy Workers for Building Literacy in Sudan with SOLO Press*, Cambridge: Cambridge International Extension College (unpublished report).

ActionAid International and the Global Campaign for Education (2005) *Writing the Wrongs: International Benchmarks on Adult Literacy*, London: ActionAid.

Adiseshiah, M. S. (1976) 'Functionalities of literacy', *Prospects* 6 (1): 39–56.

Aikman, S. (2001) 'Literacies, languages, and developments in the Peruvian Amazon', in B. Street (ed.), *Literacy and Development: Ethnographic Perspectives*, London: Routledge.

Aikman, S. and E. Unterhalter (2005) *Beyond Access: Transforming Policy and Practice for Gender Equality in Education*, Oxford: Oxfam.

ALBSU (1982) *Making the Most of Tax Forms*, London: Adult Literacy and Basic Skills Agency.

ALBSU (1985) *Adult Literacy: The First Decade 1978–1985*, London: ALBSU.

Allman, P. (1988) 'Gramsci, Freire and Illich: their contribution to education for socialism', in T. Lovett (ed.), *Radical Approaches to Adult Education*, London and New York: Routledge.

Amnesty International (2004) *It's in Our Hands: Stop Violence Against Women*, London: Amnesty International.

Ananda, S. (2000) 'Equipped for the Future Assessment Report: How Instructors can Support Adult Learners through Performance-Based Assessment', Washington DC: National Institute for Literacy.

Archer, D. and S. Cottingham (1996) 'Regenerated Freirean Literacy through Empowering Community Techniques', London: ActionAid.

Ashfar, H. (1985) *Women, State and Ideology: Studies from Africa and Asia*, Basingstoke: Macmillan.

Ashraf, M., M. El Gindy, and A. Sabri (2005) 'Capacity enhancement for lifelong learning', in the 'Report of the Meeting of Literacy Experts, Achieving Literacy for All', BMENA and Member States of the G8, British Council: Cairo.

Barton, D. (1994) *An Introduction to the Ecology of Written Language*, Oxford: Blackwell Publishing.

Barton, D. and M. Hamilton (1998) *Local Literacies: Reading and Writing in One Community*, London: Routledge.

Barton, D. and R. Ivanic (1991) *Writing in the Community*, London: Sage.

Baynham, M. (1993) 'Code switching and mode switching: community interpreters and mediators of literacy', in B. V. Street (ed.), *Cross-cultural Approaches to Literacy*, Cambridge: Cambridge University Press.

Baynham, M. and M. Prinsloo (1999) 'New directions in literacy research', *Language and Education* 15 (2-3): 83–91.

Bebbington, A. (1999) 'Capitals and capabilities: a framework for analysing peasant viability, rural livelihoods and poverty', *World Development* 27 (12): 2021–44.

Bell, B., with F. Affolter and S. Shukla (2005) 'Literacy and Community Empowerment Program: Internal Evaluation of the Literacy Component', Boston, MA: EDC for USAID.

Besser, S., G. Brookes, M. Burton, M. Parisella, Y. Spare, S. Stratford, and J. Wainwright (2004) 'Adult Literacy Learners' Difficulties in Reading: An Exploratory Study', London: National Research and Development Centre for Adult Literacy and Numeracy.

Bobbitt, F. (1918) *How to Make a Curriculum*, Boston: Houghton Mifflin.

Boserup, E. (1970) *Women's Role in Economic Development*, New York: St Martin's Press.

Bown, L. (1991) 'Preparing the Future: Women, Literacy and Development. The Impact of Female Literacy on Human Development and the Participation of Literate Women in Change', London: ActionAid.

Bown, L. (2004) 'Afterword: reading ethnographic research in a policy context', in A. Robinson-Pant (ed.), *Women, Literacy and Development: Alternative Perspectives*, Abingdon: Routledge.

Bransford, J. D., A. L. Brown, and R. R. Cocking (1999) *How People Learn: Brain, Mind, Experience, and School*, Washington DC: National Academy Press.

British Council (2002) *Nigeria Community Education*, Abuja Nigeria: The British Council.

Bruner, J. (1983) *In Search of Mind: Essays in Autobiography*, New York: Harper and Row.

Brydon, L. and S. Chant (1989) *Women in the Third World: Gender Issues in Rural and Urban Areas*, Aldershot: Edward Elgar Publishing Limited.

Canieso Doronila, M. L. (1996) *Landscapes of Literacy: An Ethnographic Study of Functional Literacy in Marginal Philippine Communities*, Hamburg: UNESCO Institute for Education.

Carlo, M.S. and E. E. Skilton-Sylvester (1994) 'A longitudinal investigation on the literacy development of Spanish-, Korean-, and Cambodian-speaking adults learning to read English as a second language', (unpublished manuscript), Philadelphia, PA: National Center on Adult Literacy.

Carr-Hill, R., A. Okech, A. R. Katahoire, T. Kakooza, A. N. Ndidde, and J. Oxenham (2001) 'Adult Literacy Programs in Uganda: an Evaluation', Washington, DC: World Bank, unpublished report.

Chambers, R. (1983) *Putting the Last First*, London: Longman Press.

Chambers, R. (2002) *Participatory Workshops: A Sourcebook of 21 Sets of Ideas and Activities*, London: Earthscan.

Chambers, R. and G. Conway (1991) 'Sustainable Rural Livelihoods: Practical Concepts for the 21st Century', IDS Discussion Paper 296, Brighton: Institute of Development Studies.

Charnley, A.H. and H. A. Jones (1979) *The Concept of Success in Adult Literacy*, Cambridge: Huntingdon Publishers.

Commission of the European Communities (1991) 'The Integration of Women in Development: Why ,When and How to Incorporate Gender into Lome 1V Projects and Programmes', Brussels: European Commission.

Crystal, D. (2000) 'Language Death', talk for Lingua Franca, Australian Broadcasting Corporation.

Department of Adult Education, Kenya (2005) 'Evaluation Practices in Literacy Programmes in Kenya: A Situational Analysis', Nairobi, Kenya: Ministry of Culture, Sports, and Gender.

Department of Education and Training, Republic of South Africa (1985) *Practical Course for Housewives and Domestics, Course 1, Part 1*, Johannesburg: Adult Education Republic of South Africa.

Desmond, S. (2006) 'Family literacy project in Kwa Zulu Natal', in UNESCO, *Synergies Between Formal and Non-Formal Education: An Overview of Good Practices*, Paris: UNLD-LIFE Publication, 330–4.

Dewey, J. (1938) *Experience and Education*, The Kappa Delta Pi Lecture Series, New York: Collier Books, Macmillan.

DfES/FENTO (2001) *Subject Specifications for Teachers of Adult Literacy and Numeracy*, Nottingham, UK.

Dighe, A. (1995) 'Deconstructing Literacy Primers', *Economic and Political Weekly*, 1 July, pp 1559–61, India.

Dighe, A. (2004) 'Pedagogical Approaches to Literacy Acquisition and Effective Programme Design', background paper for Education for All Global Monitoring Report.

Dighe, A. and U. Vyasulu Reddi (2005) *Women's Literacy and Information and Communication Technologies*, available at: www.cemca.org/CEMCA_Womens_Literacy.pdf (last accessed June 2007).

Dighe, A., I. Patel, P. Krishnan, A. Razzack, S. Saxena, and I. Sen (1996) *Deconstructing Adult Literacy Primers*, New Delhi: National Institute of Adult Education.

Doe, S. and J. McCaffery (2001) 'Integrating Literacy and Conflict Resolution', report on training workshop 'Rebuilding Communities in Sierra Leone', Education for Development, UK, Development Initiatives, and ABC-Development, Sierra Leone (unpublished).

Doe, S., J. McCaffery, and K. Newell-Jones (2004) *Integrating Literacy and Peacebuilding: A Guide for Trainers and Facilitators*, Reading: Education for Development.

Dutcher, N. (1998) 'Eritrea: Developing a programme of multilingual education', in J. Cenoz and F. Genesee (eds.), *Beyond Bilingualism: Multilingualism and Multilingual Education*, Clevedon, England: Multilingual Matters.

El Bushra, J. (2000) 'Rethinking gender and development practice for the 21st century', in C. Sweetman (ed.), *Gender in the 21st Century*, Oxford: Oxfam.

Ezeomah, C., J. McCaffery, J. Pennells, and K. Sanni (2006) 'Participation and relevance in nomadic education: a case study of the adult literacy and teacher education components of the nomadic education programme component of the Nigeria Community Education Programme', in C. Dyer (ed.), *The Education of Nomadic Peoples: Current Issues, Future Prospects*, Oxford: Berghahn.

Fagan, W. T. (1992) *Monitoring Literacy Performance: Assessment and Diagnostic Tasks*, Montreal, Quebec: Les Editions de la Cheneliere Inc.

FENTO (2002) *Guidance on using the subject specifications for teachers of adult literacy (and numeracy) at Level 4 in conjunction with the Standards for teaching and supporting learning*, FENTO, UK.

Fingeret, H. A. (1991) 'Meaning, Experience and Literacy', *Adult Basic Education* 1 (1): 4–11.

Fordham, P., D. Holland, and J. Millican (1998) *Adult Literacy: a Handbook for Development Workers*, Oxford: Oxfam.

Fowler, E. and J. Mace (2005) *Outside the Classroom: Researching Literacy with Adult Learners*, Leicester: National Institute of Continuing and Adult Education.

Freire, P. (1970) *Pedagogy of the Oppressed*, Harmondsworth: Penguin.

Freire, P. (1972) *Pedagogy of the Oppressed*, Harmondsworth: Penguin.

Freire, P. (1992) *Pedagogy of the Oppressed*, Harmondsworth: Penguin.

Freire, P. and D. Macedo (1987) *Reading the World and the Word*, Westport CT: Bergin and Garvey.

GALAE (2005) Survey reported in 'Report of the G8 BMENA Meeting of Literacy Experts Cairo 24 Sept 2005', p 46, Cairo, The British Council.

GALAE and British Council (1997) *Aswanta: Stories from Egypt*, London and Cairo: British Council and GALAE.

Geary, N. (2001) 'Eight Hundred Stories for Dong Development: A Bilingual Education Pilot Project in Guizhou province, China', paper presented at the 'Sixth Oxford International Conference on Education and Development', Oxford, UK, 19–21 September.

Gifford, B. R and M. C. O'Connor (1992) *Changing Assessments: Alternative Views of Aptitude, Achievement and Instruction*, Kluwer Academic Publishers.

Gramsci, A. (1968) *The Modern Prince and Other Writings*, New York: International Publishers.

Grundy, S. (1987) *Curriculum: Product or Praxis?* Lewes: Falmer Press.

Hallouda, M. (2005) 'Utilising Information and Communication Technologies', paper presented at the conference of the BMENA and Member States of the G8, Report of the Meetings of Literacy Experts, British Council, Cairo.

Harris, T. L and R. E. Hodges (eds.) (1995) *The Literacy Dictionary: The Vocabulary of Reading and Writing*, Newark, DE: International Reading Association.

Hassan, Z. (2005) 'A Decade of Learning and Action', in *Education Action Issue 19*, London: ActionAid.

Heath, S. B. (1982) 'What no bedtime story means: narrative skills at home and school', *Language in Society* 11: 49–76.

Hope, A. and S. Timmell (2003) *Training for Transformation*, London: ITDG Publishing.

Human Resources and Social Development Canada (2001) 'International Adult Literacy Survey – January 2001', available at: www.hrsdc.gc.ca/en/cs/sp/hrsd/prc/publications/research/2001-002538/page06.shtml (last accessed July 2007).

Hunter Carman, S. and D. Harman (1985) *Adult Illiteracy in the United States: A Report to the Ford Foundation*, Columbus, OH: McGraw-Hill.

Hussain, M. A. (2005) Speech given at the conference of the BMENA and Member States of the G8, Report of the Meetings of Literacy Experts, British Council, Cairo.

Ives, D.(1976) 'Fishing at Newhaven', in A. Hemstedt and J. McCaffery (eds.), *Brighton Writing*, Brighton: Friends Centre.

Jeffs, T. J. and M. K. Smith (1990) *Using Informal Education: An Alternative to Casework, Teaching and Control?* Milton Keynes: Open University Press.

Jeffs, T. J. and M. K. Smith (1999) *Informal Education: Conversation, Democracy and Learning*, Ticknall: Education Now.

Kabeer, N. (1994) *Reversed Realities: Gender Hierarchies in Development Thought*, London: Verso.

Kelly, S., L. Soundranayagam, and S. Grief (2004) 'Teaching and Learning Writing: A Review of Research and Practice', London: National Research and Development Centre for Adult Literacy and Numeracy, available at: www.nrdc.org.uk (last accessed June 2007).

Khan, Q. (2005) 'Bilingualism and adult literacy', in *Achieving Literacy for All, Report of the Meeting of Literacy Experts*, Cairo: DFID.

Kolb, D. (1984) *Experiential Learning: Experience as the Source of Learning and Development*, New Jersey: Prentice Hall.

Krauss, M. (2000) 'Preliminary suggestions for classification and terminology for degrees of language endangerment', in M. Brenzinger (ed.), *The Endangered Languages of the World*, presented at the Colloquium 'Language Endangerment, Research, and Documentation – Setting Priorities for the 21st Century', 12–17 February 2000, Karl-Arnold-Akademie, Bad Godesberg, Germany.

LABE (Literacy and Basic Education) (2003), 'The LITKIT: Resource File for Instructors/Facilitators of Adult Literacy and Numeracy', Kampala and London: LABE and Education Action International.

Lamour, C. (1997) 'Women in Parliaments of the World: 1997', available at: www.aph.gov.au/library/pubs/rn/1996-97/97rn41.htm (last accessed June 2007).

Lankshear, C. with J. P. Gee, M. Knobel, and C. Searle (1997) *Changing Literacies*, Buckingham: Open University Press.

Lavender, P., J. Derrick, and B. Brooks (2004) 'Testing, Testing 1, 2, 3… Assessment in Adult Literacy, Language and Numeracy', a NIACE policy discussion paper, Leicester: NIACE.

Le Roux, W. (1999) 'Torn Apart: A Report of the Educational Situation of San Children in Southern Africa', Windhoek, Namibia: WIMS.

Learn and Teach (1983) 'The story of Nokukhanya Luthuli', *Learn and Teach* Number 9, Johannesburg.

Limage, L. (2004) 'Literacy Practices and Literacy Policies: Where has UNESCO Been and Where Might it be Going?', presentation at ESRC Seminar on 23 January 2004, background paper available at: www.education.ed.ac.uk/hce/ABE-seminars/papers/ABE5-Limage_BkgdDiscuss.pdf (last accessed June 2007).

Lind, A. (2004) 'Beyond Access: Developing Gender Equality in Adult Education', Norwich: University of East Anglia.

Literacy South (1997) 'Phenomenal Changes: Stories of Participants in the Portfolio Project', Durham NC: Literacy South.

Lucas, N., H. Casey, S. Loo, J. McDonald, and M.Giannakaki (2004) 'Research Review – Initial Teacher Education Programmes for Teachers of Literacy, Numeracy and ESOL 2002/3: An Exploratory Study', London: National Research and Development Centre.

Lytle, S. L. and M. Wolfe (1989) 'Adult Literacy Education: Program Evaluation and Learner Assessment', Information Series no. 338, Columbus: ERIC Clearinghouse on Adult, Career, and Vocational Education, Center on Education and Training for Employment, The Ohio State University (ERIC Document Reproduction Service No. ED 315 665).

Mace, J. (2005) 'Events, practices and values', in E. Fowler and J. Mace (eds.), *Outside the Classroom*, Leicester: NIACE.

Mace, J. (1992) *Talking About Literacy: Principles and Practice of Adult Literacy Education*, London: Routledge.

Mace, J., J. McCaffery, and J. O'Hagan (2006) 'Adult Basic Education in Ireland: Towards a Curriculum Framework', London: National Research and Development Centre (unpublished).

Maddox, B. (2004) 'Language policy, modernist ambivalence and social exclusion: a case study of Rupendehi District in Nepal's Tarai', *Studies in Nepali History and Society* 8 (2): 205–24.

Maddox, B. (2005) 'Education for Rural People in Sub-Saharan Africa Livelihood Approaches', background paper for seminar at the University of East Anglia, (unpublished).

Malone, D. (2003) 'Developing curriculum materials for endangered language education: lessons from the field', *International Journal of Bilingual Education and Bilingualism* 6 (5): 332–48.

Matshumi, M. (1983) 'Sloppy goes shopping with his family', in *Learn and Teach*, Number 9, Johannesburg.

Mayo, M. (1997) *Imaging Tomorrow: Adult Education for Transformation*, Leicester: NIACE.

McCaffery, J. (1999) 'Personal and Political: Mainstreaming Gender', unpublished presentation at Communication Across Sectors: Gender and Literacy in Development, Nottingham, British Association for Literacy in Development.

McCaffery, J. (2004) 'Closing the gap: issues in gender-integrated training of adult literacy facilitators – possibilities, progress and resistance', in A. Robinson-Pant (ed.) *Women, Literacy and Development: Alternative Perspectives*, Oxford: Routledge.

McCaffery, J. (2005) 'Using transformative models of adult literacy in conflict resolution and peacebuilding processes at community level: examples from Guinea, Sierra Leone and Sudan', *Compare* 35 (4): 443–62.

McCaffery, J., F. Obanubi, and K. Sanni (1999a) 'Second Stage Instructor Training', Nigeria: British Council.

McCaffery, J., F. Obanubi, and K. Sanni (1999b) 'Alternative Approaches to Literacy: Applying New Literacy Studies to the Development of a LOCAL Approach to Literacy in Four Minority Communities in Nigeria', paper presented to the Oxford International Conference on Education and Development.

Merrifield, J., U. Coleman, and O. McDonogh (2001) *Issues and Opportunities in Assessment*, Dublin: National Adult Literacy Agency.

Millican, J. (2006) 'Evaluation of a REFLECT Programme in The Gambia', (unpublished).

Moser, C. (1989) 'Gender planning in the third world: meeting practical and strategic gender needs', *World Development* 17 (11): 1799–825.

Moser, C. (1999) *Improving Literacy and Numeracy: A Fresh Start*, Sudbury DFEE, cited in Lucas *et al.* 2004: 8.

Moser, C. (2005) *An Introduction to Gender Audit Methodology: Its Design and Implementation in DFID Malawi*, London: Overseas Development Institute, available at: www.odi.org.uk/PPPG/Poverty_and_Inequality /publications/cm_gender_audit_methodology.pdf (last accessed 30 September 2006).

Moser, C. and C. Levy (1986) 'A Theory and Methodology of Gender Planning: Meeting Women's Practical and Strategic Gender Needs', Gender and Planning Working Paper Series, No 11, DPU, University College London.

Musa Yuguda Bello, Malam Gúnda Auta, Umaru Ahmadu Bubari, Abdullahi Abubakar, Sanusi Ahmed, aminu Isa Lushi (1997) *Dalilaji Egguki Fulbe Daga Ndumille Yahu Go Shedille Kala Hitadefu,* Community Education Programme, Lagos, British Council.

Mwiria, K. (1993) 'Kenyan women adult literacy learners: why their motivation is difficult to sustain', *International Review of Education* 39 (3): 183–92.

NALA (2005) *Mapping the Learning Journey*, Dublin: National Adult Literacy Agency.

NCSALL (1998) 'US Adult Literacy Program Practice: A Typology Across Dimensions of Life-contextualized and Dialogic/Monologic', Harvard Graduate School of Education, NCSALL Reports No. 2, The National Center for the Study of Adult Learning and Literacy.

Newell-Jones, K. (2004) 'Service Delivery in Difficult Environments: Review of Small-scale Educational Interventions on Literacy and Conflict Resolution/Peace-building in Guinea, Sierra Leone and South Sudan', unpublished report for DFID.

Newell-Jones, K. and J. McCaffery (2007) 'Rebuilding communities: the contribution of integrated literacy and conflict resolution programmes', *Critical Literacies: Theory and Practices* 1 (1) available at: www.criticalliteracy.org.uk/images/journal/v1issue1/jonesmccaffery.pdf (last accessed August 2007).

NFE A&E (2002) *Manual of Operations*, Section 2, NFE A&E LSDS Learning Process, Philippines.

NICHD (National Institute of Child Health and Human Development) (2000) 'Report of the National Reading Panel – Teaching Children to Read: An Evidence-based Assessment of the Scientific Research Literature on Reading and its Implications for Reading Instruction', available at: www.nichd.nih.gov/publications/nrp/smallbook.htm (last accessed May 2006).

Nirantur (1997) *Windows to the World: Developing a Curriculum for Rural Women*, New Delhi: Nirantur.

Nussbaum, M. (2000) *Women and Human Development*, Cambridge: Cambridge University Press.

Oakely, A. (1972) *Sex, Gender and Society*, London: Temple Smith.

OECD and Statistics Canada (2000) 'Literacy in the Information Age: Final Report of the International Adult Literacy Survey', Paris: OECD, available at: www1.oecd.org/publications/e-book/8100051e.pdf (last accessed June 2007).

Office of the Deputy Prime Minister (1999) *Gypsies and Travellers*, London: ODPM.

Okech, A. and the Country Project Team (2005) 'Evaluation Practices in Adult NFE and Literacy programmes in Uganda: A Situational Analysis', Paris: UNESCO Institute of Education.

Omolewa, M. (2000) 'The Language of Literacy', final remarks delivered at a strategy session on 'Literacy for All: A Renewed Vision for a Ten-Year Global Action Plan', organised on behalf of the EFA Forum by the UNESCO Institute for Education (UIE), the International Literacy Institute (ILI), ISESCO, ActionAid, and SIDA, available at: www.iiz-dvv.de/englisch/Publikationen/Ewb_ausgaben/55_2001/eng_Omolewa.html (last accessed June 2007).

Ouane, A. and C. Glanz (2005) 'Why First Literacy in Mother Tongue is Advantageous in Multi-lingual Settings: Findings from a Stock Taking Research on Sub-Saharan Africa', background paper for Education for All Global Monitoring Report.

Ouane, A., M. A. de Armengol, and D. V. Sharma (1990) *Handbook on Training for Post Literacy and Basic Education*, Hamburg: UNESCO.

Overseas Economic Co-operation Fund (1991) *Guiding Principles on Women in Development*, Tokyo: OECD.

Oxenham, J. (1980) *Literacy, Writing, Reading and Social Organisation*, London: Routledge and Kegan Paul.

Oxenham, J. (2004) *In Support of Adult Basic Education with Literacy in Indonesia, Ghana, Bangladesh, Senegal, and Côte d'Ivoire, 1977-2002*, Washington, DC: World Bank.

Oxenham, J. and R. Hamed (2005) 'Lessons from a Project on Capacity Enhancement for Lifelong Learning (CELL)', Egypt, Social Research Centre, American University in Cairo.

Premsrirat, S. and D. Malone (2003) 'Language Development and Language Revitalization in Asia', paper presented at the International Conference of the Summer Institute of Linguistics.

Prenderville, P. (2004) *Developing Facilitation Skills: A Handbook for Group Facilitators*, Dublin: Combat Poverty Agency.

Purcell-Gates, V., S. Degener, E. Jacobson, and M. Soler (2001) 'Taking Literacy Skills Home', NCSALL Volume 4, Issue D, www.ncsall.net.

Rao, A. (1991) 'Introduction', in A. Rao, M. B. Anderson, and C. Overhol (eds.), *Gender Analyis in Development Planning*, New York: Kumarian.

Rao, N. and A. Robinson-Pant (2003) 'CONFITEA thematic review: adult learning and indigenous peoples', paper read at CONFITEA mid-term review.

Rassool, N. (1999) *Literacy for Sustainable Development in the Age of Information*, Clevedon: Multilingual Matters.

Resnick, L. B. and D. P. Resnick (1992) 'Assessing the thinking curriculum: new tools for educational reform', in B. R. Gifford and M. C. O'Connor, *Changing Assessments: Alternative Views of Aptitude, Achievement and Instruction*, Kluwer Academic Publishers.

Riddell, A. (2001) 'Review of 13 Evaluations of REFLECT', London: ActionAid International, International Reflect Circle.

Ringold, D., M. A.Orenstein, and E. Wilkins (2004) *Roma in an Expanding Europe, Breaking the Poverty Cycle*, Washington DC: World Bank.

Rogers, A. (1986) *Teaching Adults*, Milton Keynes: Open University Press.

Rogers, A. (1992) *Adults Learning for Development*, London: Cassell and Reading: Education for Development.

Rogers, A. (1994a) 'Women, Literacy and Income Generation', Education for Development Occasional Paper, Reading.

Rogers, A. (1994b) 'A New Approach to Post Literacy Materials', Education Research Paper No. 10, London: Department for International Development.

Rogers, A. (2000) 'Literacy comes second: working with groups in developing societies', *Development in Practice* 10 (2): 236–40.

Rogers, A. (2003) 'Training Adult Educators in Developing Countries', background paper for Education for All Global Monitoring Report 2006, Paris: UNESCO.

Rogers, A. (2005) 'Adult Learning and Literacy Learning for Livelihoods', available at: www.uea.ac.uk/care/Recent_Writing/COLLIT4.pdf (last accessed June 2007).

Rogers, A. and P. Taylor (1998) *Participatory Curriculum Development in Agricultural Education: A Training Guide*, Rome: FAO.

Rogers, A., B. Maddox, J. Millican, K. Newell-Jones, U. Papen, and A. Robinson-Pant (1999) 'Re-defining Post Literacy in a Changing World', DFID Serial Paper 29, Education Research Report.

Sabatini, J. P., L. Ginsburg, and M. Russell (2002) 'Professionalization and certification for teachers in adult basic education', in *Annual Review of Adult Learning and Literacy* Volume 3, John Wiley & Sons, Inc., and the Office of Educational Research and Improvement, available at: www.ncsall.net/?id=493 (last accessed June 2007).

Sabri, A. and M. El Gindy (2003) 'The CELL approach and its operationalisation, appendix 3', in 'Report on the Training of GALAE Central Training Cadre', Cairo and Manchester, British Council, unpublished.

Scribner, S. and M. Cole (1981) *The Psychology of Literacy*, Cambridge, MA: Harvard University Press.

SEAMEO-INNOTECH (Southeast Asian Ministers of Education Organization, Regional Center for Educational Innovation and Technology) (2006) 'Case study on non-formal education in the Philippines', in UNESCO 2006.

Sen, A. (1990) *Development as Freedom*, Oxford: Oxford University Press.

Sen, A. (1997) 'Human capital and human capability', *World Development* 25 (12): 1599–961.

Shah, S. Y. (2004) 'Approaches to training grassroots level workers in literacy and adult basic education: the Indian scenario', in Singh and McKay 2004.

Singh, M. and V. McKay (2004) *Enhancing Adult Basic Education: Training Educators and Unlocking the Potential of Distance and Open Learning*, Hamburg: UIE.

Skutnabb-Kangas, T. (2000) *Linguistic Genocide in Education – or Worldwide Diversity and Human Rights?* Mahwah, NJ: Lawrence Erlbaum Associates.

Snow, C. E. (2002) 'Reading for Understanding: Toward an R&D Program in Reading Comprehension', Santa Monica, CA: RAND, available at: www.rand.org/pubs/monograph_reports/MR1465/index.html (last accessed June 2007).

Sommers, M. (2002) 'Children, Education and War: Reaching Education for All (EFA) Objectives in Countries Affected by Conflict', Conflict, Prevention and Reconstruction Working Papers, paper no.1.

Stascz, B. B., R. C. Schwartz, and J. C. Weeden (1994) 'Writing our lives: an adult basic skills program', in M. Radencich (ed.) *Adult Literacy: A Compendium of Articles from the Journal of Reading*, Newark DE: International Reading Association.

Stock, A. (1982) 'The United Kingdom: becoming and staying literate', *Prospects* 12 (2): 221–32.

Street, B. V. (1984) *Literacy in Theory and Practice*, Cambridge: Cambridge University Press.

Street, B. V. (1985) 'Adult literacy in the UK: a history of research and practice', draft.

Street, B.V. (1993) *Cross-Cultural Approaches to Literacy*, Cambridge: Cambridge University Press.

Street, B. V. (2001) *Literacy and Development: Ethnographic Perspectives*, London: Routledge.

Street, B. V. (2003) 'Literacy and development: challenges to the dominant paradigm', in A. Mukherjee and D. Vasanta (eds.), *Practice and Research in Literacy*, Research in Applied Linguistics Series, Delhi and London: Sage Publications.

Street, B. V. (2006) 'Contexts for literacy work: the 'new orders' and the 'new literacy studies'', in J. Crowther, M. Hamilton, and L.Tett (eds.), *Powerful Literacies*, Leicester: National Institute of Adult Continuing Education.

Swift, D. (2006) 'Adult literacy in sector wide reform: is this the way forward for adult literacy?', in B. V. Street (ed.) *Fresh Hope for Literacy: A Critical Reflection on Literacy for Life, EFA Global Monitoring Report*, London: British Association for Literacy in Development and UK Forum for International Education and Training.

Taylor, P. (2000) 'New Perspectives, New Curricula: a Case Study of Participatory Curriculum Development in Forestry Education in Vietnam', discussion paper prepared for the 'Forestry Education Workshop',Vietnam, April.

The Sector Skills Council for Lifelong Learning, www.lluk.org/home/home.html.

Thompson, Ekundayo J. D. (1999) 'Kenya Post-Literacy Project: Three Years On, 1996–1999', Nairobi: German Agency for Technical Co-operation (GTZ).

Training Adult Learning South Africa (ALSA),
www.aldsa.org/directory/training.html.

Tusting, K. and D. Barton (2003) 'Models of Adult Learning: A Literature
Review', London: National Research and Development Centre for Adult
Literacy and Numeracy, available at: www.nrdc.org.uk.

Tyler, R. W. (1949) *Basic Principles of Curriculum and Instruction*, Chicago:
University of Chicago Press.

UNDP (1995) *Human Development Report 1995*, New York: Oxford University
Press.

UNDP (2000) *Human Development Report 2000*, New York: Oxford University
Press.

UNDP (2004) *Human Development Report 2004 – Cultural Liberty in Today's
Diverse World*, available at: hdr.undp.org/reports/global/2004/ (last
accessed June 2007).

UNDP (2005) *Human Development Report 2005 – International Cooperation at
a Crossroads: Aid, Trade and Security in an Unequal World*, available at:
hdr.undp.org/reports/global/2005/ (last accessed June 2007).

UNESCO (1965) 'Final Report of the World Congress of Ministers of
Education on the Eradication of Illiteracy', Tehran.

UNESCO (2000) 'Education for All – Dakar Framework for Action', available
at: www.unesco.org/education/efa/ed_for_all/dakfram_eng.shtml
(last accessed June 2007).

UNESCO (2003/4) 'Gender and Education for All: The Leap to Equality',
Education for All Global Monitoring Report, Paris: UNESCO.

UNESCO (2005a) 'Literacy for Life 2006', Education for All Global Monitoring
Report, Paris: UNESCO.

UNESCO (2005b) 'Report of the Sixth Meeting of the Working Group on
Education for All', Paris: UNESCO.

UNESCO (2006) 'Synergies between Formal and Non-formal Education',
Paris: UNESCO.

UNESCO Education Sector Position Paper (nd) 'The Plurality of Literacy and
Its Implications for Policies and Programmes', available at:
www.unesco.cl/medios/biblioteca/documentos/plurality_literacy_
implications_policies_programmes.pdf?menu=/esp/atematica/alfayeduja/
docdig/ (last accessed June 2007).

Unterhalter, E. (2005) 'Fragmented frameworks? Researching women, gender, education and development', in S. Aikman and E. Unterhalter (eds.), *Beyond Access: Transforming Policy and Practice for Gender Equality in Education*, Oxford: Oxfam.

Vorhaus, J. (2006) 'What is good practice in skills for life?', *Reflect* 6, London: National Research and Development Centre for adult literacy and numeracy.

Vygotsky, L. (1978) *Mind in Society*, Cambridge, MA: Harvard University Press.

Wadsworth, Y. (1997) *Everyday Evaluation on the Run: a Hands-on Guide to Program Evaluation*, St Leonards, NSW, Australia: Allen and Unwin.

Wagner, D., R. L. Venezky, and B. Street (1999) *Literacy: An International Handbook*, Boulder, CO: Westview Press.

Watahomigie, L. J. and T. L. McCarty (1994) 'Bilingual/Bicultural education at Peach Springs: A Hualapai way of schooling', *Peabody Journal of Education*, 69 (2): 26–42.

Wenger, E. (1998) *Communities of Practice: Learning, Meaning and Identity*, Cambridge: Cambridge University Press.

West, C., P. McLaren, P. Leonard, and P. Freire (1992) *Freire: A Critical Encounter*, London: Routledge.

World Bank (1985) *World Development Report*, Oxford: Oxford University Press.

World Education (2006) 'Exploiting the synergy between them for the benefit of both World Education's integrated education strengthening and adult literacy program', in UNESCO, 'Synergies Between Formal and Non-formal Education: An Overview of Good Practices', Paris: UNESCO.

Yasser el Sirafi (2005) 'Mobile ICT Clubs', a presentation at the BMENA and Member States of the G8, *Report of the Meetings of Literacy Experts*, British Council, Cairo.

Index

ActionAid 97, 98, 210, 220
  REFLECT programme 15, 97, 210
Adult Basic Education Training
  (ABET) 214
adult education 12, 13, 16
adult learning, theory of 70, Chapter 12
*Adult Literacy: A Handbook for
  Development Workers* 187
Afghanistan 34, 147
Africa, literacy in 9–10, 11, 12, 14,
  19–20, 30, 39, 48, 66, 68b, 90
    disparity in education in 22
    literacy programmes in 122, 145, 146
alphabetic approach 44
Arab states, literacy in 10
Arnstein Ladder 178–9f
Asia
literacy in 14, 22, 90
  literacy programmes in 144–7
assessment Chapter 16
  of achievement 234, 236, 245ff
  assessing reading 243–5
  assessing writing 243–5
  assessment plan, developing 241–2
  'folk models' of assessment 242
  for learning 233–4, 235
  performance or authentic
    assessment 247–8
  portfolio assessment 248–50
  quality assurance 234
  self assessment, learners' 233

Australia 6, 11, 50, 194, 204
autonomous 38, 46, 59, 73, 258–9

Bangladesh Rural Action Council
  (BRAC) 210
Bangladesh 20, 47, 98, 210
bilingualism and bi-literacy 126–7
Bolivia 11
Botswana 22, 224
Brazil 11, 224
Burundi 98, 99

Cambodia 11
Canada 85
capabilities 24, 80–1
CARE programme 210
CELL (Capacity Enhancement for
  Lifelong Learning, Egypt) 79–80, 96,
  181–2b, 220
China 132, 204
cloze exercises 241b, 245b
Combat Poverty (Irish NGO) 217
Community Education Programme,
  (DFID project, Nigeria) 39, 77, 87,
  96, 102, 217, 228
community literacies 75ff
Community Literacy Project Nepal
  (CLPN) 19, 48, 75–7, 195, 222
community of practice 153–4, 155
critical reflection and literacy 103–4
    training of facilitators for 216, 259

Cuba 204
culture and training 227–8
curriculum 29, 54, 65, 73, 118, 121, 122,
  130, 146, 149b, Chapter 13
  defining 169
  design 3, 4, 149, 152, 170, 171
  development 176–7
  and gender 18, 29
  and learners 173
  materials selection and production
    178
  participatory curriculum
    development (PCD) 178
  reform 138b
  selecting and organising learning
    experiences 177–8
  and syllabus 169–70
  ways of looking at 171–5

Dakar Framework for Action 12–13,
  19, 22
DFID (Department for International
  Development, UK) 69, 75, 77, 79, 80,
  116
disability and literacy 256–7
  Braille 256
  sign language 129, 162, 256

easy reading material for new learners
  194–5
  guidelines for creating 194–5
  and real materials 188–93, 195, 197
Education for All see EFA
educator 173
  cultural, language, and gender issues
    227–9
  and curricula 173–4, 180
  qualifications of 225–6
  training 15, Chapter 15
  working situation 211–13
EFA (Education for All) 7, 16, 47–8

Dakar Framework for Action 19, 22
  Global Monitoring Reports 9, 13,
    16, 47, 262
Egypt 16, 30, 61, 72, 79–80, 88, 96, 102,
  120, 131
  national literacy programme 128,
    131, 132, 212
  see also CELL
'Equipped for the Future' framework,
  USA 33
'equivalency education' (Indonesia)
  54b
ESOL (English for Speakers of Other
  Languages) 166
Ethiopia 11, 95
ethnography 11, 262
European Commission 25
European Union 127
evaluating literacy programmes
  Chapter 11, 135, 136–8
  accountability 139–40
  evaluation planning 135, 141–8
  formative 136
  summative (impact/outcomes) 136–7
EWLP (Experimental World Literacy
  Programme) (UNESCO) 37, 59–60

facilitator/learner ratios 47–8
facilitators 39, 47, 78, 81, 82, 86, 94, 95f,
  103, 108, 109, 111, 115, 128, 131, 175, 199,
  203, 204, 207ff, 217, 226, 247, 250, 262
  and curricula 170, 174, 175b
  defined 5
  and local languages 131, 227–8
  and local needs 85, 101
  and resources 46, 186, 188
  training 109, 119, 120, 136, 142,
    148–9, 152, 160, 175, 180, 213ff,
    218, 220, 221, 222, 225, 229
  tutors as 247
  women as 91, 131–2, 229

FENTO (Further Education National Training Organisation, UK) 226
Freire, Paulo 4, 40, 59, 87, 92–4, 97, 125, 156–7, 167, 188, 259
    Freirian approach 44, 100, 174
funding for literacy programmes 77, 78, 101, 109, 115, 116, 118, 121, 140, 230, 262

GAD (Gender and Development) 23, 25–6, 27–8, 29, 116
Gambia, literacies in 128
gender 2, 3, Chapter 3, 76, 223, 255
    concepts 22–3
    gender and curriculum development 181–3
    gender bias 229
    gender difference in language use 132–3
    gender disparity in education 21–2, 85, 131–2, 256
    gender equality 23, 28, 30
    gender integration 84–5
    gender issues and training trainers 228–9
    gender and literacy 10, 145
    gender and power 28
    gender roles 23, 27, 131
    gender-specific language 131–3
    mainstreaming 18–19
    policy approaches to gender 24b
    practical and strategic gender needs 26–8
    training 227–8
    UN and gender equality 12–13
gender-integrated programmes 115–16
Global Monitoring Report see EFA
global North see North
global South see South
government policy and literacy 7, 255
Gramsci, Antonio 88
Gypsies, UK 10, 227

HIV/AIDS 13, 146
human rights 125
    literacy as a human right 7

IALS (International Adult Literacy Study) 35, 36, 51b, 232, 236, 238, 241b
ICT (information and communication technology) 15–16, 262
ideographic approach 44
ideological approach to literacy 48, 73–4, 89
income generation 15, 61, 65, 70, 81, 118, 153, 195, 211
India
    literacy in 11, 12
    literacy programme 132–3, 204
Indonesia 54b, 64–5, 65b–66b
information technology 68, 69, 204
International Benchmarks on Adult Literacy (EFA) 47–8
International Decade for Literacy (1990–2000) 11
International Literacy Year (1990) 11
international policies 8, 262–3
Internet 69
Iran 73
Ireland, Republic of 215, 239b
    literacy training 190, 239
Israel 120, 124

Jamaica 22
Jordan 10

Kenya 116
Kenya Adult Education Project 201
    literacy programmes in 149b, 195
    post-literacy project 202b
Kerala, South India, literacy in 9
knowledge
    acquiring and organising 157–8
    memory and structuring knowledge 158

types of 226

language 255
  choice of 128
  creating orthography for oral
    languages 129
  gender difference and 132–3
  gender-specific 130–3
  language and training 227–8
  language policies 194
  languages of power 123, 125, 132–3
  minority 9, 89, 123, 124, 126–7, 129,
    130, 131, 219, 256, 257, 263
  mother tongue 126ff, 194, 227, 240
  regional language variations 128–9
'language experience' 154, 157, 166,
  241b, 245b
Latin America, literacy in 14, 204
learner 15, 36, 48, 49 54b, 58ff, 63,
  82–3, 101, 116, 135, 161, 162, 169,
  186, 209, 214, 216, 219, 233, 262
  acquiring knowledge 157–9, 160,
    162–3, 164–7, 172–3, 177, 188–9,
    239, 243, 246
  apprenticeship 155
  cultural and other background 86,
    113, 167, 227, 247
  and curricula 154, 169, 170–1,
    173–4, 178, 180, 181b–183b, 184,
    237, 250
  developing learner-orientated
    materials 73, 111–12, 154, 187,
    191, 197, 204, 205, 214, 215, 223
  engaging learners' interest 65b–66b,
    83, 85, 94, 112, 115, 116, 130, 140,
    146b, 171, 173, 249–50
  and gender issues 131–3, 229
  and language 126ff, 212, 257
  learning environment 62, 65b 112,
    114, 115, 121, 144, 154–5, 157, 173
  learning from experience 156–7

memory 158
needs and motivations 3, 39, 50, 52,
  59, 61, 62b, 65, 67, 111–112, 140,
  143, 144b, 168, 175, 183b, 184, 218,
  233
  and planning of literacy
    programmes 29, 65b, 111, 116,
    172, 174, 175, 176, 177, 216, 234,
    235, 249, 260
scaffolding 154
self assessment 233, 235, 240, 249,
  250
see also facilitators, LGMs, tutors
learning group 5, 39, 65b, 115, 121,
  142, 145, 155, 157, 160, 192, 238, 239,
  242, 249, 250, 252
learning literacy Chapter 12
learning materials 35, 48, 54b, 62b, 65,
  82, 130, 138b, 145, 149, 175, 178, 202,
  204
learning to read 160–3
learning to write 164–7
Lesotho 22
LGMs (learner-generated materials)
  48, 101, 102, 103, 114–15, 130, 191,
  199–201, 203–4, 247
  use in literacy programmes 201
    Nepal 203–4
    Sudan 203
literacy 15
  adapting literacy to local context 59
  applying literacy 70, 74–5
  competency-based approaches
    49–52, 214
    Australian approach 50
    UK approach 49, 50
  competency-based programmes 214
  concepts of literacy 34–40
  definition of literacy 11, Chapter 4
  family literacy 66–8
  key principles 254ff

language of Chapter 10
literacy for change 87–8
literacy for liberation 59, 87, 92–3
literacy for oppression 87, 92–3
male and female literacy 10–11
materials used 188
mother-tongue literacy 125
multiple literacies 9, 38–9
planning for literacy Chapter 9
questions of power and access 89ff, 254, 255–7, 258
radical literacy 104
relative levels 9–10
resources for literacy Chapter 14
statistics 9–10
technology and literacy 129
as a tool for empowerment 397
training methodologies 213ff
transfer of between languages 9, 126, 129
types of 32–3
understanding literacy 33, 41, 44
universal, as international goal 12–13
and poverty reduction 7
uses of literacy 87
visual literacy 44
work-based literacy 68–9
literacy design
assessing Chapter 16
building capacity for assessment 250
literacy educators
described 207–11
selection 212–13, 223
training of Chapter 15
literacy group 5, 8, 78, 89, 93, 101, 102, 116, 126, 155, 170, 208, 209, 217, 281
post-literacy group 63
literacy and power 89–93
literacy providers 77, 112
literacy as skills 34, 35–6, 41, 171, 186, Chapter 5, 75, 139, 257

criticism of approach 36
failure of skills-based programmes 257–8
primer-based approach 43–8, 214
syllabic approach 44–5, 45f
whole word approach 46
literacy as social practices (social contextual approaches) 35, 38–9, 41, Chapter 7, 138, 258–9
criticism of approach 39
descriptors 72–3
literacy for livelihoods 80–1
literacy programmes and pre-planning 76–7
social literacies 73
testing literacy 245–7
literacy as tasks (functional approach) 34, 37–8, 41, Chapter 6, 138, 258
criticism of approach 37–8
functional literacy 57–8, 64–5, 75
in Indonesia 65b, 144b
spread of concept 60–2
weakness of functional approach 258
literacy as tool for critical reflection and social change (radical approach) 35, 39–40, 41, 138, Chapter 8, 259
capacity for enabling participants 259
criticism of approach 40
'Literacy for Life' (UNESCO report) 9, 13, 16, 262
'Literacy and Community Empowerment Program', Afghanistan 34, 147
LOCAL (Learner Oriented Community Adult Literacy) 39, 77–9
local materials, use of in literacy and numeracy learning 81–3

Mali 67b, 239–40
MDGs (Millennium Development Goals) 2, 7, 13, 19, 22, 256

men and literacy 6–7, 18, 19, 109, 116
  and learning 153
  disadvantages faced by 26
  gender awareness 29–30
  gender issues and tutoring 229
  strategic gender needs of 22, 103
mentoring 132
metacognition (self-monitoring)
  159–60
Mexico 11, 204
Middle East, literacy in 10, 22, 90
military and literacy programmes 37,
  61
Millennium Development Goals
  see MDGs
minority groups and literacy 12, 36,
  89, 110, 117b, 130, 138b, 219, 227,
  256, 257
monitoring of literacy programmes
  16, 29, Chapter 11, 256, 260, 261
Morocco 10
multilanguage literacy
  Nigeria 127
  South Africa 128
  Sudan 128–9
multilingual policy, inclusive 133–4

Namibia 11
Nepal 12, 48, 121, 198, 199, 203–4
  see also Community Literacies Project
New Literacy Studies (NLS) 38, 73–5,
  262
New Public Management 36
New Zealand 6, 11, 204
newspapers, use in literacy 48, 83, 101,
  115, 121, 189, 190, 193, 195, 198, 204,
  243
NGOs (non-government
  organisations) 3, 29, 48, 103, 117,
  130, 208, 215
  NGO literacy staff 210
Nicaragua 88, 92, 94, 103, 120, 211–12,

217
Nigeria 11, 30, 39, 72, 77–9, 88, 91, 94,
  96, 101, 102, 127, 166
  languages in 127
  learner-generated material 200
  literacy programmes in 132, 144b,
  222
  women 103–4, 131, 132
Nirantur, resource group, Delhi, India
  132–3, 182–3b, 210
nomadic pastoral people and literacy
  9, 11, 28, 79, 88, 200, 227
North (global North) 6, 35, 72, 82, 90,
  93, 116, 262
numeracy 6, 7, 14, 15, 33, 53, 62b, 66b,
  68, 73, 99f, 138b, 182b, 207, 210,
  212–13, 215, 262, 263

Organisation for Economic
  Co-operation and Development
  (OECD) 35
organisational frameworks for literacy
  7, 8f
organisational needs analysis 69
orthography creation for languages
  129–30

Pakistan 10t, 14, 21, 84, 213
Papua New Guinea 130
participatory action research (PAR)
  241b
participatory curriculum development
  (PCD) 178–80
  gender considerations in
  curriculum development 181–3
participatory learning and action
  (PLA) 241b
participatory rural appraisal (PRA) 15,
  78, 79–80, 87, 92, 94–7, 100, 103, 109,
  114, 145, 262
  training and 216, 319
pastoralists, sub-Saharan Africa 227

pedagogy 226
Peru 11
Philippines 61–62b, 235, 236, 238
    alternative education system 250
phonics 162–3
phoneme awareness 162
planners
    and assessing literacy learning
        Chapter 16, 251
    and choice of languages in multi-
        lingual areas 133–4
    and context of programmes 119
    and critical reflection 104–5
    and curriculum design 183–4, 193
    and gender mainstreaming 29–30
    planning gender-integrated
        programmes 116–17
    identifying stakeholders 109–10
    and implications of evaluation and
        monitoring 149–50, 262
    and learning to read and write
        167–8
    and literacy as skills 54
    and literacy as tasks 70–1
    and local community 110–111
    and mapping literacy usage 112–13
    and needs assessment 108–9, 118–22
    and outcomes 118
    planning for literacy Chapter 9
    purposes of planning 118
    and resources 119ff, 205
    and scale of programmes 122
    and scope and sustainability 114–16
    and social practice 85–6
    and training programmes 229–30
    understanding learners 111–12
policy
    approaches 23ff, 24t
post-conflict literacy programmes 96,
    217
    post-conflict situation 81, 100, 209
    post-conflict states and societies

124, 213
post-literacy 63–4, 67b, 69–70, 71, 127,
    195, 202–3
poverty 7, 8
    poverty reduction 9, 13, 24ff
power
    disparities within society 257
    making visible 89
    relationships 36, 255–7
PRA see participatory rural appraisal
praxis 156–7, 171, 174–5
primers 43–7, 99, 188, 192–4, 214, 217,
    257, 257
    advantages and disadvantages of
        45–6, 48
    and competency-based approach 49
    limitations of 192–3, 194
    and training 213, 214
problem solving 158–9
psycho-social method 87, 93, 217, 219

radical pragmatism 100–2
radio and literacy programmes 204
reading for understanding 160ff
    comprehension 163–4
    examples of assessment 244b
    fluency 163
    process of reading 243
    technical skills required 161–2, 167
    and writing 166–7
reading schemes 81–4
real materials approach 83–4, 115–16,
    188–91, 195, 198–205
reasoning 158–9
REFLECT Mother Manual 97, 218
REFLECT programme (ActionAid) 15,
    40, 87, 93, 97–100, 210, 217–18, 262
    Kwa Zulu Natal family literacy
        project 240
    and mapping of community 97–8
    training and 219
resources for literacy Chapter 14

Roma 11
San – Southern Africa 12
Sandinistas 88, 92, 93, 94, 120, 211–12
Saudi Arabia 181
scaffolding as learning process 154, 163
school equivalency 52–3
school tests, standardised 232
scribing 76, 121, 199
self-monitoring (metacognition) 158, 159–60
Senegal 63
Sierra Leone 94, 96, 98–9, 100, 102, 121–2
SIL International 129–31
Skills for Life 36, 56
SOLO (Sudan Open Learning Organisation) 94, 203b, 223
South (global South) 6, 35, 39, 43, 72, 93, 116, 262
    literacy primers in 43
    literacy programmes 248
    literacy as social practice 258
    literacy testing 247
South Africa 52, 68, 90, 112, 133b, 166, 195
    Adult Basic Education Training 214
    apartheid era literacy material 91–2
    choice of English as a national language 124
    Kwa Zulu Natal family literacy project 240
    languages in 124, 127, 128, 133
    literacy programmes in 191, 198, 204
special education 52–3
stakeholders 109–11, 115, 176, 178–9, 181
statistics 9–12, 18–19, 234, 242
student 15, 53, 67b, 93, 115, 120, 121, 131, 161, 171, 172, 181, 188, 191, 216, 221, 237, 242, 246

planners and 47
requirements of 82, 126, 128, 130, 132, 163, 164, 165, 173, 175, 191, 212, 249
student writing movement 73, 87, 91, 100–2, 103, 166, 199–201
    see also learner
Sudan 81, 85, 91, 95, 96, 100, 102
    languages in 128–9, 228
    post-literacy project 202
    training trainers 228
    see also SOLO
Swahili 133
syllabic pairs 44
syllabus 169–70

Tanzania 98, 133, 224
teacher 154, 211
    training teachers 168
    see also facilitator, tutor
Teaching Adults (Rogers, 1986) 176
testing of students 144, 232, 235b, 250
tests
    curriculum 237
    designing and application 245–7
    use of 35, 36, 39, 49, 52, 79, 145, 182, 189, 233, 236–7, 238, 239, 241b, 242, 251
trainers and their trainers 223
    ideology and methodology of 221
    literacy educators training and supporting Chapter 15
    qualifications 211
    recruitment of 211–12
    selection 212–13
    types of educator 207–11
training courses
    cultural issues in training 227–8
    gender issues 227–8
    language issues 227–8

training methodologies for literacy 212ff
  for critical reflection,
    transformation and change
    programmes 216–18
  for skills-based and competency-
    based programmes 213
  for social practice programmes 216
  for task-based literacy programmes
    215
  methods and styles 221–3
  models of training 220
  post-initial training support 222–3
  training frameworks 224
  tutors 29, 54b, 55, 73, 80, 82, 85, 86,
    101, 105, 112, 120, 129, 143, 144,
    148, 154, 155, 165, 187, 190, 191,
    195, 198, 207, 208, 209, 211, 212,
    213, 233, 243, 243, 244b, 247, 248,
    250, 260, 261
  defined 5
  framework for teaching 49, 52, 65,
    121, 199, 204, 205, 234, 235, 239, 251
  training of tutors 86, 140, 148, 149,
    160, 171, Chapter 15, 242, 257, 258,
    259, 262
  see also facilitator

Uganda 137–138b, 145
  gender issues and training 228
  government literacy programme 218
UK 36, 50, 53, 58, 70, 87
  Access to Higher Education courses
    53
  adult literacy 36, 195, 199, 215
  Adult Literacy and Basic Skills Unit
    (ALBSU) 60
  literacy campaign in 15, 68, 82, 87,
    100, 183, 190, 225
  literacy and gender policies 22
  numeracy campaign 15
  status of women in 20, 21, 22
  training programme 160, 166, 167,

    211, 221, 226
  Welsh teaching in 124–5
UNESCO 9–10, 12, 58, 79, 128, 219,
  223, 256
  Education and Planning Division 7
  Education for All Global
    Monitoring Report 'Literacy for
    Life' 9, 13, 16, 262
  estimate for literacy 9
  EWLP (Experimental World
    Literacy Programme) 37, 58–9
  General Conference, 1978,
    definition of functional literacy 3
  priorities for monitoring and
    evaluating literacy programmes
    137b
  see also EFA
United Arab Emirates 10, 22
University of the Western Cape, South
  Africa, training programmes 225–6
USA 36, 52, 58, 82, 126, 204
  assessment of levels of literacy 237
  literacy programmes 61
  NCSALL 189, 190

vocational training 61

Welsh language 124–5
women
  conditions faced by 20, 28, 90–1,
    103–4
  disadvantages faced by 22ff
  exclusion from workforce 21, 28, 91
  and learning 153
  and literacy 6–7, 18–19, 22, 34,
    89–91, 109, 116
  and literacy programmes 22, 27,
    84–5, 110, 116–117, 136, 210
  self-esteem 27, 85, 229
  strategic gender needs of 103
  varying social conditions 28, 85
  see also Nirantur programme,

gender disparity
'Women in Development' (WID)
  framework 18, 23, 25, 26
women's literacy, male attitudes
  towards 27, 90
women's rights 27
writing
  learning how to write 164ff
  as a process 165, 243
  and reading 166–7
  and thinking 165–6

Yemen 10, 210, 213
Yo, sí puedo, Cuba 15, 204, 262

ZPD ('zone of proximal development')
  154